STUDIES IN POLITICAL ECONOMY
Volume I: The Interwar years and the 1940s

STUDIES IN POLITICAL ECONOMY

VOLUME I: THE INTERWAR YEARS AND THE 1940s

Donald MacDougall

ISBN 978-1-349-02165-9   ISBN 978-1-349-02163-5 (eBook)
DOI 10.1007/978-1-349-02163-5
© Sir Donald MacDougall 1975
Softcover reprint of the hardcover 1st edition 1975

First published 1975 by
THE MACMILLAN PRESS LTD
London and Basingstoke
Associated companies in New York
Dublin Melbourne Johannesburg and Madras

SBN 333 15711 7

Typeset in Great Britain by
PREFACE LIMITED
Salisbury, Wiltshire

Contents

Introduction

This is the first of two volumes containing a selection of studies in political economy made over the past thirty-five years or so. I call them studies in 'political economy' because the majority of them attempt to use economic analysis (and usually a quantitative approach) to illuminate real problems of policy that have arisen both in the United Kingdom and elsewhere during this period. I have omitted some purely theoretical studies such as my very first article on 'The definition of prime and supplementary costs'.[1]

A good many of the studies were inspired by current controversy but I hope they will be of more than historical interest. First, many of the problems discussed are still very live issues today. Those that are not may well arise again; for history tends to repeat itself. Secondly, in the course of exploring particular problems I have, I believe, developed some techniques and methods of analysis which have proved to be of general and lasting interest.

After a good deal of thought I decided to divide the studies between the two volumes largely on a chronological basis. Thus, most of the studies in the first volume were written in the 1930s and 1940s, and those in the second volume mostly in the 1950s and 1960s.

THE INTERWAR YEARS

The first study in this volume, published in 1938, is about the British trade cycle of the 1930s. It came to be written in the following way. Section F of the British Association decided in 1935 to produce a book on 'Britain in Recovery' to follow a previous volume on 'Britain in Depression'. I was appointed Assistant Secretary of the research committee in charge of the publication and, in addition to organising the contributions of other authors, was asked to prepare a general survey to go at the beginning of the book. I decided, in fact, to cover the whole of the cycle of 1929–37. Where appropriate I went further back into the 1920s and, where possible, brought the story up to the early part of 1938, thus including the beginning of the downturn in that year.

[1] *Economic Journal,* September 1936.

The piece I wrote was based mainly on published statistics but also, to a lesser extent, on some of the other contributions to the volume which dealt with the fortunes of particular industries as well as with more general developments in, for example, the foreign exchanges, commercial policy, industrial relations and the various regions of the country. I have decided to reprint it here, despite its considerable length, for a number of reasons. It is, so far as I know, the only account of its kind of what might perhaps be called the last 'classic' trade cycle in Britain. Cycles since then have been shorter and, of course, there has been intervention along broadly Keynesian lines. I am one of those who believe that some economic history is a necessary part of an economist's training and, whether or not the 1930s are yet part of 'history', I would like to think that a reading of things such as my account of this particular cycle is a useful, and perhaps necessary, background and complement to the study of macro-economic theory and of econometrics. I feel, too, that economists and econometricians should not be brought up to believe that history begins in 1955 (the first year for which there are official quarterly national income figures in Britain), or even later.

The study, incidentally, illustrates the way in which economists were obliged to piece together the various fragments of information in the days before formally comprehensive statistics of national income and expenditure became available. (There were some estimates by Colin Clark, and some of these are quoted, but they mostly did not go beyond 1935.)

This piecing together of different bits of information had its advantages, because the different stories that they sometimes told made one aware of the uncertainties involved in describing past economic developments, and cautious in drawing conclusions. We still in Britain have, for example, our three measures of gross domestic product whose divergent movements help to keep us on our guard, but in other respects we may sometimes take our enormously improved statistics too much at their face value, and fail to look sufficiently at how they are compiled and the raw data behind them.

The first study is concerned not only with the macro-economics of the cycle but also with developments in the various industrial sectors: both longer-term trends between the peaks of the cycle (1929 and 1937) and how various industries were affected by the cycle itself. It also shows, for example, what a major contribution was made by house-building to the early stages of the recovery up to 1935, no doubt reflecting very cheap money and the big fall in import prices which greatly increased the real incomes of those who managed broadly to maintain their money incomes during the depression. (The analysis of this problem used a primitive type of input—output analysis although I am not sure whether this term had yet been invented.) The price indices are also broken down into their various components. I venture to suggest that the value of studies of this kind, covering more recent periods, would be enhanced by the inclusion of such a disaggregated analysis.

The next two studies were made shortly before the war for the Royal Commission on the Geographical Distribution of the Industrial Population (the Barlow Commission). My Professor at Leeds, J. Harry Jones, was a member, and he asked me to analyse some statistics prepared for the Commission by the Ministry of Labour and the Registrars General.

Study 2, on interwar changes in the location of industry, reaches the conclusion that the slow economic growth, between the wars, of the depressed areas in the West and North of Britain can be almost wholly explained (with the notable exception of Mid-Scotland) by the heavy concentration in these areas of the older industries destined to decline, and not by a slower growth in them of the more rapidly expanding industries, which in general grew as fast (in percentage terms) in the depressed areas as elsewhere. This suggested that there might be nothing inherently disadvantageous in their location. Conversely, the rapid growth of the South-East reflected its favourable industrial pattern at the beginning of the period; there was no significant tendency for individual industries to grow faster in that part of the country.

I have reprinted this study partly because of the inherent interest of the findings (which exploded some popularly held myths) and partly because it developed techniques which I do not think had been used before, and which have since been used a good deal by students of regional economics. In particular, I compared the *actual* increase in the insured population in each area with what I called the *'hypothetical'* increase that would have occurred if each industry had expanded (or contracted) in the area at the same rate as in the country as a whole. I believe this is now sometimes called the 'shift-share' method of analysis. The interesting result was that the two rates were very similar in nearly every area, one notable exception (as already mentioned) being Mid-Scotland where the actual rate was well below the hypothetical one. The pattern of industry in that area corresponded broadly with that of the country as a whole at the beginning of the interwar years; yet the Scottish rate of growth between the wars was well below the national average. Why Scotland was the odd man out is a puzzle which I am not sure has yet been resolved.

I also tried to distinguish 'local' industries from 'basic' industries — the former serving mainly local markets, and the latter sending part of their production outside the region. A strange result here was that, in general, the 'local' industries did not expand proportionately faster in the rapidly expanding, prosperous areas as might have been expected on the grounds that their size must depend largely on the size of the population and on its purchasing power. This seemed to cast doubt on the idea of a local or regional multiplier. I suppose one possible explanation is that in declining areas, where job opportunities were few, workers were forced into relatively low paid occupations, such as retail distribution, while in prosperous areas like London there were more lucrative opportunities in other industries. Another factor that may be relevant is that London and the Home Counties, the most rapidly growing area, was better endowed with 'local' industries at the beginning of the period than were the other areas.

Study 3 deals with another aspect of the geographical distribution of population, and asks the question to what extent, and in what senses, Britain became more 'urbanised' between the wars. The concept of growing urbanisation is a difficult one, and I believe the study makes a contribution to an understanding of it and to the methodology to be used in studying the relevant statistics. The results are also of interest in themselves. One of the main conclusions is that, while Britain became more urbanised between the wars in the sense that the proportion of the population living in large urban centres increased, this can be explained largely by the growth of towns through the processes of natural increase and spreading; smaller towns simply became larger towns. There was not, in addition, as many had supposed, any considerable migration into the larger towns from the rest of the country.

THE WAR

As is evident from the first three studies in this volume, a good deal of my work before the war consisted of economic analysis based on the interpretation of statistics (though it was hardly econometric work as now understood). I think this served me in good stead when, shortly after the outbreak of war, I started to work under Professor Lindemann, later Lord Cherwell, in Winston Churchill's Statistical Section. This started in the Admiralty, where Churchill was appointed First Lord in 1939; in May 1940, when he became Prime Minister, it was transformed into the Prime Minister's Statistical Section, and the scope of its work greatly enlarged.

Study 4 describes the working of the Section up till its demise on the change of Government in July 1945. (It also discusses the pros and cons of such an institution — a perennially controversial issue). In the early years the only objective was, of course, the winning of the war. The Section was involved, not only in 'micro-', but also in many important macro-economic decisions, and it is interesting to recall that the main instruments — at least after direct taxation had been raised to the limit and Lend—Lease had removed the balance of payments problem — were not financial, as in peace-time, but direct controls. Instead of operating through public expenditure, fiscal and monetary measures, and the exchange rate, we had rationing, allocation of materials, direction of manpower and manpower budgets, shipping programmes and complete control of the allocation of ships and what went into them.

THE EARLY POSTWAR YEARS

Towards the end of the war we concentrated more and more on postwar problems. One of those in which I became most interested, apart from that of achieving a high level of employment, was the balance of payments. (The two were of course closely interrelated.) There was, first, the problem of getting the volume of exports up from 30 per cent of the pre-war level, to which it had fallen during the war, to perhaps 175 per cent, so as to pay for essential imports. This huge increase (which in the event was achieved by the mid-1950s) was required to make good the net loss of overseas investment income resulting from the war, to correct the pre-war current account deficit, and to allow for higher Government expenditure abroad, a possible deterioration in the terms of trade and a level of national output which it was hoped would be substantially higher than before the war, partly as a result of much fuller employment. There was also the closely related question of what sort of international trade and monetary regime would be most conducive to British interests.

The last five studies in this volume are concerned with these problems. They are closely interrelated and should be read together.

During the latter part of the war and the early postwar years there was heated controversy about Britain's foreign economic policy. I was in favour of working, with the United States, for the widest possible acceptance of international agreements on the lines of Bretton Woods and the proposed International Trade Organisation (I.T.O.), which later became the G.A.T.T. I regarded this as in the British interest. But there were others to whom this course was anathema. To quote from the Conclusion to Study 5:

> Our foreign trade problem is so great, they argue, that we must
> forswear no weapon in our armoury. We must reserve the
> *unconditional* right to restrict imports; to vary the value of the
> pound; to buy from countries only if they will buy from us; to
> exploit Empire sentiment to the full by maintaining and extending
> Imperial Preference; to use our bargaining power as a large
> importer; to subsidise our exports; and possibly to build up an
> economic bloc, centred on London, from which the United States
> would be excluded.

Most of these arguments were discussed at the time in very
general, dogmatic terms. My main contribution to the debate was, I
suppose, to analyse them in a *quantitative* context — in the light of
facts, figures and orders of magnitude. Also, I made the apparently
obvious point again and again that, if Britain were to insist on the
right to do exactly what she wanted, other countries must be
expected to do the same. There would then be an international
free-for-all in which trade could hardly be expected to expand, and
this would have serious consequences for the economic prosperity of
the United Kingdom.

I think my analysis has stood the test of time (although, for
example, I underestimated the speed at which restrictions on German
and Japanese industry would be relaxed and the subsequent great
success of these countries in expanding their production and trade).
Certainly, whatever may have been the shortcomings of the I.M.F.,
the I.B.R.D., and the G.A.T.T., world production and trade have
expanded at an unprecedented rate since the war. And however
disappointing Britain's economic performance may have been,
compared with that of other industrial countries, I judge that her
difficulties would have been much greater if she had gone in for the
sort of international free-for-all which seemed to me to be advocated
by some of my opponents in the debate.

My first contribution was a short article on 'Britain's Bargaining
Power' published in March 1946. (One reason I decided to return to
University life from Government service after the war was that, had I
stayed, I should not have been allowed to publish this article. I like
to think that we are more liberal nowadays.)

An amplified version of the article (which may also be of interest
for its discussion of methodology in the measurement of bargaining
power) is reprinted as Study 8, and the implications for policy are
further discussed in Study 5. My detailed analysis of the figures by
country and by commodity showed, in my view, that Britain's
bargaining power as a large importer was far smaller than was

sometimes claimed. This meant that if we had attempted, in a 'Schachtian' manner, to use our bargaining power to force other countries to take our exports (as some were advocating), our success would at best have been very limited. Moreover, in a world where this sort of behaviour was permitted, we should very probably have lost out to the United States whose bargaining power was, as I attempted to show, considerably greater than our own. This is obvious now, but it was not generally recognised at the time. Many regarded Britain as the world's really big importer, especially of primary products, and there was a popular fallacy that the United States was a self-sufficient, highly protectionist country that imported practically nothing.

(My analysis also suggested that there was little future in the idea of an economic bloc of countries, centred on London, from which the U.S. would be excluded. Though superficially attractive it seemed to me that, given the hard facts of the real world, this would be a very small bloc indeed which could not possibly have met Britain's need for a rapid growth of exports and for plentiful supplies of primary products.)

Another reason why I was against a world in which trade was conducted to a large extent on the basis of bilateral arrangements (as was the case after the war over quite a large part of the world)[2] was that this would very considerably limit the amount of multilateral trade, which I regarded as of great value and importance, both for the world as a whole and for Britain in particular. Here again I tried in Study 7 to demonstrate in concrete terms the value to the world of multilateral trade, and Study 5 contained an estimate of its importance for the United Kingdom. In the 1920s, before the spread of bilateralism in the 1930s, something like one-quarter of all international trade was multilateral, i.e. the sum of all the bilateral balances between pairs of countries represented one-quarter of world trade. Calculations reported in Study 5 showed that about one-quarter of Britain's international transactions on current account was multilateral; and the countries with which she had a favourable balance spent nearly three times as much on her exports as was necessary to balance their receipts from her; in other words, no less than two-thirds of Britain's exports to them depended on their willingness to run 'unfavourable' balances with her. These figures seemed to show conclusively the dangers, for a country like the United Kingdom which needed a vast increase in its exports, of a world system that would cut down multilateral trade.

[2] Study 7 in Vol. II describes some of the complexities involved in breaking out of such a system in early postwar Europe.

This was the main reason why I favoured acceptance of the general principle of non-discrimination. In Study 7, however, I discussed, in a largely theoretical manner, possible circumstances in which a departure from discrimination might lead to a greater volume of world trade: for example, where there is a large-scale disequilibrium in the balance of payments between one part of the world and another, which cannot be corrected on a non-discriminatory basis without restricting world trade and employment to unnecessarily low levels; or where discrimination might be justified on grounds of convenience of negotiation when an attempt is being made to increase international trade. But I emphasised that the existence of such circumstances did not mean that we should abandon the general principle of non-discrimination and permit discrimination in all circumstances. Rather should we seek to agree a code of international behaviour under which discrimination was allowed only in certain carefully defined circumstances and within carefully prescribed limits. It was particularly important at the time of writing that, in applying discriminatory practices for good reasons, the world should not allow discrimination to get out of hand.

This article is reprinted here, not simply because of its contemporary relevance, but because it was one of the early contributions to the theory of discrimination in international trade which influenced subsequent writings,[3] and would still be relevant in any reconsideration of international rules on trade and payments (and to the implications of recent oil price rises).

Another topic of controversy in this period (and also later during the debate on whether Britain should enter the Common Market) was what was then called Imperial Preference. One of the main concerns of the opponents of the proposed International Trade Organisation was that it might lead to an erosion of these preferences, and would certainly prevent their extension. But, rather surprisingly, no systematic attempt at all had been made to quantify their importance, and I therefore set out to remedy this gap in our knowledge. Though the first results were not published until 1952,[4] and the final results only in 1954, I have included the latter in this volume (as Study No. 9), even though the date is in the 1950s rather than the 1940s.

The research showed that, so far as Britain's total exports to the

---

[3] See, for example, Professor Meade's *The Balance of Payments*, 1951, p. x. I myself developed the analysis further in *The World Dollar Problem*, Chapter XVI and Appendix XVIA.

[4] *Economic Journal*, September 1952. See Vol. II, Study 1.

Commonwealth were concerned, the Ottawa Agreements of 1932 raised the average margin of preference from 5 per cent to 10–11 per cent, but that by 1953 the figure had come back again to about 6 per cent, partly as a result of tariff changes and partly because of the large rise in prices which had reduced the *ad valorem* incidence of specific margins. The average preference on U.K. imports from the Commonwealth was raised by the Ottawa Agreements from 2–3 per cent to 10–12 per cent and had since come down to about 6 per cent.

I reckoned it unlikely that the remaining preferences could make a difference of more than, say, 5 per cent in Britain's total exports to the world as a whole. These figures confirmed my previous impression that, while Commonwealth preferences in the postwar world were by no means insignificant and should not be bargained away lightly, neither should a refusal to limit or reduce them be allowed to stand in the way of a wider agreement which gave Britain important advantages, especially as the preferences were likely to be steadily eroded in any event.

My position on Britain's foreign trade problem, as it appeared in the early postwar years, is mostly brought together in Study 5 (and in Study 6 which is my reply to a comment on this study by Mr. – now Lord – Balogh, one of my most formidable opponents at the time). Study 5 was published in March 1947. It had the distinction of being one of only two (very long) articles in the issue of the *Economic Journal* of that date, the other being a memoir of Lord Keynes. This gives some indication of the importance then attached to Britain's foreign trade problem. Plus ça change . . .

I have already described how in this article I cast doubt on the strength of Britain's bargaining power as a large importer, and attempted to quantify the importance to Britain of multilateral trade. I also answered the claim of some people at the time that we could easily dispense with a large part of our imports – by growing most of our food, by cutting out luxuries, a large part of our manufactured imports and so on. I showed in quantitative terms how this would entail extreme austerity. I showed, by reference to past experience, how severely an intensification of trade barriers could reduce world trade, how a reduction in barriers might be expected to increase it, and how vital it was that a country in our position should secure a large expansion of world trade, because otherwise we should be faced with the task of achieving an impossibly large increase in our share of that trade for our exports.

I also gave one of the earlier demonstrations (rather a crude one), based on the experience of the interwar years, that changes in our prices relative to those of our competitors *could* bring very substantial changes in our exports; and that a reduction in the exchange value of sterling could, despite what many were arguing, improve our balance of payments. I therefore emphasised the need to preserve the right to depreciate sterling, and also, in view of the experience of the 1930s, the desirability of an international agreement, such as Bretton Woods, to prevent unwarranted competitive depreciation.

But I also expressed the view that, in the special circumstances then prevailing (i.e. in 1947), Britain's international payments and receipts could not be balanced at any rate of exchange. For this reason I welcomed the proposed rule that countries in balance of payments difficulties should be permitted to impose temporary import restrictions while this right should in general be denied to others.

Given all this, it is not surprising that I should have supported international codes of rules on the lines of Bretton Woods and the I.T.O. I was acutely aware that most prewar international economic conferences had done little more than pass pious resolutions on the virtues of free trade which had had no practical results. The early postwar conferences seemed to me much more promising because they had not insisted on rigid doctrines. They recognised that there must be exceptions, carefully controlled, to general principles. Thus 'I.T.O. and I.M.F. neither insist on complete non-discrimination, nor allow full freedom to discriminate. They neither impose a rigid gold standard nor allow full freedom to devalue. They neither insist on free trade nor allow unlimited restriction.'[5] This type of rule seemed to have much more chance of success.

The rules were by no means ideal in all respects. For example, while I supported the principles of the scarce currency clause, I thought — rightly as it turned out — that it needed revision; and in 1951 I was a member of a United Nations group of experts which recommended changes in the operation of some of the rules.[6] But, by and large, they seemed to make good sense from an international point of view and also to be in Britain's interest given the problems confronting us. I believe that my general support has proved justified, at least so far as most of the past quarter of a century or so is concerned.

---

[5] Study 6, p. 185.
[6] The report of the group was entitled 'Measures for International Economic Stability'.

Part One: The Interwar Years

1 The British trade cycle of 1929-37[1]

INTRODUCTION

There exists no one measure that indicates adequately the course of a business cycle. There are many possible indices of activity, while any attempt to measure changes in general economic well-being is confronted with many difficulties. The various indices of activity and prosperity do not always move in the same way or in the same degree, and in order to obtain a general picture it is necessary to examine the changes that have taken place from various points of view.

An attempt will be made, in the first section of this chapter, to describe briefly the movements during the period 1929–37 of some of these general indices, as revealed by the available statistics. A description of changes in employment, unemployment, and output is followed by a discussion of the effects of changes in the terms of trade and the import surplus. Finally, an attempt is made to trace the course of consumption during the period.

In the second main section of the chapter a general picture is given of the varying fortunes of the different industries by an examination, first, of the employment statistics and, secondly, of certain relevant indices of production and activity. In the last section is given a brief account of price and wage movements.

It is hoped that the chapter, which describes the whole period from 1929, may provide some sort of a background for the more detailed studies of the recovery period that fill the rest of the book.

[1] Introductory chapter in 'Britain in Recovery,' published by the British Association in 1938. There are several quotations from later chapters, but page references to these chapters have been deleted to avoid confusion with pages in this volume.

A. GENERAL INDICES OF ACTIVITY AND PROSPERITY

I. EMPLOYMENT, UNEMPLOYMENT, AND OUTPUT

1. Employment

The level of employment is frequently taken as a criterion of the economic situation. The course of insured employment is illustrated in Diagram I by the *Economist* index of employment, which is corrected for seasonal fluctuations. It is seen that employment reached a peak in the summer of 1929, when the number of insured persons in employment was higher than ever before.[2] During 1930 there was a severe fall, but this was checked in 1931, and at the end of that year there was a slight improvement, associated partly with the departure from the gold standard.[3] Employment fell again during 1932 and reached its lowest level in the autumn, about three years after the peak period in 1929. From that time employment expanded steadily for five years and encountered no marked setback until the autumn of 1937, although some slackening of the rate of expansion was noticeable during the latter half of 1934 and the beginning of 1935. The 1929 level of employment appears to have been regained somewhere about the autumn of 1934 or the spring of 1935, and it may therefore be said that, so far as insured employment is concerned, the depression meant a pause of at least five years.

1929–32. Insured employment fell from the peak month of 1929 (September) to the worst month of 1932 (also September) by between 11 and 12 per cent, while if the monthly average for the two years is compared the fall is seen to be between 8 and 9 per cent. It is possible, however, that the fall was greater in insured employment than in employment as a whole. There was no doubt a considerable fall in employment among persons under 16 and over 65 years of age, while agricultural employment also fell (though relatively no more than all insured employment),[4] but employment among domestic workers and other uninsured employees may well have increased. 'Employment' among independent workers and employers, moreover, is likely to be less affected by a depression than employment among insured workers. Indices (2) and (3) in

---

[2] September was the peak month, according to the Ministry of Labour's estimates.
[3] The effects were probably most felt in the textile industries. For a discussion of the largely temporary stimulus given to the cotton, wool textile, iron and steel, and coal-mining industries, the reader is referred to p. 344, 363, 271, and 164 of *Britain in Depression.*
[4] See Table XIV, p. 38.

DIAGRAM I

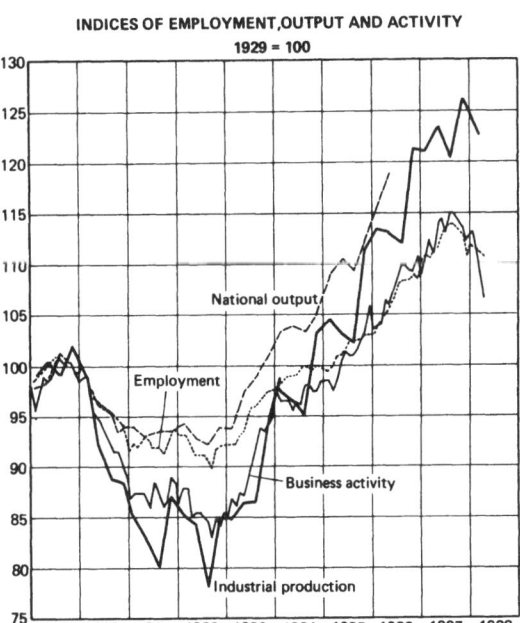

INDICES OF EMPLOYMENT,OUTPUT AND ACTIVITY
1929 = 100

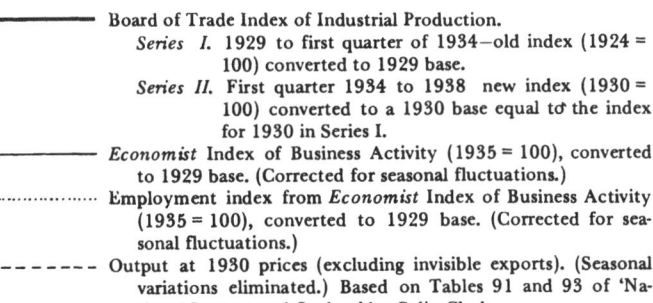

———— Board of Trade Index of Industrial Production.
    Series I. 1929 to first quarter of 1934—old index (1924 =
        100) converted to 1929 base.
    Series II. First quarter 1934 to 1938 new index (1930 =
        100) converted to a 1930 base equal to the index
        for 1930 in Series I.
———— *Economist* Index of Business Activity (1935 = 100), converted
        to 1929 base. (Corrected for seasonal fluctuations.)
··············· Employment index from *Economist* Index of Business Activity
        (1935 = 100), converted to 1929 base. (Corrected for sea-
        sonal fluctuations.)
— — — — Output at 1930 prices (excluding invisible exports). (Seasonal
        variations eliminated.) Based on Tables 91 and 93 of 'Na-
        tional Income and Outlay,' by Colin Clark.

Table I, which are based on Mr. Clark's estimates, suggest that the fall in employment among all wage and small salary earners was only some 4 or 5 per cent, while the proportionate fall in the number of all occupied persons in work was possibly even smaller. (If women working at home were also considered to be 'employed,' the proportionate fall in employment in the widest sense would appear to have been very small indeed.) It should be emphasized, of course, that the figures quoted take no account of short-time working among employers and employees, but it is true, nevertheless, that the fall in total employment after 1929 was relatively smaller than the fall in insured employment.

1929–37. Over the whole period from 1929 to 1937 insured employment increased by between 12 and 13 per cent. Total employment possibly rose somewhat less, as the proportion of the occupied population within the unemployment insurance scheme is said to have been increasing year by year, even before taking account of the various extensions of the Act.[5] The movements of indices (2) and (3), however, suggest that employment as a whole may well have increased by as much as 10 per cent, though probably not by more. This is a rather surprising result, as the population increased over the whole period by only about 3½ per cent, while even the number aged 15 to 64 did not increase much more quickly.

2. Unemployment

For some purposes we are interested in changes, not in employment, but in unemployment, which measures the degree of wastage of the nation's available human resources. There are many difficulties in the measurement of changes of this sort. Some are theoretical. What human resources are in fact 'available'? Some are statistical. These are discussed below in the section by Mr. Robinson. The general movements are, however, clear. Unemployment increased enormously between 1929 and 1932. Both the number and the proportion of insured persons unemployed more than doubled. In 1932 over one-fifth of all persons insured against unemployment were out of work; but if a wider definition than the number of insured persons were given to 'the nation's available human resources,' the proportion would no doubt be somewhat smaller,[6] while if women working at home were included, it would be smaller still.

[5] See Minutes of Evidence taken before the Royal Commission on the Geographical Distribution of the Industrial Population. Tenth Day. Questions 2464–2481.
[6] According to Mr. Clark's definitions and estimates, between 16 and 17 per cent of the 'occupied' population were out of work in 1932. (*Op. cit.*, Table 94.)

TABLE I
General Indices (1929 = 100)

	1929	1930	1931	1932	1933	1934	1935	1936	1937
Employment									
(1) Insured persons in employment	100	96	92	91	95	99	102	107	112
(2) All wage-earners, and salary-earners earning less than £250 p.a., in work	100	97	95	96	97	101	104	—	—
(3) All occupied persons in work	100	98	96	96	98	101	104	—	—
Unemployment									
(4) Insured persons unemployed	100	158	217	227	206	174	162	139	117
(5) Insured persons unemployed: per cent of all insured persons	10.3	15.8	21.1	21.9	19.8	16.6	15.3	12.9	10.6
Output and Activity									
(6) Board of Trade Index of Production: 'old' series	100	92	84	83	88	99	—	—	—
'new' series	—	92	—	—	—	98	105	115	123
(7) London and Cambridge Economic Service: Annual Index of Production	100	92	84	85	93	104	110	118	124
(8) London and Cambridge Economic Service: Quarterly Index of Production	100	89	76	77	82	92	98	107	112
(9) National output of goods and services (excluding 'invisible' exports)	100	96	93	93	98	104	110	—	—
(10) Business Activity — *Economist* Index	100	94	89	85	90	97	102	108	114

(1), (4), (5) Ministry of Labour; persons aged 16–64; excluding agriculture; monthly average; Great Britain.

(1) A deduction is made for those directly involved in trade disputes, and for sickness, etc.

(4), (5) Excluding those directly involved in trade disputes. No extra allowance made for sickness, etc. (The index of *registered* unemployment moves somewhat less violently than index (4).)

(2) Based on Clark, *op. cit.*, Table 28, U.K.

(3) Based on Clark, *op. cit.*, Table 94, U.K.

(6) See note below Diagram 1 for method of conversion.

(7), (8), (10) Converted to 1929 base. (7) 1937 figure provisional.

(9) Based on Clark, *op. cit.*, Tables 91 and 98.

Note. An index of insured persons in employment for the United Kingdom, and with no deduction for sickness, etc., is strictly necessary for comparison with the indices of employment based on Mr. Clark's figures ((2) and (3).) Such an index would not, however, be greatly different from the index given (1), and its use would not affect the main conclusions reached in the text.

1932 was the worst year both for insured employment and for insured unemployment, and after that year unemployment was reduced steadily until the autumn of 1937, when there was a considerable setback. Whereas, however, employment appears to have regained the 1929 level probably in 1934 or 1935, the same is not true of unemployment. The statistics, taken as they stand, suggest that only in the better months of 1937 were the available resources being used as fully as in 1929. The unemployment percentage for the year 1937 was indeed greater than the percentage for any of the years 1924, 1927, 1929, and only slightly lower than for the years 1925 and 1928. Total insured unemployment, also, was higher in 1937 than in 1929. These figures contain many statistical difficulties and are not representative of employment as a whole, but they do suggest that only for a brief period, at the very end of the recovery movement, were the available human resources being used again as fully as during most of the period 1924–29 (excluding, of course, 1926, the year of the General Strike).

3. Output

Changes in the volume of what is produced may differ from changes in employment. We may expect to find both secular and cyclical changes in output per head. The Board of Trade index of production is shown in Diagram I, and the method of linking up the 'old' and the 'new' indices is described in the note below the diagram. Movements of the old index, adjusted for seasonal variations, are shown in the table on p. 9. The general movements of the index are similar in direction to those of the employment index. The unadjusted index reaches a peak in the last quarter of 1929, and the adjusted index in the third quarter. The fall is severe during 1930, but is checked in 1931, and there is a slight recovery at the end of that year which is not wholly seasonal. The index falls again to its lowest level in the third quarter of 1932, and subsequently rises steadily throughout the recovery period, although there is some evidence of a slackening in the rate of expansion during parts of 1934 and 1935. The reversal of the movement in 1937 is seen, not in a fall in the index between the third and fourth quarter, but in a very much smaller rise than in the other recovery years, while between the last quarter of 1937 and the first quarter of 1938 there was a marked fall.

1929–32. The Board of Trade index of production fell, between 1929 and 1932, by about 17 per cent. The London and Cambridge Economic Service annual index (which includes house-building and

TABLE II
Board of Trade Index of Industrial Production: Adjusted for
Seasonal Variations (1924 = 100)
From *Board of Trade Journal*, 28th March, 1935

	Quarter			
	I	II	III	IV
1928	107.7	103.8	103.9	106.1
1929	108.8	112.2	114.6	111.6
1930	109.5	103.3	103.1	96.7
1931	93.2	92.3	92.6	95.2
1932	93.6	94.5	90.7	93.0
1933	93.3	96.9	100.2	102.8
1934	108.6	110.5	109.9	113.6

agriculture) fell by 15 per cent, and the quarterly index (which is less representative) by 23 per cent. (See Table I.) These figures almost certainly exaggerate the fall in the whole national output, where this is given any reasonably comprehensive definition. None of the indices purports to cover the output of many consumers' services which, according to the employment figures shown in a later section, was steadily expanding throughout the period. An index that covered these services would clearly show a smaller fall than the other less comprehensive indices. If we also decided to include in the national output the use of durable consumers' goods, the fall would appear even smaller. The wider the definition, in this respect, the smaller will the fall appear to have been. An index of national output of goods and services is shown in Table I and Diagram I. It is based on Mr. Clark's figures, and covers industry, agriculture, transport, and services. The use of dwelling houses is considered to be part of the national output, but the use of other durable consumers' goods, such as private motor cars, is not. (No deduction is, of course, made for maintenance and depreciation.) The fall in this index from the highest quarter in 1929 to the lowest quarter in 1932 is only about 9 per cent, and the fall between the year 1929 and the year 1932 only 7 per cent. In a later section it will be suggested that the level of consumption was probably well maintained throughout the depression. It seems fairly easy to reconcile this with a fall of only 7 per cent in the national output, although we might have very serious doubts of its validity when faced with figures showing a fall of from 15 to 25 per cent in production in a narrower sense.

1929–37. It is extremely difficult to measure the change in output between 1929 and 1937. The Board of Trade index is not continuous over the whole period. The 'new' index shows a rise, between 1930 and 1937, of 33 per cent. The 'old' index (which did not cover building) fell between 1929 and 1930 by 8 per cent. If we choose to link up these figures, we find a rise of 23 per cent over the whole period. The L.C.E.S. quarterly index rose by only 12 per cent, but this index does not cover building, and is unrepresentative in other ways. The annual index rose in line with the Board of Trade index. The more complete index of the national output fell less after 1929 than the other indices but also rose more slowly between 1932 and 1935. It seems probable that it would show a rise of something like 20 per cent over the whole period, i.e. roughly the same as the proportionate rise in the two other main indices. (Employment in the 'service' industries, as will be shown in a later section, increased relatively to all insured employment.) We may therefore perhaps think of an increase in the 'real' national output of the order of 20 per cent.

4. Output per head

It must always be remembered that any index of 'real' output, where more than one commodity is included, must necessarily take the form of a (weighted) average of indices relating to different types of output. For this reason alone any measure of changes in output per head has a very limited meaning and must be interpreted with caution.[7] We have seen, also, that the various indices of employment and of output, though moving, on the whole, in the same direction, do not move in the same degree. This should make us even more cautious. Only the most tentative generalizations may be suggested.

In the first place, it seems probable that output per person in work, however we may define it, increased over the whole period. On any reasonable and comparable definitions, employment can hardly have increased by more, nor output by less, than 15 per cent. We may also say that output per head of the population increased more than output per person in work. It seems likely, moreover, that most

---

[7] It should also be remembered that most indices of output are partly based on indices of employment.

of this increase in output per head came during the recovery period. It is obvious that output per head of the population, and per person available for work, fell between 1929 and 1932; and the indices suggest that there was at least no increase in output per person in work during that period. No attempt will be made to make more ambitious generalizations than these.

5. Conclusions

All the indices of employment and output that we have considered, and also the *Economist* index of business activity (which is shown in Diagram I), show a fall from a peak in the autumn of 1929 to a low point in the autumn of 1932. They also show that this fall was checked during 1931 and that there was a slight, but temporary, recovery at the end of that year. After 1932 there was a steady rise in all the indices until the autumn of 1937, when there is evidence of a setback. Most of the indices suggest that the recovery was least rapid during parts of 1934 and 1935.

We may say that the 1929 levels of employment, output, and activity were regained at some time during 1934 or 1935, although it was possibly not until 1937 that the available resources were being once more utilized as fully as during the pre-depression period.

We have seen that the indices most commonly quoted probably exaggerate the fall in employment and output betwee 1929 and 1932, and also the degree of wastage of human resources during the depression.

Finally is seems probable that output per person in work increased over the whole period, and that the increase came wholly during the recovery. It is certain that output per head of the population fell between 1929 and 1932 and increased considerably between 1929 and 1937.

II. TERMS OF TRADE AND THE IMPORT SURPLUS

I. For some purposes we may be interested in changes, not in the home output of goods and services, but in the 'final outcome or result of the national labour, including (that is) the volume of goods obtained for that part of the product which is exported to foreign countries,'[8] i.e. in the quantity: home output *minus* exports *plus* imports, or, in the case of this country, home output *plus* what may

---

[8] Haberler, *Prosperity and Depression*, p. 165.

TABLE III
Foreign Trade and the Net National Income

	Exports of U.K. Produce			Retained Imports	
	Net National Income* £ millions	£ millions	As Percentage of Net National Income	£ millions	As Percentage of Net National Income
1924	4035	801	20	1137	28
1929	4384	729	17	1111	25
1932	3844	365	9	651	17
1933	3962	368	9	626	16

*Clark, *op. cit.*, Table 37; and see Chapter 1 for definition.

Note. According to further estimates of the net national income in 1934 and 1935 by Mr. Clark (*op. cit.*, p. 90), and tentative estimates for 1936 and 1937 by the *Economist* (Budget Supplement, 9th April, 1938, p. 12), it would appear that the values of imports and exports respectively formed roughly the same proportions of the net national income throughout the period 1932–37.

The table is intended to convey only a very general impression. It may legitimately be objected that the percentages shown are of doubtful significance. For a discussion of the problems involved, see Dr. E. C. Snow's paper in the *J.R.S.S.* for 1931, entitled 'The Relative Importance of the Export Trade.' Dr. Snow there estimates that the wages, salaries, and remuneration of capital in the export trade represented nearly 24 per cent of the corresponding total for industry, agriculture, and other services in 1924. He also suggests that the fall in the gross value of exports between 1924 and 1930 may exaggerate the true decline in the amount of labour, etc., employed in export.

perhaps be called the 'real' import surplus (of goods and services).[9,10] Changes in this "final outcome of the national labour" may differ from changes in home output when there are unequal proportionate changes in home output and the real import surplus respectively. This real import surplus will increase, other things being

[9] It is, of course, impossible to measure this 'real' import surplus quantitatively. It is possible, however, to correct the annual total values of visible imports and visible exports for changes in average values (the Board of Trade makes such corrections), and to find a series by subtraction which may be said to represent changes in the 'real' (visible) import surplus. (Dr. E. C. Snow has suggested the use of such a method. See *J.R.S.S.*, 1931, pp. 388–9.)

There are admittedly many theoretical difficulties in the method of approach adopted in this section, but it is believed to be less unsatisfactory than other possible methods, and the general conclusions reached in the text are believed to be correct.

[10] Changes in the money import surplus are the net results of changes in the balances on account of (i) international capital movements, (ii) international gold movements, and (iii) income on international investment of all kinds. There may be a case for regarding only movements in the net income from overseas investment as important, but for the purpose of this review we shall discuss movements, from year to year, in the import surplus, for whatever reason they may have taken place.

equal, (i) if the money value of the import surplus increases, or (ii) if there is a general fall in the prices of both exports and imports, or (iii) if average import prices fall relatively to average export prices. Conversely, the real import surplus will decrease if the opposite changes take place.

Notable changes of all three types have taken place during the period under review and the importance for this country is considerable. Table III, which shows the values of visible exports and imports respectively as percentages of the national net income,

DIAGRAM II
(See Table IV)

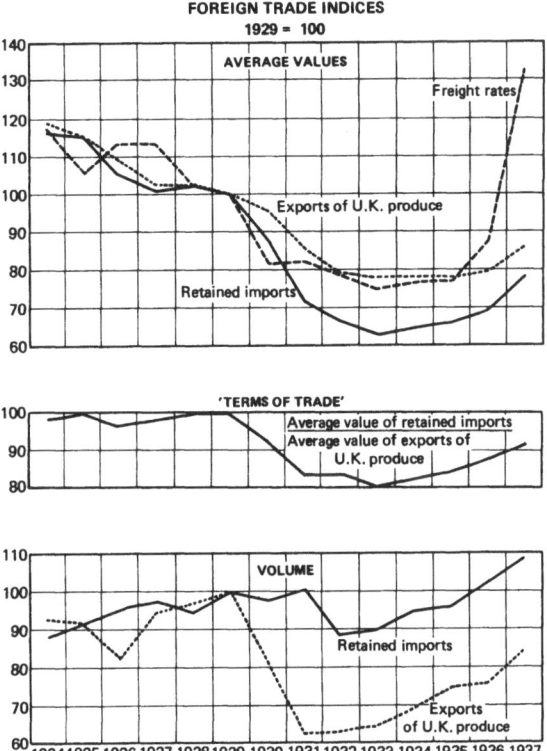

FOREIGN TRADE INDICES
1929 = 100
AVERAGE VALUES
Freight rates
Exports of U.K. produce
Retained imports

'TERMS OF TRADE'
Average value of retained imports
Average value of exports of U.K. produce

VOLUME
Retained imports
Exports of U.K. produce

1924 1925 1926 1927 1928 1929 1930 1931 1932 1933 1934 1935 1936 1937

suggests that foreign trade, though possibly of declining significance
in our national economy, still plays an important part. It follows that
changes in the relation between the volume of imports and the
volume of exports is worthy of consideration.

2. The terms of Trade

The Board of Trade has calculated indices of the average values
of (visible) imports and exports. These are shown in Table IV,

DIAGRAM III
(See Table V)

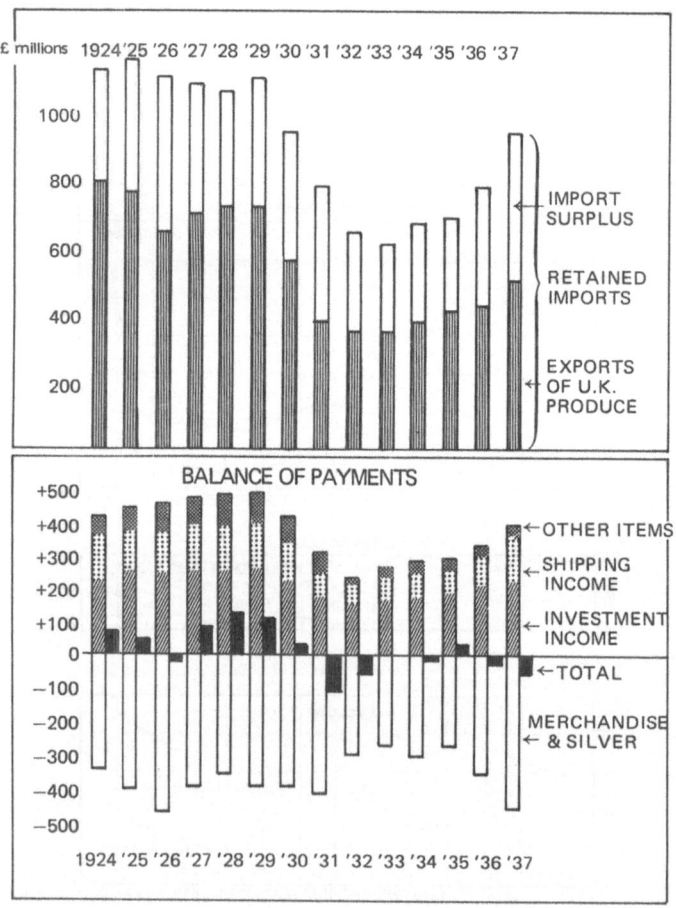

which explains the method of conversion,[11] and in Diagram II. They suggest that, so far as visible exports and imports are concerned,[12] little change took place between 1924 and 1929 in the terms of trade (i.e. in the index representing changes in the ratio: average value of imports ÷ average value of exports). Both indices fell together. During 1930, however, import prices fell much more rapidly than export prices, so that the terms of trade moved in our favour. This tendency continued, though in less marked degree, until 1933.[13] Some explanation may be found by a study of the price indices shown in a later section. It is well known that our imports consist primarily of raw materials and foodstuffs and our exports of manufactured products (coal being an important exception). A reference to Diagram IX below shows that the prices of basic materials and of foodstuffs fell much more markedly during the years of falling prices that followed 1929 than did those of manufactured products.[14] After 1933 the terms of trade moved against us, the tendency being most marked during the period of rapidly rising prices which began about the middle of 1936. During the latter part of 1937, however, the fall in raw material prices, together with the maintenance of the prices of manufactured products, combined to check and reverse the movement. Between the third quarter of 1937 and the first quarter of 1938 average import prices fell markedly while average export prices continued to rise.

One is tempted to describe the experience of this country as typical of the experience, during the course of a trade cycle, of any highly industrialized country that depends to a large extent on imports for its supplies of foodstuffs and raw materials. The terms of trade will move in its favour during the downswing and against it during the recovery. This was the experience of the United Kingdom, not only between 1929 and 1937, but also during the period

---

[11] Particular attention is directed to Note 2 below Table IV, which suggests that the conclusions reached in the text are independent of the particular method adopted in linking up the available indices.

[12] Throughout this section the terms 'visible imports and exports' refer to retained imports and exports of U.K. produce, i.e. re-exports are excluded.

[13] The annual indices do not show the relatively small improvement in the terms of trade during 1931 as compared with 1930. Reference should be made to the quarterly figures.

[14] The Board of Trade indices of the average value of imports of food, drink, and tobacco, and of raw materials, fell more rapidly during the years to 1932 than did the corresponding indices relating to both exports and imports of manufactures. Incidentally, they also fell more rapidly than the indices of average values of *exports* of food, drink, and tobacco, and of raw materials (the price of coal was relatively well maintained). See *Bank of England Statistical Summary*, November, 1934, p. 137, for diagrams.

TABLE IV

Foreign trade: Indices of volume and average value and of freight rates (1929 = 100)

		1924	1925	1926	1927	1928	1929	1930	1931	1932	1933	1934	1935	1936	1937
Average Value															
Retained Imports (based on 1924 quantities)	(a¹)	117	115	105	101	102	100	88	–	–	–	–	–	–	–
(based on 1930 quantities)	(b¹)	115	–	–	–	–	88	71	66	63	65	66	69	–	–
(based on 1935 quantities)	(c¹)	–	–	–	–	–	85	–	–	–	–	66	69	79	–
Exports of U.K. Produce (based on 1924 quantities)	(a¹)	119	116	109	103	103	100	95	–	–	–	–	–	–	–
(based on 1930 quantities)	(b¹)	115	–	–	–	–	95	85	80	78	78	78	79	–	–
(based on 1935 quantities)	(c¹)	–	–	–	–	–	91	–	–	–	–	78	78	79	86
Average Value of Imports ÷ Average Value of Exports (Terms of Trade')	(a)	98	100	97	98	100	100	92	84	84	80	82	85	87	92
Freight Rates	(a)	117	106	113	113	102	100	82	82	78	75	76	77	87	132.5
Volume															
Retained Imports (based on 1924 average values)	(a¹)	88	91	95	98	95	100	98	–	–	–	–	–	–	–
(based on 1930 average values)	(b¹)	89	–	–	–	–	98	100	88	90	95	96	96	108	–
(based on 1935 average values)	(c¹)	–	–	–	–	–	102	–	–	–	–	96	96	102	109
Exports of U.K. Produce (based on 1924 average values)	(a¹)	92	92	82	94	97	100	82	–	–	–	–	–	–	–
(based on 1930 average values)	(b¹)	95	–	–	–	–	82	63	63	64	69	75	76	76	–
(based on 1935 average values)	(c¹)	–	–	–	–	–	86	–	–	–	–	75	75	76	83

(a) *Economist* index of tramp shipping freight rates. The Chamber of Shipping index moves in much the same way as the *Economist* index, but shows a somewhat greater fall after 1929 and subsequently a rather greater rise.

Notes.(1) Board of Trade indices of the average value and volume of imports and exports during the period 1924–37 are available in three series—

(a) 1924–30, based on 1924 quantities and average values respectively (1924 = 100).

(b) 1924 and 1930–36 based on 1930 quantities and average values respectively (1930 = 100)

(c) 1930 and 1935–37 based on 1935 quantities and average values respectively (1935 = 100).

In all cases, these series have been multiplied by factors necessary—

(i) to convert the 1929 figures in series (a) to 100, to obtain series (a¹);

(ii) to convert the 1930 figures in series (b) to the value of the 1930 figures in the corresponding series (a¹), to obtain series (b¹);

(iii) to convert the 1935 figures in series (c) to the value of the 1935 figures in the corresponding series (b¹), to obtain series (c¹).

The figures in italics are shown to the nearest whole number, as also are the converted indices are shown to the nearest whole number, as also are the terms of trade index and the freight rate index, but the diagrams are drawn from more 'accurate' figures.

(2) It is believed that the general conclusions reached in the text would not be altered if other methods of linking up the series were adopted. In particular, the comparison of *relative* movements in the indices referring to exports and imports respectively is little affected. For example, in comparing the years 1930 and 1935, we find that the falls in the average value of *both exports and imports* appear greater in the series (b¹) (which are based on 1930 quantities) than in the series (c¹) (which are based on 1935 quantities). The falls in volume, on the other hand, *of both exports and imports*, appear greater in the series (c¹). For a full discussion, see the *Board of Trade Journal*, 4th March, 1937.

1919–24.[15] Over the whole period from 1929 the position of this country appears, on balance, to have improved, only part of the advantage gained during the years to 1933 having been lost during the recovery. An apparent secular trend was thus continued, because the terms of trade during the period 1924–29 represented an 'improvement,' so far as it can be measured, of some 15 per cent on 1913.[16] The terms of trade in 1913, moreover, were probably more favourable than in most other pre-war years after 1900, while there is also some evidence of a steady 'improvement' in the terms of trade during the last twenty years of the nineteenth century.[17]

So far we have considered only visible exports and imports, and it is necessary to take account of shipping services, this country's most important invisible export (if, as seems correct for this analysis, income from overseas is excluded). It is improbable that our general conclusions require much modification. Shipping income is relatively unimportant in relation to the value of visible exports. The net earnings of British shipping[18] in both 1931 and 1936 were, according to the Chamber of Shipping estimates, between £70 and £75 million, while exports of United Kingdon produce were valued at about £390 million in 1931 and £440 million in 1936. A general index of the average value of exports (including shipping services) would thus differ little from the Board of Trade index (which refers to visible exports only) unless movements in the average value of shipping services diverged considerably from movements in average visible export prices.

The freight rate indices published by the *Economist*, 'Lloyd's List,' and the Chamber of Shipping refer to tramp shipping only, and may not be representative of shipping as a whole. It is hoped, however, that despite this and other difficulties, they are adequate for our present purpose. A marked fall in freight rates during 1929 was checked in 1930 and 1931, and a comparison of the year 1929 with the years 1931 to 1933 suggests that freight rates had fallen more than average export values but less than average import values. It is unlikely that our general conclusion regarding the improvement during this period in the terms of trade need be modified.

[15] See John Inman, 'The Terms of Trade,' *The Manchester School*, 1935, Vol. VI, No. I, for a discussion.

[16] See Inman, *op. cit.*, pp. 47–50, for a discussion.

[17] See Taussig, *International Trade*, and *Economic Journal*, March, 1925.

[18] I.e. gross earnings of British shipping employed in the foreign trade, less expenditure abroad. The Board of Trade figures for net shipping income include disbursements by foreign ships in British ports. For details, see *Board of Trade Journal*, 17th February, 1938, and the paper read before the Royal Statistical Society by Mr. L. Isserlis on 21st December, 1937, entitled 'Tramp Shipping, Cargoes and Freights.'

From about the middle of 1936 freight rates rose very rapidly until September, 1937, after which there was a strong reaction. It appears likely that this rise in freight rates offset considerably, if not completely, the tendency we have noted for the terms of trade to move strongly against this country during 1936 and most of 1937. Between 1936 and 1937, for example, we find that the index of the average value of exports increased by 8 per cent as against 14 per cent in the case of imports. On the other hand, 'the freight indices published by the *Economist*, "Lloyd's List," and the Chamber of Shipping show average increases in the rates in 1937, as compared with 1936, of 52, 51, and 55 per cent, respectively. These index numbers relate to tramp shipping. For tanker tonnage there was an increase of similar or greater magnitude but liner rates are believed not to have advanced to the same extent, though showing a considerable improvement on 1936.'[19] It is quite possible that changes of this order of magnitude necessitate some revision of our general conclusions. The movement of the terms of trade against us during the last two years of the period was much less marked than is sometimes imagined, if we take account of shipping services.[20] Moreover, the improvement over the whole period from 1929 to 1937 was perhaps somewhat greater than is suggested by the Board of Trade indices.

It is necessary to have some idea of the order of importance of changes in the terms of trade for the economy as a whole. The Board of Trade indices show a relative fall, between 1929 and 1933, of something like 20 per cent in average import prices as compared with average export prices. We may perhaps be allowed to think of a '20 per cent improvement in the terms of trade.' Exports of United Kingdom produce were 17 per cent and 9 per cent of the net national income and retained imports 25 per cent and 16 per cent, in 1929 and 1933 respectively. We might perhaps expect the change in the terms of trade to have affected the net national income by something of the order of 5 per cent or less. An estimate by Mr. Colin Clark is in conformity with this rough guess. Between 1929 and 1933 he estimates that real income per person in work (including

[19] *Board of Trade Journal*, 17th February, 193 , p. 231.
[20] The following very rough calculation is presented for what it is worth. Giving weights of 6 and 1 to visible exports and shipping services respectively (on the basis of the estimate given in the text of their relative importance in 1936), and assuming that the increase in the average value of shipping services between 1936 and 1937 was only 40 per cent, we find an increase of about 13 per cent in the average value of exports (including shipping services) as against 14 per cent in the case of visible imports. It should also be remembered that the value of imports includes freight charges, and 68 per cent by value of our total imports was carried in British vessels in 1936. (*Board of Trade Journal*, 17th February, 1938, p. 230)

income from overseas) decreased by about 2 per cent, if no account is taken of changes in the terms of trade. Allowing for changes in the terms of trade, he finds an increase of about 3 per cent over the same period.[21]

3. The Import Surplus

We have seen that between 1929 and 1933 the terms of trade moved in our favour and that at the same time there was a fall in the prices of both imports and exports. Between 1933 and 1937 opposite movements were taking place. If the money value of the import surplus had remained constant, then the real import surplus would have increased between 1929 and 1933 and fallen between 1933 and 1937, i.e. it would have moved in general in a direction opposite to that followed by home output. The 'final outcome of the national labour' would have fluctuated less markedly than home output.

We should perhaps expect this tendency to have been offset by a fall during the depression in income from overseas investment (and so in the money import surplus), and a corresponding rise during the recovery. Investment income, according to the Board of Trade estimates, did in fact fall from £250 million in 1929 to £150 million in 1932, while the item 'Commissions, etc.,' fell from £65 million to £25 million.[22] There was, however, no corresponding decline in the money import surplus. The visible import surplus actually rose between 1929 and 1931, while shipping income fell heavily. The result was a fall in the balance on current account from +£103 million in 1929 to −£104 million in 1931. The abandonment of the gold standard in September, 1931, and the subsequent imposition of tariffs, etc., was indeed followed by a marked reduction in the money import surplus in 1932[23] which considerably reduced the

[21] Clark, *op. cit.,* p. 208, Table 94. The details are:

	1929 £	1933 £	Change £
Real net income per person in work (including income from overseas)	226.0	221.9	− 4.1
Ditto—at consumption prices (i.e. including effect of terms of trade)	221.9	228.8	+ 6.9

[22] This item includes both interest payments on short-term investments and payments for various services rendered, including merchanting commissions on overseas produce, brokers' commissions, and insurance remittances. The item 'is of an ambiguous nature, but seems to partake more nearly of the nature of the income from property than from "export of services".' (Clark, *op. cit.,* p. 92.)

[23] The fall in the volume of imports was especially marked in the case of manufactured products. Indices of volume of retained imports (1930 = 100):

	1931	1932
Food, etc.	108	104
Raw materials	94	96
Manufactures	102	65
Total	103	90

TABLE V
United Kingdom Imports and Exports: Balance of Payments
(Million £'s)

	1924	1925	1926	1927	1928	1929	1930	1931	1932	1933	1934	1935	1936	1937[1]
Total Values														
Retained Imports	1137	1167	1116	1095	1075	1111	957	797	651	626	680	701	787	954
Exports of U.K. Produce	801	773	653	709	724	729	571	391	365	368	396	426	441	522
Balance of Payments														
Net Transactions on Current Account														
(Board of Trade Estimates)														
Merchandise	−337	−393	−463	−386	−352	−382	−386	−407	−286	−258	−284	−275	−346	−432
Silver	−2	+2	—	—	−1	+1	—	−2	−2	−5	−10	+14	+1	−10
	−338	−392	−463	−387	−352	−381	−386	−408	−287	−263	−294	−261	−345	−443
Government Transactions[2]	−25	−11	+4	+1	+15	+24	+19	+14	−24	−2	+7	−2	−3	−4
Shipping Income	+140	+124	+120	+140	+130	+130	+105	+80	+70	+65	+70	+70	+85	+130
Investment Income	+220	+250	+250	+250	+250	+250	+220	+170	+150	+160	+170	+185	+205	+220
Commissions, etc.	+60	+60	+60	+63	+65	+65	+55	+30	+25	+30	+30	+30	+30	+35
Miscellaneous	+15	+15	+15	+15	+15	+15	+15	+10	+15	+10	+10	+10	+10	+10
	+410	+438	+449	+469	+475	+484	+414	+304	+236	+263	+287	+293	+327	+391
Total	+72	+46	−14	+82	+123	+103	+28	−104	−51	—	−7	+32	−18	−52

[1] Provisional.   [2] Including items on capital account.

negative balance on current account, but the net reduction in the total import surplus between 1929 and 1932 was small. (The visible import surplus fell by about £100 million, but shipping income fell by £60 million.)

Between 1929 and 1931 the real import surplus rose enormously,[24] and the fall in home output was offset to a considerable extent. Prices fell greatly, the terms of trade improved and, despite a fall in investment income (in the widest sense), the total money value of the import surplus (taking into account the fall in shipping income) showed a marked increase. Between 1931 and 1932 there was a large reduction in the monetary value of the import surplus, and despite a further fall in prices it seems certain that the real surplus also fell considerably.[25] The 'final outcome of the national labour' must have fallen more than home output, which showed only a small decline. Between 1929 and 1932, however, the net fall in the money import surplus does not appear to have been sufficient to offset the 'favourable' factors (the fall in prices and the improvement in the terms of trade), and the real import surplus increased.[26] The net result was a definite mitigation of the effects of the depression.

Between 1932 and 1933 there was some further fall in prices and some improvement in the terms of trade, but the money import surplus also fell slightly and there was little change in the real import surplus. During the whole period 1932 to 1935 the total money import surplus remained fairly constant, despite a continuous rise in investment income. (The result was a change in the balance on current account from −£51 million in 1932 to +£32 million in 1935.) Meanwhile there were no appreciable net changes either in average values or in the terms of trade. The real import surplus thus

---

[24] According to the indices of volume, the volume of imports was maintained, while the volume of exports fell by between 35 and 40 per cent. The excess of visible imports over visible exports (both being valued on the basis of 1924 average values) increased from £429 million in 1929 to £556 million in 1930, and (on the basis of 1930 average values) from £386 million in 1930 to £548 million in 1931. If we choose to link up these Board of Trade estimates, they suggest that there was a rise of between 80 and 90 per cent in the 'real' *visible* import surplus between 1929 and 1931, while if the decline in shipping income were taken into account the rise in the *total* real import surplus would probably appear to have been greater.

[25] The volume of visible exports was maintained, while the volume of visible imports fell by some 12 per cent. The 'real' visible import surplus in 1932 (on the basis of 1930 average values) was over 20 per cent smaller than in 1931.

[26] The indices show a fall of 12 per cent in the volume of visible imports as against 37 per cent in the volume of visible exports, but as imports are more important than exports we cannot definitely say that the 'real' import surplus increased. If, however, we link up the Board of Trade estimates in the manner indicated in the last footnote but one, we obtain a figure of over 40 per cent as the rise in the real *visible* import surplus. If we took account of shipping, the rise in the *total* real import surplus might appear to have been greater.

remained steady. As, at the same time, home output was increasing, it follows that the 'final outcome' must have risen less rapidly.

During the last two years of the recovery period prices were rising more and more rapidly, while the terms of trade continued to move against us. Between 1935 and 1936, however, these forces appear to have been more than offset by a marked rise in the total money import surplus, and it is probable that the real import surplus rose in line with home output.[27] Between 1936 and 1937, on the other hand, it is doubtful whether the rise in the money import surplus (approximately half of the rise in the visible money import surplus was offset by a marked rise in shipping income) was sufficient to do more than offset the rise in prices and the adverse movement in the terms of trade.[28] Such conclusions as can be drawn from these primitive calculations seem to be that the 'final outcome' rose in line with home output during the earlier part of the last two years of recovery, but lagged behind during the period of very rapidly rising prices. A more marked divergence in the movements of the two quantities was prevented only by a rapid rise in the money import surplus. This rise was greater than the rise in investment income, and the balance on current account declined from +£32 million in 1935 to −£52 million in 1937.

4. Conclusion

The analysis has been a dangerous one, but it is believed that certain broad conclusions may be stated that are not affected by theoretical difficulties. The real import surplus increased enormously between 1929 and 1931. The total money import surplus increased markedly while prices were falling and the terms of trade rapidly improving. The real import surplus fell between 1931 and 1932 as a result of a sharp cut in the money import surplus, but on balance showed a considerable increase between 1929 and 1932. The effects of the depression were thus mitigated and the 'final outcome of the national labour' fell less, between 1929 and 1932, than home output,

[27] According to the indices of volume, the volume of visible imports showed a considerably greater proportionate rise than the volume of visible exports, and therefore, as visible imports are more important than visible exports, we are justified in thinking of a definite increase in the real visible import surplus. On the basis of 1935 average values the real visible import surplus, as defined, appears to have risen by some 15 per cent, i.e. at least in the same proportion as home output.

[28] The volume of visible imports showed an appreciably smaller proportional rise than the volume of visible exports, and the real visible import surplus, on the basis of 1935 average values, appears to have shown only a very small increase. It is hard to say what would be the result of taking shipping services into account.

although the fall in the 'final outcome' between 1931 and 1932 was greater than that in home output.

During most of the recovery period the real import surplus definitely lagged behind home output, which must therefore have risen proportionately more than the 'final outcome'. After 1933 prices were rising and the terms of trade moving against us, while the money import surplus failed to increase appreciably until the last two years of the period, when prices began to rise more rapidly than before.

The full effects of the various forces we have discussed were thus that the 'final outcome of the national labour' fluctuated less widely than home output, while over the whole period from 1929 to 1937 it seems not unlikely that the former quantity increased more than the latter.[29]

During the years after 1929 the annual volume of imports was, on an average, about the same as during the years 1924 to 1929. The volume of exports, on the other hand, was considerably lower. This change was made possible, despite a fall in income from overseas investment (including short-term interest), by three developments. First, the terms of trade were more favourable; secondly, prices in general were lower; and thirdly, while a positive balance on current account was normal during the earlier years, a negative balance was more common during the years after 1929.

III. CONSUMPTION

1. We have seen that employment, in the widest sense, fell between 1929 and the trough of the depression in 1932 by only perhaps 4 or 5 per cent. So far as it is possible to measure such changes quantitatively, we may think of a fall in the national output, including non-industrial output of goods and services, of the order of 7 or 8 per cent, but we have seen that the 'final outcome of the national labour,' which allows for the increase that took place in the real import surplus, must have fallen even less. It was, moreover, the industries producing capital goods (and goods for export) that suffered most severely, and it is therefore quite conceivable that the volume of consumption was maintained and even increased throughout the period.

---

[29] This judgment involves a measurement of the change in the somewhat nebulous real import surplus over a period of eight years, and is even more dangerous than those judgments that concern changes over shorter periods. It may be noted, however, for what it is worth, that the real visible import surplus, as defined, increased by between 60 and 70 per cent between 1929 and 1937.

2. A considerable body of evidence supports this hypothesis. We have seen that the prices of imported foodstuffs fell rapidly after 1929 and it is clear, in the first place, that most wage-earners remaining in full employment benefited by rapidly falling retail prices, especially of foodstuffs, while money wages were relatively well maintained. This point is further discussed in the section on prices and wages. It is possible that the official index exaggerates the fall in the cost of living, which is of course a difficult concept, because of the large weight given to food. For the same reason the rise after 1933 may be exaggerated. The official wage index, on the other hand, probably overstates the rise in wages during the recovery. (See p. 76.)

TABLE VI

	1929	1930	1931	1932	1933	1934	1935	1396	1937[1]
(1) Wage Rates	100	100	98	96	95	96	97	99	103
(2) Cost of Living	100	96	90	88	85	86	87	90	94
(3) 'Quotient' (1) ÷ (2)	100	104	109	109	112	111	111	111	110
(4) Retail Food Prices	100	94	85	82	78	79	81	84	91

[1] Provisional.

(1), (2), and (4). Ministry of Labour indices (converted to 1929 base).
(3). More 'accurate' figures used than shown in (1) and (2).

DIAGRAM IV
(Reproduced by permission of the *Economist*)

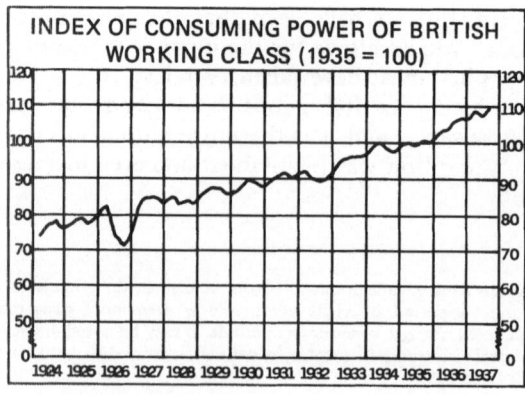

INDEX OF CONSUMING POWER OF BRITISH WORKING CLASS (1935 = 100)

It is more difficult to generalize about the consuming power of the working class as a whole. Large sums, it must be remembered, were paid out to a growing number of unemployed, while unemployment was increasing more rapidly than employment was declining. The movements of an index, compiled by the *Economist*, of 'the total real income of the insured population, employed and unemployed together,'[30] suggest that the general movement was steadily upwards. The rate of increase prevailing between 1924 and 1929 does not even appear to have been seriously checked, except possibly in 1932. The index, as the *Economist* emphasizes, gives only a very rough indication of changes in the consuming power of the working class. It refers only to the section of the population covered by Unemployment Insurance and not to the working class as a whole, while 'its chief defect is that it makes no allowance either for overtime or for such short-time as does not appear in the unemployment returns.' It does, however, suggest the possibility that the consuming power of the working class as a whole was increasing fairly steadily.

An index of expenditure on consumption by persons with annual incomes of less than £250, based on Mr. Clark's figures,[31] points to the same broad conclusion, when taken in conjunction with the official cost of living index. It moves as follows:

1929	1930	1931	1932	1933	1934	1935
100[32]	98	97	94	96	100	104

A very rough comparison of the *Economist* index with that showing changes in the numbers insured against unemployment suggests that the consuming power *per head,* i.e. per actual or potential worker, remained roughly the same between 1929 and 1932, although it is obvious that undue weight must not be attached to the result of such a primitive calculation.[33] The distribution of consuming power, however, became more unequal, those remaining in work gaining at the expense of those thrown out of employment and of those recruits to the labour market who failed to find jobs.

During 1933 the cost of living was still lower than in 1932, while employment was expanding rapidly and unemployment declining.

[30] *Economist,* 1st January, 1938, pp. 13–14. 'The index has been calculated on the basis of the official indices of wage rates and of the cost of living, of the monthly returns of employed and unemployed, and of the returns of sums paid by various agencies to the unemployed.'
[31] *Op. cit.,* Table 12; and p. 251 for definition and method of calculation.
[32] Based on last two quarters.
[33] Some of the statistical difficulties involved are discussed in the section on 'Employment and Unemployment,' by Mr. Robinson.

The indices of consuming power advanced considerably and there can be little doubt that consuming power per head of the working class increased also. The rate of recovery was somewhat slower during parts of 1934 and 1935, but the cost of living remained low and consuming power probably continued to expand. During the remainder of the period until the summer of 1937 the cost of living was rising (and the rise became rapid during 1936 and 1937) but employment and wages were also rising. (Mr. Ramsbottom's wage index, which makes no allowance for overtime earnings, etc., rose as quickly during 1936 as the cost of living index.)[3 4] Consuming power expanded steadily.

During the last quarter of 1937 occurred the first serious setback to employment since the recovery began in 1932. Meanwhile the cost of living continued to rise, although the movement after the middle of 1937 was probably largely seasonal,[3 5] and despite a further rise in wage rates it is possible that consuming power suffered a setback. Broadly speaking, this was the first time during the whole period after 1929 that a marked fall in employment had been accompanied by a marked rise in the cost of living, although it must be remembered that money wage rates were also rising rapidly.

It seems probable, then, that working class consumption expanded fairly steadily throughout the period, but that there may have been some check in 1932 and during the last few months of 1937. During 1930, 1931, and 1932, consumption *per head* was quite possibly maintained, although this meant that some gained at the expense of others. During the rest of the period it seems not unlikely that consumption per head increased.

3.   About those with higher incomes it is more difficult to generalize. Profits form an important part of such incomes, and several relevant figures are shown in Table VII. According to the first index it would appear that profit earning power was immediately and seriously affected by the decline in activity that began at the end of 1929. The general recovery, again, which began at the end of 1932, seems to have had an immediate effect on profits. In short, profits moved very much in line with general business activity and the decline during the depression was severe.

As far as the investor is concerned, however, there is some lag between the earning and the distribution of profits, even when interim dividends are paid. The second index shows the other side of

---

[3 4] See Diagram XII.
[3 5] See Section on 'Cost of Living' below.

TABLE VII
Profits, 1929–37

	1929	1930	1931	1932	1933	1934	1935	1936	1937
(1) Profits *earned* during year (1929 = 100)	100	86	72	70	77	89*	99*	113*	..
(2) Profits *reported* during year (1929 = 100)	100	99	77	63	63	74	86	97	113
(3) Percentage of profits reported during year paid out in dividends	81	82	90	93	88.5	80	78	74	72

*Provisional.

(1) Lord Stamp's general index of aggregate profits (converted to 1929 base): based on *Economist* data and figures of profits assessed to income tax. The index numbers are entered against the years in which, approximately, the profits were made.

(2) *Economist* chain index of total profits after debenture interests based on company reports published during the calendar year.

(3) *Economist* sample.

the story. A large part of profits reported during any calendar year is earned during the previous year,[36] and the lag between the two series is very clear. In view, however, of the practice of declaring interim dividends, and of numerous other difficulties, it is impossible to measure at all accurately the lag between the earning and the distribution of profits.

There may have been some maintenance of dividends, after profit earning power had fallen, for the reason just discussed. A more important reason, however, was the attempt to maintain dividends either by reducing the proportion of profits not distributed, or actually by drawing on reserves previously accumulated. The importance of this policy is illustrated by the figures in the last row of the table.[37] The effect of falling profits on dividends was greatly mitigated and conversely the rise in profits was not allowed to have its full effect on dividends. Over the whole period there seems to have been a tendency towards increasing self-sufficiency in finance. Thus, of the profits reported during 1937 and analysed by the

[36] In a discussion of company reports published during 1937, the *Economist* (15th January, 1938) writes: 'Nearly 70 per cent of the profits in last year's sample were, in fact, *reported* before June 30th and were largely *earned* before March 31st, 1937.'
The *Bank of England Summary* publishes the *Economist's* figures of profits reported. 'The year ending with the third quarter is shown because in general it is probably more representative than any other four consecutive quarters of profits made in the previous calendar year.' (*B.E.S.S.*, October, 1937.)
[37] So far as hidden reserves are diminished during a depression and increased during recovery and prosperity, changes in the proportion will be even more marked.

Economist, 28 per cent were not distributed, as compared with 19 per cent in 1929.[38]

The fall in dividends was postponed and mitigated for the reasons discussed. Interest payments and other income from the ownership of property may be expected to fluctuate less widely than profits, although it must be remembered that the rate of interest was falling throughout a considerable part of the period and that many conversions were successfully carried out, especially during 1932 and the succeeding years. We should expect higher salaries, also, to fluctuate less than profits, and in general it would seem unlikely that the higher incomes fell by nearly as much as the 30—35 per cent suggested by the indices of profits.

TABLE VIII
Persons with Incomes over £250
Indices (1929 = 100)

	1929	1930	1931	1932	1933	1934	1935
Spendable Income (after paying taxes)	100	86	74	69	79	84	92
Consumption Expenditure	100*	98	91	91	89	90	99

*Based on last two quarters.

Based on Clark, *op. cit.,* Table 112; and see pp. 250—51 for definition and method of construction.

However, Mr. Colin Clark's figures of the spendable incomes (after paying taxes) of persons with incomes of over £250 a year show a drop of about 30 per cent between 1929 and 1932. On the other hand, expenditure by such persons on consumption goods and services shows a much smaller decline during the depression. 'Up to the beginning of 1931,' he writes, 'they continued spending at practically the 1929 level, although their incomes had heavily diminished. There was then a fairly rapid fall in the level of consumption of about 10 per cent. This level of consumption persisted till the end of 1934, two years after the rise in incomes had begun. During 1935 and 1936 there has been a rapid increase in consumption.'[39]

[38] The reports of 2279 companies, issued during 1937, were analysed by the *Economist,* as compared with 1770 companies in 1929.
[39] Clark, *op. cit.,* p. 254.

The lag referred to between changes in income and expenditure respectively may be the result partly of the lag between the earning and distribution of profits. 'Consumption' in the quotation refers to expenditure on consumption and, although we have no consumption price index applicable to the richer classes, it is probable that the 10 per cent fall in expenditure would be offset to a considerable extent by lower prices. The possibility must, however, be recognized that a price index applicable to consumption by the richer classes might fall considerably less than the Ministry of Labour cost of living index (which fell by 15 per cent between 1929 and 1933). It may be that many goods and services bought by the richer classes have conventional prices. Again, it has been suggested that, in view of the large expenditure by the rich on personal services, a wage index is more applicable than a retail price index. (The various wage indices fell by only 5 per cent during the depression,[40] although it is doubtful whether this figure has much relevance.) The rich, again, spend a smaller proportion of their income on food, the prices of which showed a relatively large fall between 1929 and 1933. Finally it must be realized that the idea of changes in the volume of consumption of the rich is an even more difficult one than that of changes in 'real' working class consumption.

On the whole we may, perhaps, conclude that consumption by the rich was comparatively well maintained during the depression, and expanded during the recovery, although there are indications that this expansion was somewhat delayed. Whether or not consumption was maintained in this way despite a fall in incomes of the order suggested by Mr. Clark's figures, and to what extent it may have meant 'living on capital,' need not concern us here.

It is interesting that consumption by the richer classes should have been so well maintained despite the great fall in security values between 1929 and 1932. Certain luxury trades no doubt suffered. Security values fell again during 1937, after a long period from the middle of 1932 during which the tendency had been steadily upwards (although gilt-edged reached their peak about the end of 1934). Despite a continued increase in declared profits, certain luxury trades were badly hit during the latter part of 1937. The Bank of England indices of retail sales showed marked increases between the last quarters of 1936 and 1937 in all the geographical divisions except Central and West End London, where the index showed a decline.

[40] See Section *C* III.

TABLE IX
Bank of England Index Numbers of Retail Sales
Average Daily Sales (1933 = 100)

Last Quarter	London, Central and West End	London, Suburban	Provincial, England and Wales	Scotland	Great Britain
1936	137	140	131	123	133
1937	134	151	142	131	142

4. It seems probable that total real consumption never fell, after 1929, much below the 1929 level. (See Table X.) It may quite easily have expanded, especially during 1930. In that year employment and prices were falling rapidly, but wages had not yet been much affected and unemployment pay was relatively good. Dividends were probably fairly well maintained, and there appears to have been no fall in expenditure by the richer classes. During 1931 and 1932 there was probably no further significant expansion. Wages fell, small savings were no doubt exhausted, and unemployment pay became less satisfactory after the changes that followed the crisis of September, 1931. The value of consumption by those in the higher income groups also fell. After 1932 the upward movement was renewed and

TABLE X
Total Consumption
Indices (1929 = 100)

	1929	1930	1931	1932	1933	1934	1935	1936	1937
(1) Total Value of Consumption	100	98	95	94	94	97	102	110	118
(2) Prices of Consumption Goods and Services	100	95	93	92	90	90	91	—	—
(3) Cost of Living (Working Class)	100	96	90	88	85	86	87	90	94.5

(1) Based on Clark, *Economic Journal*, June, 1937; 'National Income and Outlay,' Table 72; and see Chapter VII for definition, method of construction, etc. Index for 1937 based on figures given in *A Commercial Barometer*, published by Messrs. Pritchard, Wood & Partners, Ltd.

(2) Based on Clark, *op. cit.*, Table 89.

(3) Ministry of Labour.

continued until 1937, when it was checked and probably reversed.[41]
These latter developments accompanied a fall in security values, a
rapid rise in the cost of living, and a decline in employment during
the last few months of the year.

In general, it was possible for working class consumption to be
maintained and increased because of the persistence of relatively
stable wage rates and large aggregate payments to the unemployed, in
the face of rapidly falling prices. The richer sections, on the other
hand, maintained their consumption, at first perhaps by living on
profits made during the immediately preceding, and more prosperous, period, and later by a reduction in saving, which may have taken
the form of 'living on capital.' A large part of this reduction in saving
was carried out on their behalf by companies, which adopted a
liberal dividend policy.

5. The following tables (XI and XII), showing certain particular
indices of consumption, rather tend to confirm our general conclusion. The volume of food imports, it is seen (Table XII),
increased rapidly between 1928 and 1931 and remained above the
1929 level in every subsequent year. Table XI suggests that the
supplies, *per head of the population,* of many foodstuffs were
maintained or increased during the depression that followed 1929.
The table includes figures for eighteen rather broad categories of
food, drink, and tobacco. It covers most of the items in the Ministry
of Labour's retail food price index, though in less detail, and includes
as well figures for the consumption of beer, spirits, tobacco, fruit,
cocoa, coffee, and poultry. In 1930 the supplies per head of only six
out of the eighteen items failed to equal or exceed the supplies per
head in 1929. In 1931 only four items failed to reach the 1929 level,
and in 1932 eight (two by the narrowest of margins). If we exclude
beer and spirits, supplies of both of which fell after 1929, the
number of 'failures' in 1930, 1931, and 1932 respectively become
four, two, and six, out of sixteen. In the case of ten items, supplies
per head equalled or exceeded the 1929 level in each of the three
succeeding years. The figures, of course, make no allowance for any
substitution of inferior qualities that may have occurred, but they do

---

[41] An index of the *volume* of retail trade, recently compiled by the *Economist,* supports this
view, although it must be remembered that the index has inevitable limitations. Its
movements suggest that 'in the first three months of 1937, the volume of retail trade was
still higher than a year earlier; but sales in the second quarter and the third quarter were no
higher than during the corresponding months in 1936. In the last quarter, however, the
index of the volume of retail turnover actually fell below the figure for the corresponding
period of 1936.' (*Economist,* 30th April, 1938, p. 243, where the method of construction
of the index is also described.)

TABLE XI

Supply of Certain Foods and Drinks and of Tobacco per Head
of Population

	Unit	1929	1930	1931	1932
1. Beef and veal	lb	69.3	*66.5*	*63.8*	*62.2*
2. Mutton and lamb	lb	28.6	28.6	30.9	33.7
3. Pigmeat and lard	lb	46.8	47.6	53.6	55.0
4. Fish	lb	43.8	48.5	45.9	*44.9*
5. Wheat and flour	lb	343	*330*	355	*340*
6. Apples	lb	27.8	*26.1*	*22.5*	*25.4*
7. Bananas	lb	10.6	10.6	11.5	12.3
8. Citrus fruits	lb	26.4	28.2	29.6	27.0
9. Refined sugar	lb	89.1	89.6	96.1	91.6
10. Cocoa	lb	2.82	*2.76*	2.96	*2.81*
11. Coffee and chicory	lb	0.910	0.927	0.941	*0.863*
12. Tea	lb	9.3	9.6	10.0	9.8
13. Beer	gallons proof	16.1	*15.7*	*13.6*	*11.0*
14. Spirits	gallons	0.277	*0.251*	*0.234*	*0.211*
15. Tobacco	lb	3.24	3.31	3.27	*3.23*
16. Milk equivalent of milk, butter, cream, and cheese	gallons	76	79	85	88
17. Eggs	number	144	153	158	149
18. Poultry	lb	4.2	4.5	4.8	4.6

Italics denote quantities smaller than in 1929.

Sources: 1—15. See *Bank of England Statistical Summary*, February, 1934.
16—18. Chapters on Agriculture in Part II of *Britain in Recovery*.
Items 3—15 refer to United Kingdom; items 1, 2, 16 to Great Britain.
Figures for items 1 and 2 refer to year ended the following 31st May.
5. Expressed as grain.
6, 8. Excluding imports of pulp and preserved fruit.
10. And preparations thereof.
13. Home production (which forms the bulk of the supply) calculated at a standard gravity of 1055°.

confirm in a general way the conclusion that the consumption of foodstuffs was maintained. Tobacco consumption, also, does not appear to have suffered, although the consumption of alcoholic drinks fell off considerably. The latter movement may have been partly secular. The consumption of beer and spirits per head has fallen steadily during the present century and, although there was some increase during the recovery period, the 1936 figures were considerably below those for 1929.[42]

[42] See the *Economist*, 26th March, 1938, for a discussion.

TABLE XII
Indices of Consumption

		1928	1929	1930	1931	1932	1933	1934	1935	1936	1937
1. Retained imports of food, drink, and tobacco (volume)—											
(a) based on 1924 average values (1924 = 100)	Index	101	105	106	—	—	—	—	—	—	—
(b) based on 1930 average values (1930 = 100)	Index	—	—	100	108	104	102	103	102	105	—
(c) based on 1935 average values (1935 = 100)	Index	—	—	100	—	—	—	—	100	102	103
2. Distributive trades — employment	Thousands	1523	1574	1608	1655	1709	1751	1782	1781	1842	1879
3. Wireless receiving licences issued during year beginning 1st April[1]	Thousands	2780	3091	3647	4620	5497	6260	7012	7618	8131	—
4. Laundries, dyeing and dry-cleaning employment	Thousands	124	129	130	134	135	139	141	141	155	163
5. Hotel, public house, restaurant, boarding-house, club, etc, service-employment	Thousands	289	304	302	314	315	332	346	358	368	379
6. Entertainment, sport, etc. — employment	Thousands	62	66	65	73	78	86	91	97	107	116
7. Private cars in use — September	Thousands	901	998	1075	1104	1149	1227	1334	1505	1675	1834
8. New registrations of private cars — year ended 30th September	Thousands	161	169	156	144	146	182	220	272	302	327
9. Motor cycles in use — September	Thousands	721	740	733	633	606	568	553	521	510	492
10. Telephone stations at 31st March	Thousands	1644	1768	1896	1996	2069	2137	2225	2388	2579	2827
11. Letters, printed papers, newspapers, and post cards delivered (year beginning 1st April)	Millions	6230	6400	6475	6540	6640	6753[2]	6935[2]	7345[2]	7690[2]	—
12. Main line railways — passenger-journeys: number	Millions	—	1187	1161	1097	1069	1084	1128	—	—	—
13. Main line railways — passenger-journeys: average length	Miles	15.78	15.78	15.32	—	15.13	—	16.65	—	—	—

All series refer to the United Kingdom, except 12 and 13 which refer to Great Britain.

Sources: 　1, 　　　　*Board of Trade Journal.*
　　　　　2, 4, 5, 6. 　　See Table XIV.
　　　　　3, 10, 11. 　　Statistical Abstract for the United Kingdom.
　　　　　7, 8, 9, 12, 13. 　Relevant chapters in Part II of *Britain in Recovery* and in *Britain in Depression.*

[1] With yearly renewal of licences the number in force at end of year is very nearly equal to the number issued during the year.
[2] Inclusive of sample packets, reintroduced in May, 1932.

Table XII shows that employment in the distributive trades expanded steadily throughout the depression, and it is doubtful whether this would have happened in the face of declining consumption. It is interesting to note, however, that employment in these trades expanded far less rapidly during the recovery, and this may denote an excessive expansion during the depression.

Certain indices of 'luxury' consumption rose throughout the period. The rate of growth in the number of wireless sets in use was accelerated during the depression years, while there was a steady expansion of employment in laundries, dyeing and dry-cleaning, in hotels, restaurants, etc., and in the entertainments and sports industries. Wireless sets were rapidly becoming cheaper and improving in quality, but the very rapid growth in their use may have been the result partly of lower prices for food and clothing combined with relatively stable wages. Considerable parts of those money incomes that were maintained at something like the pre-depression level must have been set free and spent, to some extent, on 'luxuries,' many of which were also becoming cheaper. It is held by some that the rise in real wages also provided an important stimulus to increased house-building activity.

There was a continuous expansion in the use of such durable consumers' goods as private cars and houses, although after 1929 new sales of cars declined temporarily, and the rate of expansion in the number in use was checked. The same thing is true of telephones. The number of motor cycles in use, on the other hand, declined steadily throughout the whole period from 1929 to 1937, 'the chief causes of the decline being the raising of the age limit for driving licences from 14 to 16 years, the high rate charged for compulsory third party insurance, and the publicity given to fatal accidents to this class of road user.' The number of letters, etc., delivered continued to increase, but the use by passengers of the main line railways fell off considerably during the depression.

Some of the series quoted are not completely satisfactory indices of consumption, but they agree in general with our conclusion that consumption was relatively well maintained throughout the depression. In the next section it will be shown that employment in the industries producing primarily consumption goods (other than the industries mentioned above) fell only slightly after 1929.

B. ANALYSIS BY INDUSTRIES

1. EMPLOYMENT

The Ministry of Labour figures of employment among persons insured against unemployment form the chief source of information regarding the course of employment in the various industries. It must be stressed at the outset that these figures should be interpreted with caution. In the first place, a large body of persons not insured against unemployment is excluded. Secondly, the classification is, in general, 'industrial' rather than 'occupational.' Thus clerical and distributive workers employed in a manufacturing industry will appear under that industry, and not under the relevant 'service' industry. Road transport workers employed by firms engaged primarily in retail or wholesale trade will appear under the distributive trades and not under road transport. Those employed in contracting work may appear under either 'public works contracting' or 'local government service.'[4 3] Despite these difficulties, however, the figures may be used fairly safely to illustrate broad tendencies.

1929–37. A brief description will first be given of the main trends over the whole period 1929–37. During this period there was an increase of 12 or 13 per cent in the number of insured persons in employment, but it is possible that the proportionate increase would appear somewhat smaller if uninsured persons were included. (See p. 6.) Given any reasonable definition of employment it seems fairly safe to think of an increase over the whole period of between, say, 8 and 13 per cent. This estimate is sufficiently accurate for the purposes of this section.

Table XIII shows the changes that have taken place in employment in the various main industrial groups into which the Ministry of Labour figures are classified. Figures relating to agriculture are also given.

There has been an absolute decrease in employment in the extractive industries (mining, quarrying, and agriculture). Employment in the manufacturing industries has increased at roughly the same rate as total employment, possibly slightly more slowly, while employment in the building and contracting, and in what are sometimes called the 'service,' industries (5–9) has increased relatively to total employment. As a result, the proportion of insured

---

[4 3] For a discussion of these points, see the Minutes of Evidence taken before the Royal Commission on the Geographical Distribution of the Industrial Population. Tenth day. Evidence submitted by Mr. Humbert Wolfe, Ministry of Labour. Questions 2464–81.

TABLE XIII
Insured Persons in Employment (Aged 16—64)
(June)

Industry Group	Numbers in Employment (Thousands)		Increase (+) Decrease (−) 1929—37	
	1929	1937	Thou-sands	Per cent
1. Fishing	26	28	+2	+11
2. Mining and Quarrying	968	794	−174	−18
3. Manufacturing	5,394	5,948	+554	+10
4. Building and Public Works Contracting	890	1,119	+229	+26
5. Transport and Distribution	2,286	2,693	+407	+18
6. Gas, Water, and Electricity Supply	153	203	+50	+32
7. Miscellaneous Serivces[1]	626	835	+209	+33
8. Commerce, Banking, Insurance, Finance	223	260	+37	+17
9. National and Local Government Services	365	446	+81	+22
All Industries and Services	10,931	12,327[3]	+1396	+13
Agriculture[2]	888	741	−147	−17

	Employment as Percentage of All Insured Employment	
	1929	1937[3]
Mining and Quarrying	8.9	6.4
Manufacturing, Building, and Contracting	57.5	57.3
'Service' Industries (5—9)	33.4	36.0

Ministry of Labour Gazette.

[1] Including hotel, boarding-house, etc., services; professional services, laundries, dyeing and dry cleaning; and entertainments, sports, etc.
[2] All employees in Great Britain on holdings of more than one acre on one day in June. Ministry of Agriculture, etc.
[3] Excluding agricultural workers, who first became insurable against unemployment in May, 1936.

persons employed in manufacturing, building, and contracting has remained about the same, at well over one-half, although if a wider definition of employment were taken this proportion would be smaller. The proportion employed in the extractive industries has declined, while the proportion engaged in the 'service' industries has increased to about 36 per cent of all insured employment. This analysis, it must be emphasized again, is based on an industrial classification, and gives no direct information as to changes in the relative importance of different occupations. The suggestion of the figures that the transport and distribution group has shown a relative increase is possibly misleading. Allowance must be made for a considerable decline in the employment of permanent railway workers (who are not included in the figures),[44] and it is doubtful whether, even after allowing for any increase in the number of road transport workers classified under other industries, the transport and distribution group has done more than keep pace with the growth of employment as a whole.

A more detailed study is necessary of the course of employment in the various industries. In Table XIV these are classified into three main groups. (See also Diagram V.) 'Declining' industries are those in which employment has declined between 1929 and 1937; industries showing a 'normal' expansion are those in which employment has increased in something like the same proportion as total employment; while industries showing a 'super-normal' expansion are those in which employment has shown a considerable increase relatively to total employment. About three-quarters of insured employment are accounted for in the table (and accompanying diagram) while figures for agriculture and railways are given that do not appear in the Ministry of Labour's statistics of insured employment. The annual figures of employment do not refer to one month only and may be regarded as fairly representative of employment during the year.[45]

There was a marked decline in employment in three important industrial groups, namely, textiles (especially cotton), coal-mining, and agriculture. Employment in shipbuilding and ship repairing (and marine engineering) also fell considerably. The numbers engaged in water transport fell somewhat, the decline being confined to shipping, while the railway companies, as we have seen, were employing considerably fewer persons in 1937 than in 1929.

Among the industries in which employment expanded absolutely but not relatively to employment as a whole we find three large groups producing primarily consumers' goods, namely, clothing; food, drink, and tobacco; and paper, printing, etc. These three

[44] Only non-permanent railway workers are insured against unemployment, and so included in the figures. The employment of such workers shows an increase between 1929 and 1937. On the other hand, the more complete employment figures published by the railway companies show a considerable decrease (see Table XIV). These figures are, of course, more comprehensive than the figures of insured employment in other industries and therefore not strictly comparable.

[45] See note below Table XIV.

TABLE XIV
Employment: By Industries
(United Kingdom)

	Numbers Employed (Thousands)			Indices[1]		
				1929 = 100		1932 = 100
	1929	1932	1937	1937	1932	1937
'Declining' Industries						
1. Cotton	480	359	361	75	75	100
2. Coal-mining	900	689	739	82	77	107
3. Agriculture[2]	888	809	741	83	91	92
4. Shipbuilding and Ship-repairing	155	66	133	86	43	202
5. Railways[3]	642	598	600	93	93	100
6. Water Transport (Shipping, Dock, Harbour, River, Canal)	234	213	227	97	91	106
7. Woollen and Worsted	206	182	199	97	88	109
'Expanding' Industries						
(a) *'Normal' Expansion*						
(i) *Little affected by depression*						
8. Clothing (including Hosiery)	632	608	675	107	96	111
9. Food, Drink, and Tobacco	474	464	527	111	98	114
10. Paper, Printing, etc.	358	374	414	112	101	111
(ii) *Greatly affected by depression*						
11. Iron and Steel Manufacture	231	146	255	110	63	175
12. Engineering (including Electrical Engineering)	687	507	779	113	74	154

Total insured in July (16—64 only) less average of unemployed in February, May, August, November. No deduction is made for direct participation in trade disputes, sickness, etc. *Bank of England Statistical Summary*, December, 1937; *Ministry of Labour Gazette.*

Employment in the industries selected (excluding agriculture and railways) represented over three-quarters of all insured employment in 1929.

[1] These indices, being calculated from the approximate figures in the first three columns, are subject to a small error.

[2] Number of workers employed on agricultural holdings of more than one acre, in *Great Britain*, on one day in June. Ministry of Agriculture, etc.

[3] Total number of persons employed by the railway companies of *Great Britain* in one week in March. The totals comprise all those receiving salaries or wages for the full week in

TABLE XIV (*continued*)

	Numbers Employed (Thousands)			1929 = 100	Indices[1]	1932 = 100
	1929	1932	1937	1937	1932	1937
(*b*) *'Supernormal' Expansion*						
(i) *Expansion throughout depression*						
13. Distributive Trades	1,574	1,709	1,879	119	109	110
14. Road Transport (including Tramway and Omnibus)	311	332	378	122	107	114
15. Miscellaneous Consumers' Services[4]	499	528	658	132	106	125
16. Gas, Water, and Electricity Supply	152	155	201	132	102	130
17. Miscellaneous Electrical Industries (Engineering; Wiring and Contracting; Cables, Apparatus, Lamps, etc.)	186	202	317	170	109	157
(ii) *Decline during depression*						
18. Building	705	605	899	128	86	148
19. Miscellaneous Metal Trades (excluding Electrical Trades)[5]	380	332	490	129	87	147
20. Motor Vehicles, Cycles, and Aircraft	228	199	335	147	87	168
All insured Industries and Services (excluding Agriculture)	10,805	9,951	12,221	113	92	123

question, together with the equivalent number of full-time workers in cases where employees were paid for less than the complete week. The figures include those employed in ancillary businesses, comprising canal, dock, quay, and marine staff, motor omnibus and passenger road vehicles staff, and hotel, refreshment-room, dining car, and laundry staff. Ministry of Transport.

[4] Hotel, public house, restaurant, boarding-house, club, etc., service; laundries, dyeing and dry cleaning; entertainments and sport.

[5] Stove, grate, pipe, etc., and general iron founding; hand tools, cutlery, saws, files; bolts, nuts, screws, rivets, nails, etc.; brass and allied metal wares; heating and ventilating apparatus; watches, clocks, plate, jewellery, etc.; metal industries not separately specified.

[6] Preliminary.

DIAGRAM V
(see Table XIV)

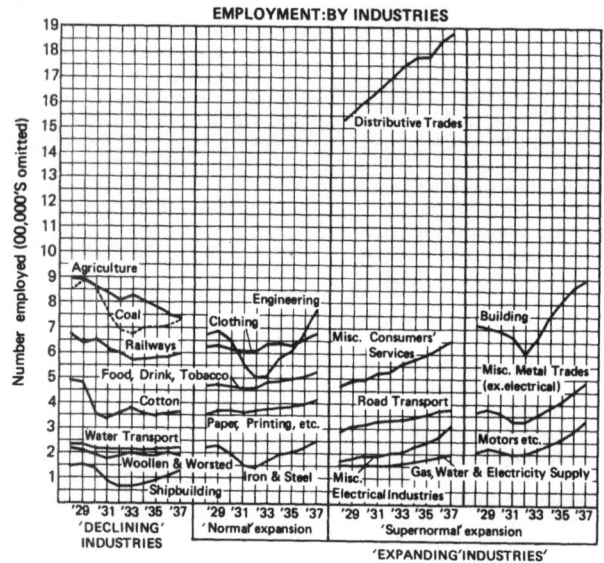

groups were affected relatively little by the depression. Two important heavy industry groups, iron and steel and engineering, also
showed a 'normal' expansion over the whole period, although they
were severely affected by the depression. The 'normal' expansion in
the large engineering group, however, conceals a decline in marine
engineering and a relatively large expansion in electrical and constructional engineering.

In the distributive trades and in road transport the increase in
employment was somewhat greater than the average, the increase in
road transport employment being, as we have seen, offset to a large
extent by the decline in railway employment. Employment in a
group of 'luxury' consumers' services (hotels, entertainments, laundries, etc.) showed a large increase. This was especially marked in the
case of those classified under 'entertainments, sport, etc.,' employment in this group increasing by about 75 per cent. There was a
marked and important expansion in the building industry and a very

rapid growth in the industries specifically connected with electricity, the latter expansion being to some extent dependent on the former. Employment in the motor vehicles, cycles, and aircraft group increased by nearly 50 per cent, and finally we find a considerable expansion in a group of miscellaneous metal trades. This group includes certain industries connected with building which showed a marked expansion, notably those producing stoves, grates, pipes, etc., and heating and ventilating apparatus. It includes also a large group of 'metal industries not separately specified,' employment in which increased rapidly. This may possibly represent an increase in the production of 'new' commodities.

The most striking features of the period suggested by the available statistics are, on the one hand, the decline in several old-established industries, notably cotton, coal-mining, and agriculture. On the other hand, we find a rapid expansion in those industries connected with building, the motor vehicle, electricity, and recreation.

1929–32. The year 1932 was, we may assume, the trough of the depression, and it is therefore convenient to consider first the period from 1929 to 1932, and then the recovery period from 1932 to 1937. The fall in employment during the first three years was highly selective. Employment actually rose in twenty out of ninety-nine industries distinguished in the Ministry of Labour figures,[46] the total increase in employment in these industries being about 300,000. The consumers' goods industries, so far as we can easily distinguish them, were relatively little affected by the depression. Employment declined only slightly in the clothing and food industries, and remained about the same in the paper and printing group. In many of the important consumers' services there was at the most a check in the rate of expansion. This is true, for example, of the hotel group, of laundries, entertainments, road passenger transport, and the distributive trades. In the last group, indeed, employment actually increased more rapidly between 1929 and 1932 than during the subsequent recovery period. The electrical industries, also, appear on the whole to have expanded, despite a decline in electrical engineering. Finally, there was a marked rise in public works contracting and local government service (especially between 1929 and 1931).

The effects of the depression were most marked, first, in the heavy industry groups, iron and steel, engineering and shipbuilding. The first two groups were subsequently successful, as we have seen, in

---

[46] In presenting certain statistics, other than employment figures, the Ministry of Labour further subdivides a small number of these industries.

staging a full recovery, while shipbuilding, in which employment fell by nearly 60 per cent, failed to recover to the 1929 level. Secondly, we find a severe fall in two of our major 'declining' industries, coal-mining and cotton, employment in which subsequently showed little recovery. Employment in this group of five large industries fell between 1929 and 1932 by about 28 per cent as compared with a fall of only 8 per cent in all insured employment. The whole group accounted for only 22 per cent of all insured employment in 1929; yet between 1929 and 1932 employment in the group fell by as much as 700,000 as against a *net* decline of about 850,000 in all industries, and a *gross* decline of considerably less than 1¼ millions. (By 'gross decline' is meant the total decline in all the seventy-nine industries, distinguished by the Ministry of Labour, that showed a fall in employment.) Considerable declines in building, textiles other than cotton, and in the motor and miscellaneous metals groups account for a further quarter of a million of the gross decline. These figures illustrate clearly the selective nature of the incidence of depression. The analysis is necessarily far from detailed, but it is believed that the broad impression gained is correct.

1932–37. During this period the only important industry to show a continued decline in employment was agriculture, but, of the other 'declining' industries, coal-mining, cotton, and railways all failed to recover significantly. What improvement there was in coal-mining employment came mostly at the end of the period. Other textile industries showed some recovery, but barely regained the 1929 level of employment.

Employment in the industries producing primarily consumption goods and services, so far as they can be distinguished, expanded less rapidly than total insured employment, which increased by nearly one-quarter. This is true of the clothing, food, and paper groups, of the distributive trades, and of road transport of both passengers and goods. Employment in the distributive trades actually increased less quickly than during the period 1929–32, and the proportionate increase between 1932 and 1937 was not much greater than in coal-mining. In the 'luxury' services group (hotels, laundries, entertainments, etc.), the proportionate increase in employment was about the same as in all insured employment. It is noteworthy, however, that employment in the entertainments and sports group (and in the industries manufacturing toys, games, and sports requisites) increased by between 40 and 50 per cent.

The expansion was most marked, first, in the heavy industries which were so badly hit by the depression, iron and steel, engineering and shipbuilding. Secondly, we find a rapid expansion in the building, motor, electrical, and miscellaneous metals groups (the expansion in the last group being associated to a large extent with the building boom). Employment in all those industries (Numbers 4, 11, 12, 17, 18, 19, 20 in the table) formed only one-fifth of all insured employment in 1932. Their expansion between 1932 and 1937, however, represented one-half of the total increase in insured employment.

The expansion in employment during the recovery period was thus very unevenly distributed, just as the decline during the earlier period was highly selective. Over the whole period the most violent fluctuations were apparent in the three heavy industrial groups — a severe fall followed by a rapid recovery. These groups were accompanied in their downward plunge by coal and cotton (two of the major declining industries) and in their recovery by several of the rapidly expanding industries, notably those connected with building, motors and aircraft, electricity and entertainment.

The importance of the part played by the building expansion in the general recovery movement is fully discussed in the chapter on building in Part II of *Britain in Recovery*. In view, however, of the importance of the subject it may be permissible to deal further with it in this section. Certain figures given in Part II will be utilized.

Employment in the building industry throughout the period constituted only 6 to 7½ per cent of all insured employment. This proportion, however, gives a false impression of the contribution of building to the recovery. The increase in building employment alone represented 13 per cent of the total increase in insured employment between 1932 and 1937, and as much as 20 per cent of the increase between 1932 and 1935. The effect of increased purchases of building materials on employment is more difficult to assess, but we may perhaps assume that the cost of materials used in building is something like one and a half times the labour cost.[47] It is maintained, moreover, that a change in house-building activity has a particularly rapid and widespread effect on other industries, especially as 'the materials used are almost entirely obtained from, and manufactured in, this country.' Finally, it is improbable that there were large stocks of materials available in the early stages of the

---

[47] Sir Harold Bellman suggests below that in the building of a *house* the cost of labour and materials respectively are in the ratio 38:62 (or 100:163). The figures relating to firms in the building *and contracting* trades that furnished returns of wages in connection with the 1930 Census of Production show a ratio of 100:154 between (*a*) wages and (*b*) the cost of materials used and amount paid for work given out. For 1924, however, on the basis of the estimated wage bill for that year given in the General Report of the 1930 Census (p. 105), the corresponding ratio is considerably lower, at 100:137.

building boom. For these reasons it seems likely that a comparatively large proportion of the value of the materials required for the increase in building activity must have been disbursed fairly quickly in wages, and so have increased employment. If we assumed that one-third was so disbursed (and this does not seem unreasonable),[48] it would follow that the increase in building employment was associated more or less directly with an increase perhaps half as large in industries connected with building materials. In other words, the increase in employment in building and the industries most directly affected may have represented 30 per cent of the total increase in insured employment between 1932 and 1935. It is of course impossible to trace the full effects of the increased purchases of materials, or to measure the various time-lags involved — every industry may be said to be affected in some degree — but it is suggested that this figure of 30 per cent gives a very rough idea of the relative importance of the increased employment, between 1932 and 1935, that might be fairly easily attributed to the expansion in building activity.

It is obvious that new houses have to be furnished and fitted, and if we included the industries affected the contribution of the building expansion to the total increase in employment would be even greater. Finally, if we take into account the indirect effect of the increased spending power that results from an increase in employment, it will be seen that the building boom must have played a very considerable part in the first three years, at least, of the recovery. This general conclusion seems to hold good, although the

[48] This is a very rough estimate of a somewhat nebulous quantity! The following data relate to firms in a small selection of trades associated with building materials that made returns of wages in connection with the 1930 Census of Production, and are given for what they are worth in the present context. (Some of the firms in one group no doubt prepared the raw materials of firms in other groups.) The figures do not tell us a great deal, and must be interpreted with caution, but they do suggest that one-third of the money spent on additional materials may well have been disbursed in wages at a fairly early stage in its journey.

Trade	Percentage of Gross Output	
	Wages Paid	Cost of Materials and Work Given Out
Brick and Fireclay	42	29
Cement	20	40
Building Materials	30	44
Slate Mines and Quarries	58	6
Wall-paper	18	42

calculations are exceedingly primitive. They are intended, first, to illustrate some of the difficulties of a satisfactory quantitative analysis, and, secondly, to serve as a rough check on an alternative analysis that will be made below.

The following table illustrates the importance of building in another way:

TABLE XV
(Gross) Value of Output of Capital Goods
(Million £'s)

	1929	1932	1935
All Capital Goods	558	496	633
All Building (including Repair Work but excluding Contracting)	243	226	307.5
As percentage of all capital goods	*44*	*46*	*49*
New Dwelling-houses	85.5	81	145
As percentage of all building	*35*	*36*	*47*

Calculated from Clark, *op. cit.*, Table 81.
(See Clark, Chapter VIII, for definitions, etc.)

It suggests that the value of all building (including repair work) represents between 40 and 50 per cent of the total value of all capital goods produced. Building is thus seen to be extremely important, in view of the general belief that recovery in the capital goods industries normally forms the main stimulus to general recovery. It should be noticed, however, that the output of new dwelling-houses represented only about one-third of the total building output in 1929 and 1932, and less than one-half in 1935. Nevertheless, the housing boom alone appears to have been responsible for nearly one-half of the increase in the total annual output of capital goods between 1932 and 1935.

The effects of an increase in building activity are obviously widespread, and it is very difficult to measure them accurately, even if the stimulus to increased consumption that results from a rise in employment be excluded. Sir Harold Bellman, in his analysis, makes use of the classification of industries associated with building adopted by the Building Industries National Council. It is, he admits, fairly wide. A study of the list of industries reveals that it includes all four of the industries classified by the Ministry of Labour as specifically connected with electricity.[49] It includes, also, many of the industries connected with the raw materials used in the production of motor cars, as will be seen by a study of the table given by Mr. Duval in the chapter on the motor industry.[50] Changes in employment in the industries chosen by the Council will therefore reflect changes, not only in the building industry, but also in the motor car and electrical industries, and in many other industries. Column D of Table XVI shows the course of employment in a group of industries which includes the building, motor car, and electrical industries, and probably most of those affected to a greater or less degree by them. It will be noted that employment in the industries classified as associated with building moves rather more in line with employment as a whole than with employment in the building industry. This is especially true of the changes between 1936 and 1937.

Whatever the merits of this particular selection of industries, it is true that, although they accounted for only about one-fifth of total insured employment in 1932, they contributed approximately one-half of the total increase in employment in each of the first three recovery years (June, 1932–June, 1935). As far as building alone is concerned, we may perhaps assume that at least one-half of the increase in employment during these years, in industries classified as associated with building (excluding building itself), may be attributed to the building boom. On this assumption the building expansion was responsible for nearly one-third of the total increase in employment during each of the first three years of the recovery, before allowing for any indirect stimulus to consumption that may have resulted from increased employment. This roughly confirms our previous estimate.

The industries selected in this way include most of those that expanded rapidly between 1932 and 1935. The only important industries in the Ministry of Labour's classification that expanded more rapidly than the selected industries as a whole (27 per cent) are as follows: (a) constructional engineering, which is connected with building; (b) shipbuilding and marine engineering which, as the following table suggests, are probably not so important as building, or even as house-building; (c) entertainments and sports; toys, games, and sports requisites.

The figures are certainly consistent with, even if they do not

[49] Electrical wiring and contracting; electrical engineering; electric cables, apparatus, lamps, etc.; and gas, water, and electricity supply.
[50] Viz. iron and steel, brass and copper, glass, paints, rubber, wire, timber.

TABLE XVI
Employment in Certain Industries
(June of each year)
(Thousands)

	A Building		B Industries Associated with Building, etc.[1]		C Motor Vehicles, Cycles, and Aircraft		D All Selected Industries (A + B + C)		E All Industries (Insured)	
	Number Employed	Annual Increase	Number Employed	Annual Increase	Number Employed	Annual Increase	Number Employed	Annual Increase	Number Employed	Annual Increase
1932	633.4	—	1138.4	—	196.3	—	1968.1	—	9,965.2	—
1933	708.3	75	1230.1	92	217.6	21	2156.0	188	10,384.9	420
1934	789.9	82	1351.6	122	242.7	25	2384.2	228	10,835.6	451
1935	843.6	54	1393.4	42	259.3	17	2496.3	112	11,054.0	218
1936	910.7	67	1499.1	106	294.3	35	2704.1	208	11,631.2	577
1937	927.3	17	1646.0	147	336.9	43	2910.2	206	12,326.8	696

[1] Including electrical industries.

TABLE XVII
(Gross) Output of Ships
(Million £s)

1929	1932	1935
59	25	38

Calculated from Clark, *op. cit.*, Table 81.

confirm, the hypothesis that building, together with the motor car, electrical, and recreation industries, played a large part in the first three years of recovery. Building alone is seen to have played a very large part. The expansion in building activity, moreover, was highly selective, especially in 1933 and, to a lesser extent, in 1934, being mainly confined to house-building, which thus played a large part in the early stages of recovery, although the direct employment involved represents a small fraction of total employment.[51]

During the last two years of the recovery period the selected industries, as a whole, made a smaller proportionate contribution to the total increase in employment. It is difficult to draw any conclusion, but this result agrees with the hypothesis that the rate of expansion in building slackened, while certain other industries expanded even more rapidly than before. This is true of the iron and steel and other metal industries, of engineering and shipbuilding, of the electrical industries, and of the motor, cycle, and aircraft group. A considerable part of the large increase in employment in this last group was associated with expanding aircraft production. It was officially stated, at the beginning of 1938, that the number of persons employed in the aircraft industry had increased from 30,000 in 1935 to roughly 90,000.[52] There can be little doubt that many of the other rapidly expanding industries just mentioned received their main stimulus from the rearmament programme, although it is impossible to measure its effect.[53]

[51] The erection of 200,000 houses, it is estimated, 'provided work for about one-quarter of the building industry'; while employment in the building industry as a whole represented only 6 to 7 per cent of all insured employment.

[52] Memorandum by the Secretary of State for Air to accompany Air Estimates, 1938. Cmd. 5677.

[53] Some idea of the order of magnitude of the rearmament programme may be obtained from the fact that total defence expenditure was £125 million greater in the financial year 1937–8 than in 1935–6, two years earlier. This figure may be compared with estimated increases of approximately £80 million and £140 million in the gross annual output of building and of all capital goods respectively between 1932 and 1935, a period of three years. (See Table XV.)

Employment in all the industries mentioned in the middle of the last paragraph[54] increased by as much as 26 per cent between 1935 and 1937. This compares with an increase of only 8 per cent in all other insured employment. Employment in the selected group of industries represented only 16 per cent of all insured employment in 1935, but contributed 38 per cent of the total increase in insured employment between 1935 and 1937.

The evidence suggests that building activity played a large part in the first three years of the recovery, and that house-building was particularly important during the earlier period. The last two years saw a more rapid expansion in total employment than any other time during the whole recovery period, and building seems to have played a less important part in this advance. Rearmament was no doubt the predominant factor.

II. PRODUCTION

I

In the accompanying diagrams are presented the Board of Trade indices of production together with certain other commonly quoted indices of activity. They tell much the same story as the employment figures. Broad comparisons may be made between the Board of Trade sub-indices for the various industrial groups and the general index of production, but it must be remembered that the latter index is itself not completely representative of the whole national output. In particular, as has been shown in the first section, the fall in the Board of Trade index between 1929 and 1932 was greater than the fall in the whole national output, largely because the index takes no account of the 'output' of various consumers' services which expanded steadily throughout the period. It must also be remembered that the movements of indices of production conceal divergent movements in the constituent series.

In this section we shall discuss briefly the indices illustrated in the diagrams and certain other statistics of production and activity. Attention will be drawn to the incomplete and unsatisfactory nature of some of the indices, while certain conclusions reached by the authors of chapters in Part II of this book will be quoted.

---

[54] Viz. iron, steel, and other metals, engineering, shipbuilding, electrical, motor, cycle, and aircraft.

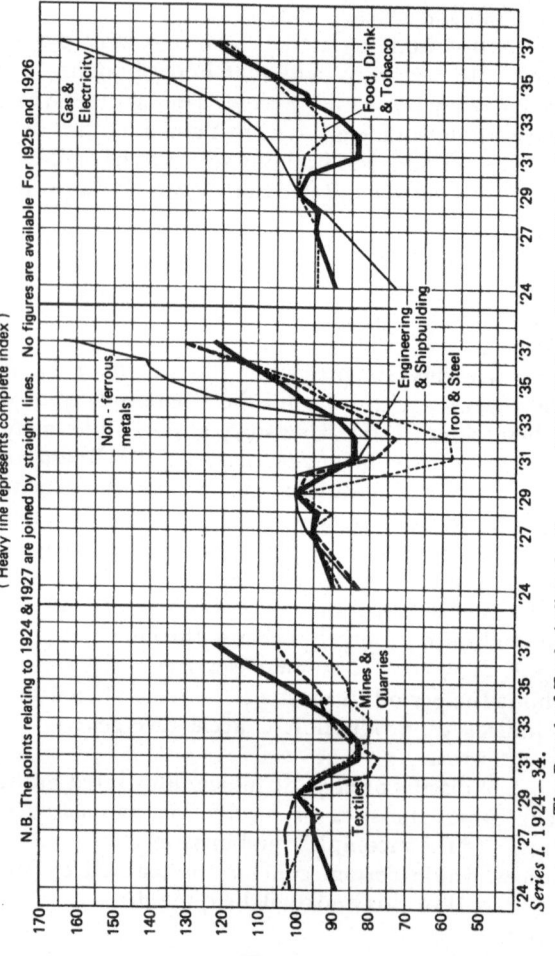

INDICES OF INDUSTRIAL PRODUCTION 1929 = 100 (BOARD OF TRADE)

(Heavy line represents complete index)

N.B. The points relating to 1924 & 1927 are joined by straight lines.   No figures are available For 1925 and 1926

% of 1929

Series I. 1924—34.

The Board of Trade indices for the years 1924—34 (base 1924 = 100) have been converted to a base 1929 = 100.

Series II. 1934—7.

The Board of Trade indices for the years 1930 and 1934—7 (base 1930 = 100) have been converted to 1930 bases equal to the corresponding 1930 indices in Series I.

Full descriptions of the method of the two index numbers are given in the *Board of Trade Journal*, 26th July, 1928, and 28th March, 1935.

Weighting is based on the results of the 1924 and 1930 Censuses of Production respectively, and there are certain other differences in the methods of construction. Of the branches of trade not covered in either index the most important are the clothing trade (other than boots and shoes) and public utility services other than gas and electricity, while the earlier index does not cover building.

DIAGRAM VII

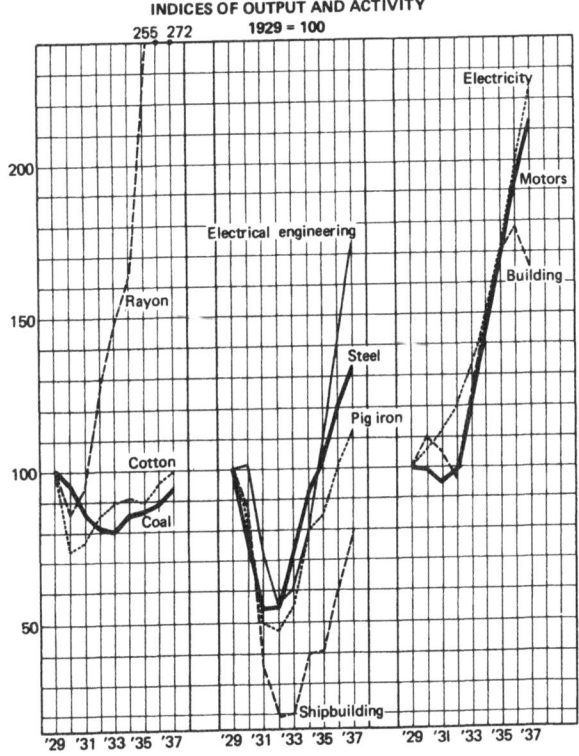

INDICES OF OUTPUT AND ACTIVITY
1929 = 100

Source: Board of Trade Journal – Unless otherwise stated.
United Kingdom – Unless otherwise stated.

Based on averages of monthly or quarterly figures of following quantities and indices—

Coal – tons of saleable coal raised.
Cotton – lb. of raw cotton delivered to mills.
Rayon – lb. of yarn and waste produced.
Steel – tons of crude steel produced.
Pig iron – tons produced.
Shipbuilding – gross tonnage of merchant vessels under construction at end of each quarter (including tonnage on which work was suspended).
Electrical Engineering – B.E.A.M.A. index of new orders.
Electricity – units of electricity generated by authorized undertakings – G.B. 1937 index based on first three quarters.
Motors – No. of vehicles produced – year ended 30th September – S.M.M. & T. Ltd.
Building – *Economist* index of building activity (see text for method of construction) – G.B.

II

1. Declining Industries

We shall discuss first our three major 'declining' industries. The output of mines and quarries failed, according to the Board of Trade index, to regain the 1929 level, despite the stimulus given to certain types of mining and quarrying by the building boom, the expansion in iron and steel production, etc. The output of coal, by far the most important mineral produced, was somewhat lower in 1937 than in 1929, and the general downward tendency of the post-war period from 1923 was thus continued. The decline, however, was much less marked in output than in employment. The annual output per person employed (including clerks and salaried persons) declined from 270 tons in 1929 to 253 in 1931, but subsequently increased steadily to 298 tons in 1936. The fall in output per person employed during the depression was partly the result of short-time working. Output per man shift showed only a very small decline from 21.69 cwt. in 1929 to 21.62 cwt. in 1931 (despite a reduction, in some of the coal-fields, in the length of the shift), and subsequently increased steadily to 23.54 ctw. in 1936 and 23.33 cwt. in 1937 (provisional).[55]

As will be seen from the following table, the decline in coal output was entirely due to the contraction in international trade. The quantity of coal shipped abroad (including bunker coal) fell severely between 1929 and 1932 and failed to show any subsequent recovery (the revival in 1937 being from the particularly low level of 1936, when the export trade was affected by sanctions against Italy). Home consumption, on the other hand, which showed an equal absolute fall, but a much smaller relative fall, between 1929 and 1932, recovered considerably from the depression level and increased over the whole period by some 9 million tons. This increase, however, failed to offset the decline in exports and bunkers.

2. The index of production for the textile industries was somewhat higher in 1937 than in 1929, but declined relatively to the general index. So far as any meaning may be attached to the statement, we may say that the output of textile goods was approximately the same in 1937 as in the pre-depression years. The index of raw cotton consumption suggests a recovery in the cotton industry to the 1929 level, but this index is misleading. 'In 1936 and 1937, although production of cotton yarn was rather greater than in 1929, produc-

---

[55] No attempt is made to explain this rise in output per head.

TABLE XVIII
Coal (Million Tons)

	Output	Shipped Abroad (Including Bunkers)*	Home Consumption†
1929	258	82	173.5
1930	244	75	167
1931	219	62	156
1932	209	57	149.5
1933	207	57	148
1934	221	57	161
1935	222	56	164
1936	228	50	176
1937	241	56	183
1929–37	−17	−26	+9

*Including coal equivalent of coke and manufactured fuel.
†These particulars relate to Great Britain only, the necessary adjustments having been made in respect of shipments to Northern Ireland.
  Source: Annual Reports on Mines and Quarries, issued by the Mines Department. (The 1937 figures are taken from the *Board of Trade Journal*, and are provisional.)

tion of cotton and rayon piece goods was only about three-quarters of the production of 1929.' Thus, despite the enormous growth in the importance of rayon, the increase in the production of cloth made wholly or partly of rayon failed to offset the decline in cotton piece goods. As in the case of coal, the decline in the cotton industry may be attributed largely to the contraction in exports. 'In 1936, home demand for cotton goods . . . was probably rather greater than in 1929.' Exports of cotton piece goods, on the other hand, failed to recover significantly from the depression level, and in 1936 and 1937 were little more than half in quantity of the exports of 1929.[56] (See Table XIX.)

In both the coal and cotton industries the recovery was limited, and almost entirely confined to the home market. Over the whole period, however, the home market failed to expand sufficiently to

[56] Exports of cotton yarn recovered more nearly to the 1929 level.

TABLE XIX
Exports of United Kingdom Produce and Manufactures

	Coal (Million Tons)	Iron, Steel, and Manufactures Thereof (Million Tons)	Cotton Yarn (Million lb)	Cotton Piece Goods (Million sq. yd.)	Woollen and Worsted Tissues (Million sq. yd.)	Motor Vehicles (Thousands)
1929	60.3	4.38	166.6	3672	155.5	42.0
1930	54.9	3.16	137.0	2407	113.8	29.8
1931	42.7	1.98	133.5	1716	86.1	24.3
1932	38.9	1.89	141.5	2197	81.8	40.2
1933	39.1	1.92	135.1	2031	94.2	51.7
1934	39.7	2.22	130.4	1994	102.2	57.6
1935	38.7	2.31	141.7	1948	109.7	68.2
1936	34.5	2.20	150.9	1917	118.0	81.7
1937	40.4	2.58	159.1	1922	122.8	98.5

offset the contraction in the export trade. These facts, together with a definite increase in output per head in coal-mining, largely explain the failure of employment in either of the two industries to recover significantly from the depression level.

3. We have seen that agricultural employment declined steadily between 1929 and 1937. The total acreage of arable land (and indeed of all cultivated land), which had fallen for many years, also continued to fall throughout the period. The London and Cambridge Economic Service index of agricultural production, on the other hand, after falling from 112.1 in 1929 (1924 = 100) to 100.3 in 1931, subsequently rose fairly steadily to 118.8 in 1937. There were indeed notable expansions in certain branches, despite the general decline in acreage and employment. The continuous decline in wheat acreage and production was arrested after 1931. Stimulated by the provisions of the Wheat Act, 1932, acreage increased by nearly one-half between the record low year of 1931 and 1934, and subsequently declined only slightly. Sugar beet production, which is indirectly subsidized, also showed a substantial expansion over the whole period. The pig industry expanded rapidly under the stimulus of special measures. 'The milk industry, because of some features of the demand for milk, and because of the operation of the marketing schemes, enjoyed relative stability during the depression. Producers increased and then began to take steps to improve their output.' The number of dairy cattle and the estimated production of milk increased fairly steadily.

The general long term tendency towards a contraction in acreage and employment was thus continued throughout the period, but certain branches of agriculture expanded, largely as a result of legislative measures. These measures helped to check the downward trend, and to restore a certain degree of prosperity to farming. Mr. Orwin writes of arable farming as follows. 'At the beginning of the decade, the plight of arable farming was serious. Except for the sugar beet crop, market prices for almost everything were below production costs, and there was every indication of a wholesale abandonment of arable farming such as had not been seen since the great depression at the end of last century. To-day, as a result of subsidies, tariffs, import regulations, and control of home production, it may be said that ploughland farming is enjoying a period of prosperity, combined with the prospect of security, such as it has not known within living memory.'

4. Consumption Goods Industries

The Board of Trade index of production for the food, drink and tobacco group showed a relatively small decline during the depression and rose over the whole period in approximately the same proportion as the general index. These movements are roughly in agreement with changes in employment. Unfortunately there is no separate Board of Trade index for the paper and printing or clothing groups, but the indices that are available suggest that the fall in output in the industries producing primarily consumers' goods, although possibly greater than the fall in employment, was relatively small.[57]

5. Heavy Industries

The indices shown illustrate in a striking manner the severe fall in activity in the heavy industries after 1929 and the rapid nature of the recovery movement. Shipbuilding nearly reached a standstill during 1932 and 1933. At the end of 1929, 1.56 million gross tons of merchant vessels were under construction. Three years later, at the end of 1932, the gross tonnage under construction had fallen by 85

---

[57] The Board of Trade index for leather, boots and shoes is not shown in the diagram. It is not representative of the clothing industry, and moreover the earlier index (1924–34) includes rubber goods. It may be noted, however, that the index fell from 1927 to 1929 but was hardly affected by the subsequent general depression, the index for 1932 being only 2 per cent below the 1929 figure.

The L.C.E.S. index of production for the paper group fell by some 14 per cent between 1929 and 1931 but had recovered by 1932 to the 1929 level.

per cent to 0.23 million.[58] The index of shipbuilding activity given refers to merchant vessels only and therefore fails to show the extent of the recovery in the industry as a whole. Naval construction expanded rapidly during the last three years of the period, the tonnage building at successive dates being as follows:[59]

Jan. 1	*Thousand Tons*
1935	139
1936	282
1937	376
1938	547

6. Changes in output in the iron and steel industry were also violent. Both the employment and the production figures suggest that the iron and steel industry advanced, over the whole period, in line with industry as a whole. This advance was achieved despite a very limited recovery in the export trade from the depression level. (See Table XIX.) In contrast to the coal and cotton industries the iron and steel industry was thus able to offset a marked decline in exports by a large expansion in production for a protected home market.

7. The Board of Trade index of production for the engineering and shipbuilding industries covers a wide field, including motor vehicle production, which declined relatively little after 1929, and ship-building and marine engineering, which, as we have seen, suffered a catastrophic fall. The complete index for the group is thus of doubtful value, as indeed are some of the other indices for a similar reason. The movements of the index of activity in the electrical engineering industry are discussed below.

8. Rapidly Expanding Industries
The indices illustrate well the rapid expansion that has taken place in three industries that have been already picked out in the previous section, namely, the building, electrical, and motor industries. Building was not included in the earlier Board of Trade index of production (for the years 1924—34), but an index for the building materials and building industries is available for the years 1930 and 1934—37. The movements of the annual index for this group of industries, and of the complete index, are shown below.

---

[58] If we exclude vessels on which work was suspended the fall is even more marked, and the gross tonnage under construction at the end of 1932 appears to have been less than 0.1 million. See *B.E.S.S.*, April, 1938, p. 50 for a useful diagram.
[59] Statement Relating to Defence (White Paper), March, 1938. Cmd. 5682.

TABLE XX
Board of Trade Indices of Production

	Building Materials and Building	Complete Index
1930	100	100
1934	133	106
1935	147	114
1936	157	125
1937	153	133

The index for building materials and building (which covers only about 30 per cent of the industries concerned) illustrates clearly the great increase in output between 1930 and 1935. The figures also suggest that building played a less important part during the last two years of the period. The building index rose less between 1935 and 1936 than the complete index, and actually showed a fall between 1936 and 1937. The *Economist* index of building activity also suggests that the rate of expansion slowed up between 1935 and 1936 and then turned into a decline. This index is not, however, completely satisfactory. It is based on the Ministry of Labour figures of the value of building plans approved by 146 local authorities.[60] Figures are not included either for the London area or for government contracts, and it is believed that government orders, in connection with the defence programme, were of considerable importance during the latter years of the period, and may have offset any decline in other types of building. There was certainly an increase in employment between 1936 and 1937 in both the building and public works contracting industries, although the increase in building employment was much less marked than in previous years. Even after general business activity had begun to decline towards the end of 1937, building and contracting activity was maintained. The *Economist* wrote, on 26th March, 1938, that 'with the exception of the coal and metal trades, there is no major branch of industry in which activity has declined so little as in building and contracting.' We may perhaps conclude that the rate of expansion of building slowed down towards the end of the recovery period while general business activity was increasing more quickly than at any previous

[60] A twelve months' moving average is calculated and the series is corrected for changes in building costs. Considerably less than one-half of the population of Great Britain lives under the 146 local authorities.

time. Building thus played a less important part during this later
period, but it is doubtful whether activity actually declined.

9. The post-war expansion in motor car production was checked
during the depression, although the decline in output was small.
After 1932, the advance was again resumed, and in 1937 more than
twice as many motor vehicles were produced as in 1929, although it
should be pointed out that the proportion of small private cars (up
to 10 h.p.) produced was very much greater.

The motor car industry was one of the few in which exports
expanded over the period. The total number of vehicles exported
more than doubled between 1929 and 1937, while the total value of
exports increased by nearly one-half. An early recovery in exports
after the abandonment of the gold standard enabled total output in
the year ended 30th September, 1932, to exceed the output of the
previous year despite a fall in production for the home market.
Exports expanded steadily throughout the recovery period, but after
1932 the main market for the rapidly increasing output was at home.

10. The Board of Trade index for the gas and electricity group rose
rapidly from 1924 to 1937. During the depression there was merely a
slowing down of the rate of increase. The rapid rise after 1929 may
be largely attributed to electricity.[61] The output of gas rose
relatively little during this period, while the output of electricity by
authorized undertakings increased by about 120 per cent between
1929 and 1937, although the increase in total output was somewhat
smaller.

The B.E.A.M.A. index of new orders in the electrical engineering
industry showed a marked rise over the whole period, but fell
severely after 1929. Employment, on the other hand, in what is
classified by the Ministry of Labour as the electrical engineering
industry declined relatively little. It is pointed out, moreover, in the
chapter on the electrical industry in Part II of *Britain in Recovery,*
that the greater part of the expenditure involved in the erection of
the Grid was allocated during the slump years, 1930—33, and that
this helped to maintain a fairly steady level of activity.

11. Finally, it may be noted that the Board of Trade index of
production in the non-ferrous metals industries, having fallen by
some 20 per cent between 1929 and 1932, rose extremely rapidly
during the recovery, and showed a very marked advance over the

[61] For a discussion, see the *Economist,* 1st and 8th January, 1938.

whole period. This movement may no doubt be largely explained by the close association[62] of these industries with the building, electrical, and motor car industries, and with armament work.

III

The indices of output and activity tell much the same story as the employment indices. We have seen in addition, in this section, some of the reasons for the decline in the coal-mining and cotton industries. Both suffered from a severe contraction in the export trade, while output per head increased considerably in coal-mining.[63] Other important exporting industries, including iron and steel, appear to have succeeded in regaining their pre-depression position in the national economy, despite a marked fall in exports, as a result of a large increase in production for a protected home market. Both the electrical and the motor car industries have been able to expand their export trade between 1929 and 1937, the increase in motor car exports being particularly marked, but the main expansion has been in the home market.

IV

1937–38. The decline in activity that began in the autumn of 1937 was not entirely general. In some industries, such as building and contracting, engineering and shipbuilding, the length of the time-lag between the placing of contracts and their completion helped to maintain activity. In the building and contracting trades, for example, the unemployment figures suggest that a high level of activity was still being maintained during the spring of 1938, despite a continued decline in the value of building plans passed. The published figures, however, exclude Government contracts, which probably helped to maintain activity. In the shipbuilding industry, the figures of tonnage commenced (which relate to merchant vessels only) reached a peak of 368 thousand tons during the second quarter of 1937, and thereafter fell sharply to 173 thousand tons in the first quarter of 1938, as compared with 253 thousand tons a year earlier. The fall in activity, on the other hand, was much less violent, and the tonnage building at the end of the first quarter of 1938 was still greater than at the same date a year earlier.

In some industries output was maintained by making for stock. Activity in the iron and steel industry expanded steadily throughout

---

[62] See Chapter XII in *Britain in Depression* for some details.
[63] No attempt is made to measure the changes in output per head in any of the other industries.

1937, and until the end of the year there was a severe shortage of supplies. During the first quarter of 1938, however, exports and home consumption were declining, while imports were increasing, and output was maintained at a high level only at the expense of a heavy accumulation of stocks. During the early months of 1938 there were signs of a decline, and the output of both iron and steel in April, 1938, was actually lower than in April, 1937. In the tinplate branch of the industry, which is dependent to a large extent on the export trade, there was a severe decline in activity which began towards the end of 1937.

Turning to consumption goods we find that the motor car industry, which produces the luxury durable consumers' good *par excellence*, was one of the first to feel the effects of the recession.[64] The very rapid expansion from 1932 came to an end during the latter part of 1937, and throughout the first half of the year beginning October, 1937, the output of private cars was running at a level about 10 per cent lower than in the previous year. In the consumption goods industries as a whole the movements in the unemployment figures during the last quarter of 1937 and the first quarter of 1938 compared unfavourably with similar movements in previous years, and some evidence is thus provided in support of the belief that consumption reached its peak in the spring or summer of 1937.[65] In many cases, however, the decline was relatively slight (and indeed much less marked than in the iron and steel and other metal industries), although the slump was severe in textiles, which are so largely dependent on international trade. The development in the export trade in general is clearly shown by the movements of the Board of Trade index of volume. The index failed to show the usual seasonal increase between the third and fourth quarters of 1937, while the fall between the last quarter of 1937 and the first quarter of 1938 cannot be wholly explained by seasonal influences. Coal-mining, however, was less affected than most industries by the general decline in business activity.

The long time-lag in certain industries between the placing of orders and their completion, and also the possibility of making for stock, render somewhat difficult any general conclusions. The main impression gained, however, is that industries connected with rearmament work were relatively little affected by the recession, and this, together with the time-lag mentioned above, no doubt helps to

[64] It is interesting to note that the volume of furniture sales, according to the index compiled by the Retail Distributors' Association, also declined markedly during the latter half of 1937.

[65] See pp. 26, 31.

explain the maintenance of a fair level of activity in many of the heavy and constructional industries. The consumption goods industries, and especially those making luxury and durable goods, seem to have been among the first affected, and this fact may perhaps be associated with the check to the expansion of consumption which appears to have occurred during the spring and summer of 1937. Industries closely connected with the export market, and especially textiles, suffered in general severely, coal-mining being an important exception.

C. PRICES AND WAGES

I. WHOLESALE PRICES

1. Introductory

An attempt will be made in this section to give a general picture of wholesale price movements during the period under review. The main movements in the various more comprehensive price indices are, in general, the same as regards the direction and order of magnitude of change. That this is true of changes from year to year is apparent from a study of the accompanying diagram (VIII), although it would appear that the more comprehensive Board of Trade indices have fluctuated somewhat less widely than the others. A more detailed sample study suggests that the movements from month to month do not usually show great divergences.

The following discussion will be based largely on movements in the official Board of Trade index and sub-indices, although reference will be made to movements in other indices. The Board of Trade index is the most representative, being based on changes in the prices of 200 commodities, as against about 100, 75, 58, and 45 in the case of *The Times, Financial Times, Economist,* and *Statist* indices respectively.[66] The Board of Trade, moreover, publishes sub-indices which are the most useful for the purposes of this survey.

It is perhaps desirable to emphasize at the beginning the obvious fact that price indices show average changes in prices. Movements in the prices of the various items show wide divergences, as is demonstrated in Table XXI.

[66] See Special Memorandum No. 61 of the London and Cambridge Economic Service (issued by the Royal Economic Society) by Mr. K. C. Smith for brief descriptions of these index numbers.

A full description of the "old" Board of Trade index (see Diagram IX, Chart A) will be found in the *Journal of the Royal Statistical Society* for March, 1921, and a description of the "new" index and sub-indices (see Charts B to F in Diagram IX) in the *Supplement to the Board of Trade Journal* 24th January, 1935.

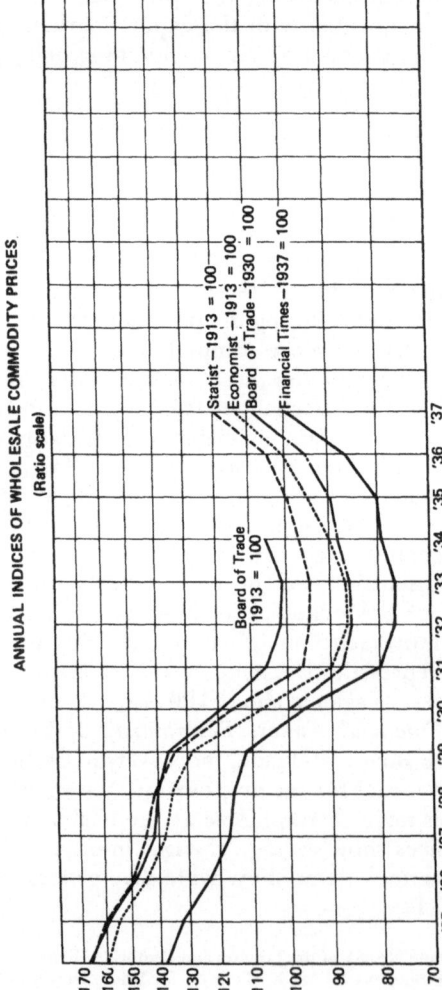

DIAGRAM VIII

ANNUAL INDICES OF WHOLESALE COMMODITY PRICES
(Ratio scale)

Statist – 1913 = 100
Economist – 1913 = 100
Board of Trade – 1930 = 100
Financial Times – 1937 = 100

Board of Trade
1913 = 100

TABLE XXI

The *Economist* Index of Wholesale Prices

(58 items)

	Percentage Change in Price of Items show-ing the Greatest Percentage	
	Increase	Decrease
Between 5th April, 1933, and 3rd Jan., 1934	+106	−125
Between 2nd Jan., 1934, and 2nd Jan., 1935	+ 83	−39
Between 2nd Jan., 1935, and 1st Jan., 1936	+ 86	−19
Between end Dec., 1935, and end Dec., 1936	+ 67	−27
Between end Dec., 1936, and end Dec., 1937	+ 38	−57

This survey will be concerned, in the main, with general movements, and only some of the more outstanding divergences will be noted. For more detailed discussions of changes in the prices of particular commodities the reader is referred to the relevant chapters in Part II of *Britain in Recovery* and *Britain in Depression*.

2. Chronology

The fall in prices from 1924, which was checked to some extent in 1927 and 1928, was resumed in 1929, and in the last quarter of that year began a very sharp fall which was continued until September, 1931, when this country left the gold standard. (See Diagram IX, Chart A.) The fall was relatively small in the index for manufactured articles, greater in the index for intermediate products, and still greater in the index for basic industrial materials. (See Diagram IX, Chart C.) A sharp rise in the index followed the abandonment by this country of the gold standard in September, 1931. The rise proved, however, to be merely temporary. Prices fell again during the first half of 1932 in sympathy with world movements, and by the middle of the year the index had fallen again slightly below the low level reached in September, 1931, before the abandonment of the gold standard.[67] A slight general recovery in August and September followed the Lausanne agreements, but was not maintained, and prices fell steadily again until the spring of 1933 when the Board of Trade index touched its lowest point of 82.7 in March, 1933, as against 83.1 in June and July, 1932, and 84.2 in September, 1931.

[67] The monthly index is based on average prices during the month, and the index for September, 1931, thus indicates a level of prices somewhat higher than that obtaining in the week before this country left the gold standard.

DIAGRAM IX

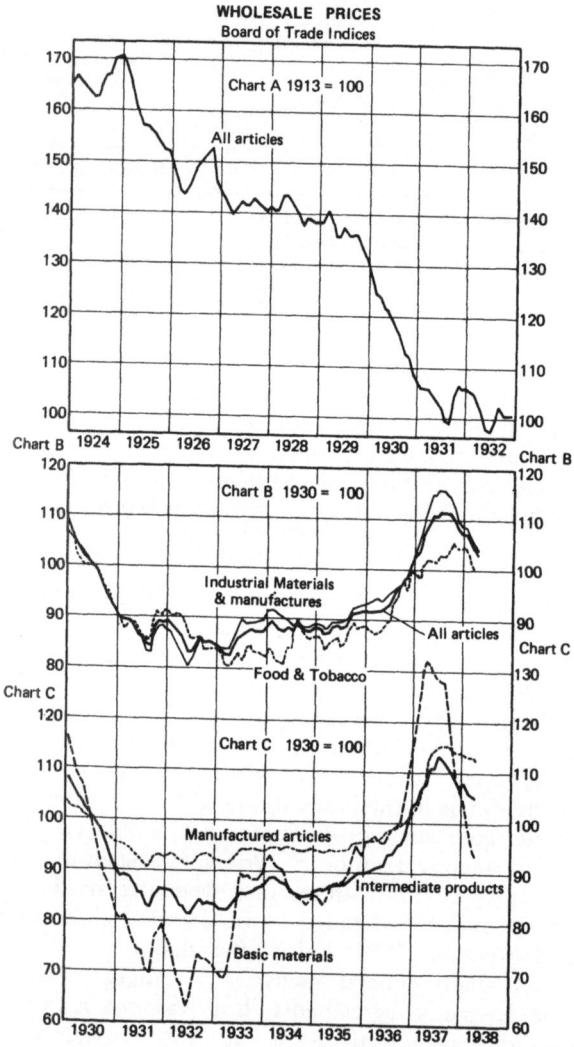

WHOLESALE PRICES
Board of Trade Indices

Chart A 1913 = 100

All articles

Chart B 1930 = 100

Industrial Materials
& manufactures

All articles

Food & Tobacco

Chart C 1930 = 100

Manufactured articles

Intermediate products

Basic materials

DIAGRAM IX (*continued*)

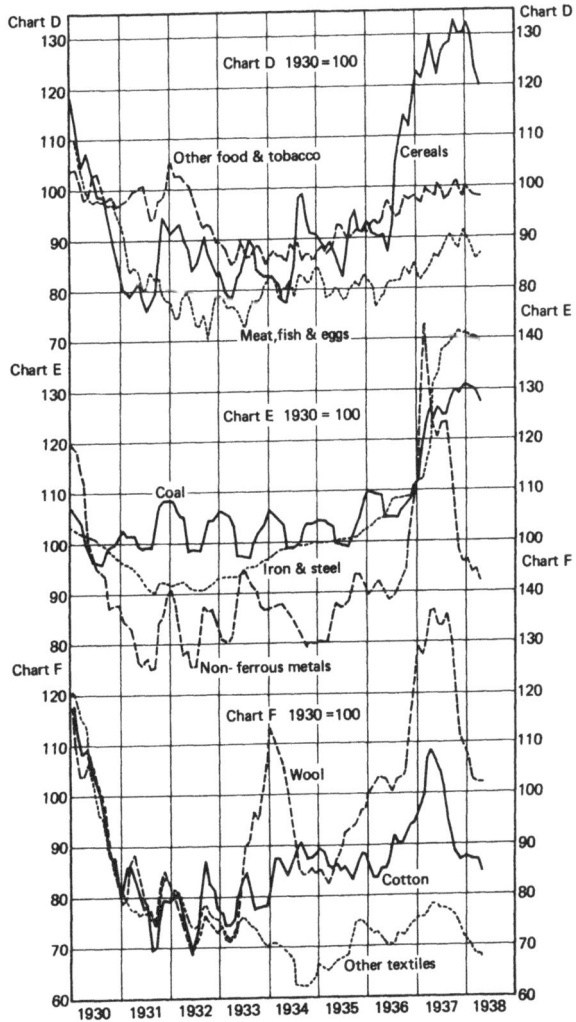

The downward fall in prices was thus definitely checked in this country in September, 1931, when we went off gold. From then until the beginning of 1933 there was no significant net fall in sterling prices,[68] while gold prices and prices in the countries that maintained the gold standard continued to fall. The following table, showing the Bank of England indices of *primary* commodity prices for certain dates, illustrates this point:

TABLE XXII
Bank of England
Index of Prices of Fifteen Primary Commodities[69]

	Week ended		
	19th Sept., 1931	11th June, 1932	7th Jan., 1933
U.K. Sterling	100	96	105
U.K. gold[70]	100	72	72
U.S. dollar	100	77	79

More comprehensive price indices for the United States, France and Germany show a similar, though less marked, fall between September, 1931 and the beginning of 1933.

The beginning of the general upward trend may perhaps be dated from the spring of 1933, but it should be noted that in the case of most industrial raw materials and manufactured articles the lowest point was reached in the middle of 1932 (or, in some cases, in the autumn of 1931). This is true of the composite index for industrial materials and manufactures, of each of the three sub-indices — basic

---

[68] The lowest points touched by the Board of Trade, *Statist,* and *Economist* monthly indices in 1931, 1932, and 1933 are shown below:

	1931		1932		1933	
	Aug.	Sept.	June	July	Mar.	April
Board of Trade (1930 = 100)	84.3	84.2	83.1	83.1	82.7	82.8
Statist (1867–77 = 100)	79.1		77.0		77.0	
Economist (1913 = 100)	85.7		80.9		81.6	

The *Statist* and *Economist* indices refer to the end of the month, while the Board of Trade index is based on average prices during the month.

[69] *Foods:* Wheat, Maize, Sugar, Bacon, Tea (U.K.), Coffee (U.S.A.).
Metals: Copper, Iron, Lead, Silver, Tin.
Other Industrial Materials: Cotton, Hides, Linseed, Rubber, Wool.
[70] Calculated by use of the French Franc exchange rate.

materials, intermediate products and manufactured articles – and of five out of the eight other sub-indices into which the index for industrial materials and manufactures is divided.[71] Recovery in the prices of foodstuffs, on the other hand, began in general later. The composite index for food and tobacco reached its lowest point in April, 1933, and was only very slightly higher a year later, in May, 1934. Turning to the sub-indices we find, indeed, that the index of the prices of cereals reached its lowest point in July, 1931, but after a jump at the end of that year it declined steadily until May 1934, when it was only very slightly above the figure for July, 1931. In the 'meat, fish, and eggs' group the lowest point was touched at the end of 1932, but in the 'other food and tobacco' group there was little recovery until the end of 1934. We may therefore make the tentative generalization that prices of foodstuffs recovered later than other prices. This generalization is, on the whole, borne out by a study of individual prices, although there are, of course, notable exceptions, as in the case of tea and bacon.[72]

In this connection it is interesting to compare the League of Nations index numbers of world production and stocks of raw materials and foodstuffs respectively. These are shown in Diagram X.[73] It would appear that, while the output of foodstuffs remained virtually stable throughout the period, that of raw materials fell off sharply between 1929 and 1932. Stocks of raw materials began to decline quite markedly in 1932, while stocks of foodstuffs continued to rise until two years later. These facts help to explain the late recovery in the prices of foodstuffs.

1933. The general recovery in prices during 1933 from the low spring level was most marked in the basic industrial materials group. Notable rises were recorded in rubber, wool, and tin prices, while food prices were less affected. An important exception was tea, the price of which was raised by artificial restriction. The rise in prices accompanied a marked improvement in the American industrial position. During this period, moreover, the dollar was rapidly depreciating, and the Bank of England index of dollar prices of

---

[71] It is not true of the 'coal,' 'other textiles,' or 'chemicals and oils' groups, but is true of the 'miscellaneous' group. (The indices for the two last groups are not shown in the diagrams.)

[72] The quarterly index numbers of average values of retained imports show a marked recovery in the raw materials group from the beginning of 1933, while the index for the food, drink, and tobacco group failed to recover until 1934.

[73] The scope of the indices of stocks is much less comprehensive than that of the production indices, but they are 'as comparable as is feasible in the present state of statistical information.' (*World Production and Prices*, 1936–7, p. 9.)

DIAGRAM X

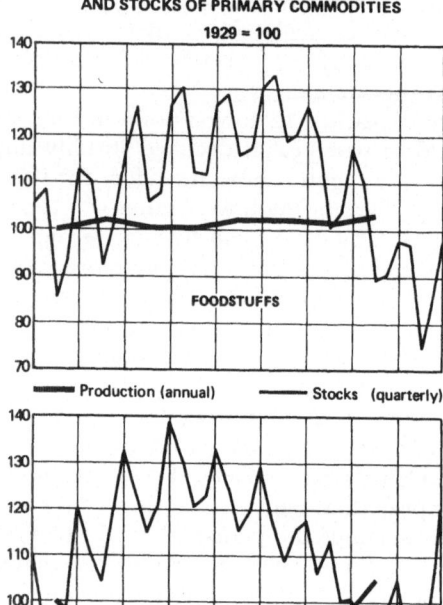

INDICES OF WORLD PRODUCTION
AND STOCKS OF PRIMARY COMMODITIES

1929 = 100

primary commodities rose from 85.5 in the week ended 15th April to 134.6 three months later, in the week ended 15th July, but subsequently fell off somewhat during the second half of the year.

1934. The comparative stability of the Board of Trade general index during 1934 masks a fall in the prices of certain raw materials, which was offset by a rise in food prices. The prices of most non-ferrous metals, with the exception of tin, fell considerably from their peak in the middle of 1933 to the end of 1934. This fall accompanied a recession in industrial activity in the United States. The price of wool also fell sharply. Among foodstuffs, we find a marked rise in the cereals group. Advances in the prices of wheat, oats, maize, and rice followed smaller world crops. Several other food prices showed marked rises on the year.

1935. During 1935 the general index rose, and the rise was accelerated in the autumn when the Italo-Abyssinian war and the applications of sanctions led to fears of a shortage of certain commodities. Prices in the non-ferrous metals and wool groups recovered again during the year.

1936–37. About the middle of 1936 the general index took a sharp upward turn, and a very rapid rise began, which continued for about a year. By the end of 1935, as is shown in the diagram, stocks of primary commodities had been greatly reduced from the abnormal depression levels. 1936 was a year of rapid recovery in many countries, including the United States. The devaluation of the gold bloc currencies in September was followed by a very marked improvement during the last quarter in France, Holland, and Switzerland.[74] Stocks of commodities were further reduced. By the autumn, according to the *Economist*, 'surplus stocks had been eliminated, and the rapid expansion of demand had practically eliminated idle capacity.'[75] A speculative boom, encouraged by prospects of heavy rearmament expenditure, began. The rise in the price of cereals began in the summer. Most other primary commodity prices followed in the autumn. Meanwhile the index for manufactured articles, which had risen only slightly from the end of 1931 to the end of 1935, began to rise markedly during 1936 and bounded upwards during the first few months of 1937. The elimination of surplus capacity, higher prices of raw materials, and shortages of labour in certain industries and districts, had their effect. The Ministry of Labour wage index, which had fallen from 98½ in the third quarter of 1929 to a low point of 94 in 1933 – a fall of only 4½ points – had recovered only to 96 by the end of 1935. During the next two years, however, the rise was rapid – to 100 in the first quarter of 1937 and 103½ in the last.

---

[74] According to the Editor of the *Statist*, 'it is not to be counted a coincidence that the devaluation of the former gold bloc currencies immediately preceded the sharp rise in prices, for these over-valued currencies had exercised a deflationary pull on the price level.' (*J.R.S.S.*, 1937, Part II.)

[75] *Economist*, 9th January, 1937, p. 53.

The index for basic materials reached its highest point in April, 1937, and began to fall rapidly in the autumn. The production of certain primary commodities had been stimulated by the rise in prices, and it became clear that a shortage of supplies was improbable. By the end of September, 1937, the index of stocks of raw materials (but not of foodstuffs) was again higher than a year earlier. By that time, moreover, it became clear that there had been a severe check to the recovery movement in many countries. Signs of a recession in activity were already apparent in the United States.

'In the light of events it is evident that the upward movement was by no means free of speculative influences which profoundly affected the later trends.'[76] In the spring the American authorities took steps to check the inflationary boom. It was announced in February that the reserve requirements of member banks would be raised. On 2nd April, a statement was made by President Roosevelt to the effect that commodity speculation was attaining dangerous dimensions and that prices were too high. The Government, he stated, would spend less on durable goods and more on consumers' goods. A sharp check was administered to the rise in prices. A rumour spread, first in April and later in June, that the dollar price of gold was to be reduced also had a depressing effect on markets, which were further affected by rumours of war.

The fall was most severe in non-ferrous metals, textiles, and rubber. Food prices, on the other hand, continued in general to rise throughout the year (although the prices of certain foodstuffs, such as cocoa, suffered a severe setback). The index of world stocks of foodstuffs at the end of 1937 was approximately the same as a year earlier, while the index for raw materials had jumped back to the 1934 level. Prices in the coal, iron, and steel groups, which had risen very rapidly during the first quarter of 1937, were maintained and increased. The index for manufactured articles, which had continued to rise for some months after the prices of basic materials had begun to fall, fell only slightly during the latter months of the year, despite a severe fall in the prices of raw materials. The steady increase in retail prices throughout 1937 may be partly explained by the absence of any significant decline in the wholesale prices of foodstuffs or manufactured articles.

The fall in prices during the latter part of 1937 was thus confined to certain commodities, notably industrial raw materials, although the rise in most other prices was, sooner or later, checked.

---

[76] *Financial Times*, 3rd January, 1938. 'Annual Finance and Stock Market Review.'

3. Conclusion

The general picture is one of falling prices until September, 1931, in which month certain prices touched their lowest point. Many other prices, however, and particularly those of foodstuffs, were destined to fall still lower.

It is impossible to define any turning point, but it may be noted that the Board of Trade general index reached its lowest level in the spring of 1933. From then until the middle of 1936 the general tendency was definitely upwards, although the rise was comparitively gradual. The rapid rise that began in the second half of 1936 was general, but the subsequent fall during 1937 was to a large extent selective, being confined largely to the prices of industrial raw materials.

The prices of manufactured articles in general remained comparatively stable throughout the period, except during the first half of 1937 when they rose rapidly. On the other hand we find violent fluctuations in the prices of most primary commodities.[77] Many schemes of control were in operation. 'It is worth remembering,' stated the *Economist* at the beginning of 1936,[78] 'that there are now restriction schemes of one kind or another affecting tin, rubber, tea, copper, lead, tinplates, wheat, sugar, silk, jute, and nitrate.' Despite the existence of these schemes, only a few of the commodities mentioned escaped a severe fall in price during 1937.

II. COST OF LIVING

The Ministry of Labour index of the cost of living for working class families is shown in the accompanying diagram, together with the indices for its main constituent groups.[79] The complete index fell rapidly during 1930 and 1931, the seasonal rise in the second half of each year being less than normal. The fall was continued until 1933, and the rise may perhaps be dated from the beginning of 1934, when (on 1st March) the index was for the first time higher than at the same date in the previous year. The rise was at first gentle, but became more marked towards the end of 1935. In 1936 the seasonal fall in the first half of the year was less than normal and in 1937 it was completely absent. The rise continued until November, 1937, but was largely seasonal in the second part of the year, the index

[77] A series of useful charts, showing movements in the prices of fourteen important primary commodities from 1927 to 1938, may be found in the *Economist* for 11th June, 1938.
[78] 11th January, 1936.
[79] The index for the 'other items' group is not shown.

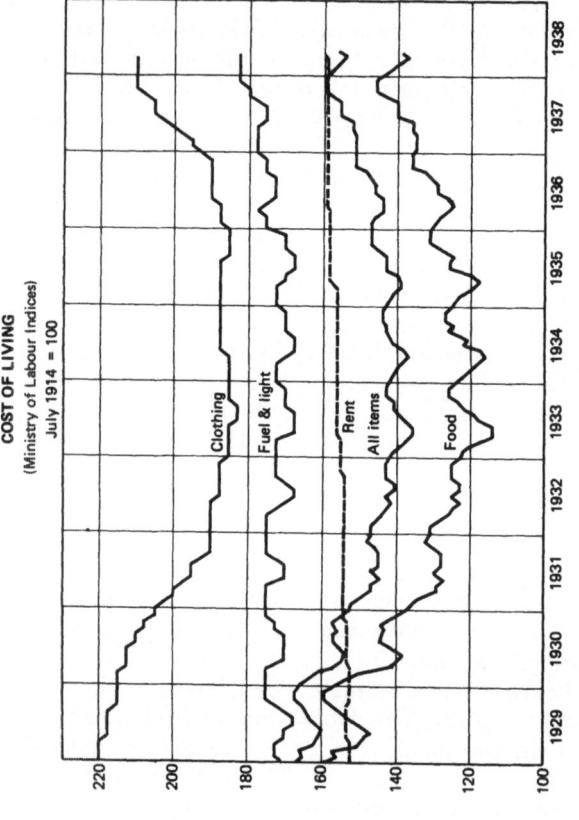

DIAGRAM XI

COST OF LIVING
(Ministry of Labour Indices)
July 1914 = 100

showing a rise approximately the same as in 1933.[80] At the beginning of 1938 there was a seasonal fall. There can be little doubt that the main force of the real upward movement was spent by the middle of 1937.

Food is given a weight of 3 out of 5 in the cost of living index,[81] and this helps to explain the supposed time-lag between changes in wholesale and retail prices. It helps to explain the continued fall in the cost of living from 1931 to 1933, after the wholesale price index had ceased to fall significantly, and the apparently late rise in the cost of living. Wholesale food prices, as we have seen, fell considerably between the autumn of 1931 and the spring of 1933, and failed to show any material recovery until 1934. The large weight given to food also helps to explain the continued rise in the cost of living in 1937, after the wholesale price index had begun to fall. Wholesale food prices, we have seen, continued to rise throughout most of that year.[82]

It may be noted also that the relatively greater fall in wholesale prices from 1929 to 1933, and the relatively greater rise from 1933 to 1937, appear less marked if we compare, not the complete wholesale and cost of living indices, but the indices of wholesale and retail food prices. This is made clear in the following table:

TABLE XXIII
Price Indices

	Change per cent	
	1929–33	1933–37
(1) Wholesale Prices	−26	+22
(2) Cost of Living	−15	+10
(3) Food Prices — Wholesale	−29	+23
(4) Food Prices — Retail	−22	+16

(1) and (3). Board of Trade. 1929–33, 'old' index: 'all articles' and 'total food.' 1933–37, 'new' index: 'all articles' and 'total food and tobacco.'

(2) and (4). Ministry of Labour.

---

[80] The Ministry of Labour index (converted to a 1924 base) rose from 87 at 1st June to 91½ at 1st November, but with the normal seasonal change removed (according to the L.C.E.S.) the index was the same at both dates (89).

[81] The index is weighted as follows: food, 7½; rent, 2; clothing, 1½; fuel and light, 1; other items, ½.

[82] On the other hand, the downward plunge of wholesale food prices from 1929 certainly appears to have begun sooner than the fall in retail food prices.

The complete index, as is shown in the diagram, fell considerably less than the food index, because the indices for fuel and light[83] and rent remained relatively stable. The latter index rose slowly but steadily from 1924 onwards, while the former was unaffected by the depression and rose during 1936 and 1937. The index for clothing also fell somewhat less than the food index between 1929 and 1933, and showed a rather smaller proportionate rise during the recovery.

DIAGRAM XII

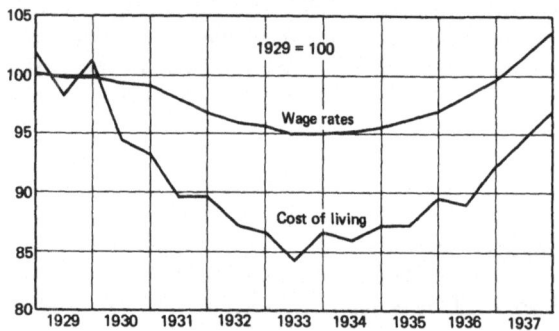

Wage Rates: Mr. Ramsbottom's index; 1934 weighting; End of June and December, 1929–34; End of December only, 1935–7; Average of End of December, 1928, End of June and December, 1929 = 100.
Cost of Living: Ministry of Labour; converted to 1929 base.

Striking movements in the prices of particular foodstuffs[84] include a very rapid fall in the average price of streaky bacon from 1s. 5½d. per lb. in 1929 to 10d. per lb. in 1932, followed by a marked rise during 1933 to an average price of 1s. 1¾d. in 1934. The price of butter fell markedly from 1s. 10¼d. in 1929 to 11¼d. in 1934, and showed only a moderate recovery during the last three years of the period. Milk prices rose steadily from 1933, but the prices of eggs, sugar, and most types of beef and mutton failed to rise significantly until late in the recovery period.

[83] The weights in this group are: 6 for coal, 3 for gas, and 0.7 for oil, candles, and matches together. No weight is given to electricity.
[84] The discussion in this paragraph refers to kinds and qualities of food usually bought by working-class purchasers, being based on the prices used by the Ministry of Labour in compiling its retail food price index. See 22nd *Abstract of Labour Statistics* and *Ministry of Labour Gazette*; and *Bank of England Statistical Summary*, April, 1938, for a useful diagram.

III. WAGES

Four indices of average weekly full-time wage rates are available for the whole period under consideration. These are (*a*) and (*b*) two indices complied by Mr. Ramsbottom of the Ministry of Labour, (*c*) the official Ministry of Labour index, and (*d*) Professor Bowley's index. The first two are the most comprehensive. Weights are used approximately proportional to the aggregate weekly full-time wages in each industry (*a*) in 1924 and (*b*) at June, 1934, respectively. Index (*b*) probably represents most faithfully the changes in average full-time weekly rates of wages over the period 1929–37. It is available at less frequent intervals than the indices (*c*) and (*d*), but seems to be the most suitable for our present purpose. It is therefore shown in the accompanying diagram, together with the Ministry of Labour cost of living index for the middle and the end of each year. Both indices have been converted to a 1929 base.

It should be emphasized that all the four available indices move closely together. This is evident from a study of the following table:

TABLE XXIV
Indices of Full-time Weekly Wage Rates

	Mr. Ramsbottom		Ministry of Labour Average for 1924 = 100 (c)	Professor Bowley Dec., 1924 = 100 (d)
	Average for 1924 = 100 (a)	Average for June, 1934 = 100 (b)		
Dec., 1928	98.9	105.3	99	99½
June, 1929	98.7	105.0	99	99½
Dec., 1929	98.6	105.0	98½	99
Dec., 1930	97.9	104.2	98	98¼
Dec., 1931	95.7	101.8	95½	96½
Dec., 1932	94.4	100.4	94	94½
June, 1933	93.9	99.8	94	94
Dec., 1933	94.0	99.9	94	94
Dec., 1934	94.4	100.4	95	94¼
Dec., 1935	95.6	101.9	96	95¾
Dec., 1936	98.6	104.7	99½	98
Dec., 1937	103.1	108.9	103½*	102¾

*Last quarter, 1937. An index for end of year would be higher. The index for the first quarter of 1938 was 105½.

Sources and Descriptions: (*a*) and (*b*) *J.R.S.S.*, 1935, Part IV, and 1937 Part I; (*c*) 22nd *Abstract of Labour Statistics* and *Ministry of Labour Gazette*; (*d*) Memoranda of L.C.E.S. (issued by R.E.S.) (No. 12 for description).

Notes: (*a*), (*b*) and (*c*) end of month; (*d*) middle of month.

All four indices fell by approximately 5 per cent between June, 1929, and June, 1933. All rose from June, 1933, to December, 1937, by between 9 and 10 per cent (the rise in index (*b*) being about 9 per cent). The rise between June, 1929, and December, 1937, was between 3 and 4½ per cent (the index (*b*) rose by about 3¾ per cent). In round numbers we may think of a fall of 5 per cent to 1933, a subsequent rise of 9 per cent to the end of 1937, and a rise of 4 per cent over the whole period.

The index illustrated falls slowly during 1929 and 1930, and much more rapidly during 1931 and 1932 to a low point in 1933. From there it rises, at first slowly, and then at an ever-increasing rate throughout the rest of the period. (The other indices move in roughly the same way,[85] but the Ministry of Labour index appears to show too rapid a rise during 1934 and 1935, and also rather too great a rise during the whole recovery period.) It is obvious from Professor Bowley's index, which is published monthly, that the rise in wages was continued throughout 1937 and the early months of 1938, even after the setback in business had begun. Professor Bowley's index (mid-December, 1924 = 100) moves as follows:

1937 Middle of		1938 Middle of	
July	100¼	Jan.	102¾
Aug.	101	Feb.	103
Sept.	101½	Mar.	103
Oct.	102	April	103¼
Nov.	102½		
Dec.	102¾		

The cost of living index fell much more between 1929 and 1933 than the wage index, and rose more quickly during the recovery, but it will be seen that during no complete calendar year was the relative rise in the cost of living index very great. Over the whole period the wage index shows a considerable relative rise.

Index numbers, prepared by Mr. Ramsbottom, of full-time weekly wage rates in sixty-five industries, are available for certain dates. These suggest, first, that the fall in wages during the depression was fairly general. Between the end of 1928 and the end of 1932, not one of the sixty-five indices showed a rise, while only fifteen escaped

---

[85] See *B.E.S.S.*, August, 1937, for a useful diagram showing the Ministry of Labour and Professor Bowley's indices from 1925.

a fall. The most marked falls were in the textile group, and some of these are shown in Table XXV. It appears also that the rise in wages during the recovery was general. Only eight of the indices failed to rise between the end of 1932 and the end of 1937. Over the whole period between the end of 1928 and the end of 1937, although the general index rose, sixteen of the sixty-five sub-indices fell, while eight more showed no change. The falls were most marked in the textile group, while nearly all the most striking rises were in the coal, metals, engineering, and shipbuilding groups. These are shown in the table, which also illustrates the rapid rise in wages that took place during the last two years of the period.

TABLE XXV

Index Numbers of Weekly Rates of Wages in the United Kingdom for Workpeople in Full Employment in Certain Industries
Average for Whole Year 1924 = 100

| | End of Year | | | | 1928–37 Change per cent |
Industry	1928	1932	1935	1937	(approx.)
Cotton	100	86	84	92	–8
Woollen and Worsted	100	84	82	89	–11
Textile Bleaching, Dyeing, and Finishing	96	82	84	91	–5
Coal-mining	87	84	84	97	+15
Iron-mining	92	90	96	121	+32
Coke-ovens	89	85	87	105	+18
Iron and Steel	92	88	94	112	+22
Engineering	104	101	104	113	+9
Tinplate	89	88	91	101	+13
Tube Manufacture	103	101	105	118	+15
Shipbuilding and Repairing	108	108	108	121	+12
Complete Index	98.9	94.4	95.6	103.1	+4

Source and Details: J.R.S.S., 1935, Part IV, and 1937, Part I.

2 Interwar Changes in the Location of Industry[1]

The present chapter contains, in considerable detail and in somewhat technical form, an analysis of statistics relating to the movement of industry and population between 1923 and 1937. It is based to a small extent upon statistics published by the Registrars General, but mainly upon statistics submitted by the Ministry of Labour to the Commission and relating to insured persons. The conclusions to which the analysis leads are interspersed with the discussion, but the outstanding facts are summarised at the end of the chapter.

I am aware of some of the dangers incurred in attempting to measure trends from the statistics for two years separated by a long interval, for the figures in one or both of the selected years may be seriously affected by temporary influences. To compare 1937 with 1923 is to assume that in each of the two years national figures are representative and that the relationship between the figures for different regions is normal. The danger of error would be particularly serious if comparisons were made between the numbers of people actually employed. The use of statistics of insured persons rather than of insured persons in employment (which, indeed, are not available in the necessary form) largely reduces the effects of temporary influences, but it is clear that these should not be used for the purpose of measuring changes in employment. For the purpose of this chapter, which is to describe broadly the trend of industry (as represented by the number of insured persons), an analysis based upon the figures for 1923 and 1937 seems to be justified.

THE DISTRIBUTION OF POPULATION

Between 1923 and 1937 the rate of increase in the number of insured workers was considerably higher than that of the population

[1] This study was prepared for Professor J. H. Jones when he was a member of the (Barlow) Royal Commission on the Geographical Distribution of the Industrial Population. It formed Chapter II of his memorandum which appeared on pp. 264—80 of the Commission's Report in 1940. It is reproduced here by permission of his daughter, Mrs. Eve Prys-Williams. Professor Jones died shortly before I was able to obtain his own permission.

as a whole. The total population of Great Britain increased by 6 per cent, the population between the ages of fifteen and sixty-four by 11 per cent, and the number of persons insured against unemployment, between the ages of sixteen and sixty-four, by 22.3 per cent. The difference between the first two rates is mainly due to the fall in the birth rate. The absolute fall in the number of children under fifteen was not wholly offset by a relatively large increase in the number of people above sixty-four years of age. The difference between the second and third rates cannot be explained so easily. In the first place it is known that during the intercensal period 1921 to 1931 the total population increased by approximately 5 per cent, the population aged sixteen to sixty-four by 9 per cent, and the gainfully occupied population between the ages of sixteen and sixty-four by 10½ per cent. It is probable, therefore, that for the period 1923 to 1937 the gainfully occupied population between the ages of sixteen and sixty-four increased more rapidly than the total population between those ages. In the second place it is clear that during the same period the insured population was increasing more rapidly than the gainfully occupied population; it must, indeed, have increased nearly twice as quickly. The increase is not a mere statistical increase to be explained by periodic extensions of the unemployment insurance scheme, for the figures for 1923 and 1937 from which the increase of 22.3 per cent is derived are comparable figures. It is clear that the proportion of the working population engaged in the insured trades increased. It is known, for example, that the number of agricultural workers (who did not become insured against unemployment until May, 1936, and therefore are not included in the statistics), as well as the number of permanent railway workers (who are not insured) declined during this period.

The disparity between the rates of increase in the total population and in the number of insured persons was not uniform throughout the country. The following table shows, for each area,[2] the difference between the rates of growth in the two classes as well as the relative growth in the insured population. From the first two columns we see, for example, that between 1923 and 1937, the total resident population of London and the Home Counties increased by 16.4 per cent, while the insured population increased by 42.7 per cent. The third column shows the rate of which the insured population has grown in each area *in relation to the total population.* Thus we see, for example, that the insured population of London

[2] The areas are those selected by the Ministry of Labour. (See paragraph 53 of Commission's Report.)

Indices, 1923 = 100	Total Resident Population 1937 (P)	Persons insured against unemployment (16–64) (ex. agriculture) 1937 (I)	(I) ÷ (P)
London and Home Counties	116.4	142.7	123
Midland Counties	110.4	128.2	116
West Riding, Notts. and Derby	105.0	115.0	110
Mid-Scotland	103.7	109.5	106
Lancashire	99.8	107.6	108
Northumberland and Durham	96.5	104.7	109
Glamorgan and Monmouth	88.8	95.7	108
Rest of Great Britain	104.5	127.8*	122*
Great Britain	106.3	122.3	115

*These high figures may be partly accounted for by the exclusion of agricultural workers from the statistics. If they were included, the rate of increase in the insured population would be more heavily reduced in the rural than in the urban areas, and so probably more heavily in the 'Rest of Great Britain' than in the seven specified areas.

and the Home Counties has grown by 23 per cent in relation to the total population of that area. In other words, the growth of the insured population, in relation to the total population, has been such that, if the total population of the area had not changed, the number insured would have increased by 23 per cent.

The table shows that in all the areas the number of insured persons has grown more quickly, or declined less quickly, than the total population[3] but it also shows that the insured population has grown, *in relation to the total population,* much more quickly in the rapidly expanding areas than in the other areas. In other words, the proportion of the total population that is insured against unemployment has increased at a higher rate in the rapidly expanding areas.[4] This may, of course, simply mean that the proportion of the gainfully occupied population that is insured against unemployment has increased more rapidly in the rapidly expanding areas, but it is unlikely that this is a complete explanation. The proportion of the

[3] There are some inaccuracies (but probably only slight ones) involved in comparing the rates of increase of the two quantities on the various areas. See Questions 2534–38 and paragraphs 5 and 6 in Appendix I of the evidence of the Ministry of Labour.
[4] In addition to this, we have seen that the proportion of insured persons in employment has increased in the two most rapidly expanding areas, and fallen considerably in Glamorgan and Monmouth. Thus the proportion of the population in insurable employment has increased more quickly in the more rapidly expanding, than in the less rapidly expanding and contracting, areas, for two reasons.

total population that is gainfully occupied has also probably increased more rapidly in the rapidly expanding areas than in the other areas.[5]

The table suggests that the relatively rapid industrial growth of the London and Home Counties and Midland areas has been facilitated, if not indeed made possible, not only by net migration into the former and the absence of net migration out of the latter but also by the entry into gainful occupations of sections of the population that had previously not been so occupied. In the less fortunate areas this may have happened only to a smaller extent, or perhaps not at all. Possibly some women and elderly men (under 65) in the less prosperous areas, who would have been employed or at least seeking employment if they had been in the more prosperous areas, have given up the attempt to find employment, while a number of young people may never have entered the unemployment insurance scheme on account of their inability to find even a first job.

There is also another possible explanation. It is probable that migration into London and the Home Counties tended to increase the proportion of the population in the age-group sixteen to sixty-four, and that it affected especially the lower part of this age-group, which contains most of the unmarried women and in which, for this and other reasons, the proportion of insured persons is highest. In the less rapidly expanding and the contracting areas net emigration may have produced the opposite results.[6]

THE INDUSTRIAL STRUCTURE
The preceding paragraphs are concerned with trends in the regional distribution of the total population and in particular of persons insured against unemployment. The next step is to relate population

---

[5] The following table suggests that this has been the case.

Changes in the total, and in the gainfully occupied, population, 1921 − 31.
Enumerated Population 1931. (1921 = 100)

Region	Total	Gainfully occupied.	
	(*T*)	(*O*)	(*O*) ÷ (*T*)
South East	109.8	116.4	106
Midland	106.9	111.5	104
Northern	103.1	106.2	103
East and South-West	102.4	104.2	102
Scotland	99.2	98.1	99
Wales	97.6	98.5	100
Great Britain	105.5	108.4	103

The above regions are the regions of the Registrars General.

[6] No attempt is made to discuss the complex nature of the effects of migration upon the age-composition of the population.

trends to industrial trends. It has been shown that the total number of insured persons increased between 1923 and 1937 by 22.3 per cent. In some industries the number increased at a higher rate and in others at a lower rate than the national rate, while in some other industries there was an absolute reduction in the number of insured persons. For the purpose of analysis the industries of the country may be divided into two main classes, namely (1) those which send part of their products to markets outside the area of production and therefore permit of geographic concentration and (2) those that are essentially local in character and are therefore to be found in all communities. The first have already been termed basic industries and the second local industries. Again, for the purpose of this analysis, industries may be divided into two groups, namely those in which the number of insured persons declined, between 1923 and 1937, either absolutely or relatively to population, and those in which the number grew at least as rapidly as the total population increased. These may be termed, for convenience, the contracting industries and the expanding industries, always remembering that the terms are used in relation to the number of insured persons as distinguished from volume of output.

During the period under consideration (1923–37) the most important of the contracting industries were coal mining; the textile industries (including cotton, wool and certain other textile industries, such as jute and lace); shipbuilding and marine engineering and iron and steel production. Employment in those industries will presently be examined. But it should be noted that other industries also contracted during the period, including the construction of carriages and carts. The number employed in railway transport and in agriculture diminished, but the statistics of the Ministry of Labour do not include the workers employed in those industries.[7] The most important industries (including both basic and local industries) in which the number of insured workers increased rapidly were the building industry, including the industries supplying building materials and those engaged in making furniture and supplying wallpaper and other products associated with housing development; the motor vehicle, cycle and aircraft industry and the road transport industries; the various electrical industries, including that supplying wireless apparatus; the silk and rayon industries; and, finally, a group of services and industries closely associated with a rising standard of living and including the distributive trades, hotels, boarding houses,

---

[7] Among railway workers only the non-permanent group are insured against unemployment, while agricultural workers were only recently brought into the insured group.

clubs; laundries and cleaners; industries providing entertainment and manufacturing toys and the requisites of various games and sports.

CONTRACTING INDUSTRIES

As a first general statement it may be pointed out that in those areas in which the chief contracting industries are located the insured population tended either to decline, or to expand less rapidly than in the country as a whole, while those areas in which the insured population increased more rapidly than in the country as a whole have apparently attracted the rapidly expanding industries. We may first consider the first part of this general statement. The following table shows, for each of a number of areas, the percentage of the total insured population that was engaged, in July 1923, in the specified contracting industries. It will be observed that, in general, the higher the proportion of the total insured population that is employed in the five declining industries the lower the rate of growth of that population.

Numbers insured in five important declining industries as per cent. of total numbers insured in each area. July 1923.*

	Great Britain	London and Home Counties	Midland Counties	W. Riding, Notts. and Derby	Mid-Scotland	Lancs.	North-umber-land and Durham	Glamor-gan and Mon-mouth
Coal-mining	11.2	0.1	8.8	21.0	10.7	6.6	37.6	51.3
Cotton	5.2	0.0	0.2	3.5	2.5	26.5	0.0	0.0
Wool	2.4	0.1	0.5	15.1	0.2	0.5	0.1	0.0
Shipbuilding and ship-repairing	2.2	0.9	0.0	0.1	7.3	1.4	8.9	2.2
Iron and steel manu-facture	2.1	0.05	2.8	3.7	3.6	0.8	2.6	5.6
Total of above 5 industries	23.1	1.1	12.3	43.4	24.3	35.8	49.2	59.1

*Calculated from Ministry of Labour, Tables IV and V, pp. 293—4 of Evidence.

It will be observed that none of the areas depended so largely upon one industry as the counties of Glamorgan and Monmouth, where more than one half of the insured population were engaged in coal mining and nearly sixty per cent were engaged in three of the five declining groups. The liability of the region to prolonged

depression is obvious from these figures. The seriousness of the
position of Northumberland and Durham is also clearly shown. But
the table does not fully reveal the situation. In the first place it does
not include all the contracting industries. Thus, for example, marine
engineering, an important industry on the North East coast and the
Clyde, is included in the Ministry of Labour evidence with constructional engineering in one industry group. Again it will be observed
that the ratios in Mid-Scotland differ from the national ratios less
than those in any other region. But Mid-Scotland comprises two
distinct industrial areas with different characteristics. Separate statistics for the western district suggest greater liability to prolonged
depression than those shown for Mid-Scotland as a whole. The West
Riding, Notts., and Derby area comprises at least two distinct
industrial areas, namely West Yorkshire, where the industrial structure is based upon wool textiles and a declining mining industry, and
South Yorkshire, Notts., and Derby, which is largely based upon a
specialised and expanding steel industry and a more prosperous
mining industry. Thus the table does not tell the full story, but it
nevertheless shows the broad connection between the rate of growth
of the insured population in an area and the degree to which that
area was dependent upon one or more of the five declining industries.[8] If we exclude the West Riding, Notts., and Derby area, it will
be seen that the lower the proportion of the insured population
attached to the five most important declining industries in 1923, the
greater was the subsequent expansion. In London and the Home
Counties, it will be noticed, the proportion attached to the five
industries was insignificant.[9]

---

[8] It is perhaps desirable to stress the limitations of regional statistics based upon regions
differently defined for different purposes and upon industries classified according to rate of
national progress. Thus, e.g., while output and employment in the coal mining industry were
seriously contracted, the regional incidence of the depression was very unequal. The West
Riding, Notts. and Derby region in the above table not only included at least two distinct
industrial areas but also two coal mining districts with differing trends. For this reason the
greatest caution must be exercised in making any general statements. Thus, e.g., while the
insured population of the region as a whole increased between 1923 and 1937 by fifteen per
cent, as compared with less than five per cent in Northumberland and Durham, and nine and
a half per cent in Mid-Scotland, which is apparently less vulnerable, it should be pointed out
that both coal mining and iron and steel production in the greater part (though not the
whole) of the Midland area escaped that decline in coal mining and iron production suffered
by the North east coast and the Clyde areas. Nevertheless, if examined with caution, the
above table is one of the most instructive in an investigation of post war trends.

[9] It must be remembered that, other things being equal, the larger the insured population in
an area the smaller may we expect the proportion in one industry or in a small group of
industries to be. This may help to explain the two extreme cases of London and the Home
Counties (by far the largest of the seven areas) and Glamorgan and Monmouth (by far the
smallest).

Having established the first part of the first general statement, namely, that in the areas in which the declining industries were located the insured population increased less rapidly than in the country as a whole, it is now necessary to examine the second part of the same statement, which is that the areas in which the insured population increased at a higher rate than in the country as a whole apparently provided a greater attraction for the expanding industries than that provided by the relatively declining areas.

To say that the relatively prosperous areas have provided a greater attraction for the expanding industries may be interpreted as meaning that they have had more than their 'fair' share in the expansion of these industries. A 'fair' share in the expansion of an industry or group of industries may, however, itself be interpreted in at least two different ways, as meaning that the total national expansion in the particular industries has been divided between the areas in proportion either to (*a*) the number of insured persons *attached to the particular industries* in each area in 1923, or to (*b*) the *total* number of insured persons in each area in 1923. For an area to have a 'fair' share in the expansion of a particular industry or group of industries in the first sense simply means that the percentage rate of increase in the particular industries has been the same in the area as in the country as a whole. On the other hand, an area may have had more than its 'fair' share, in the second sense, even if the percentage rate of increase in the particular industries has been no higher, or indeed lower, than in the whole country, simply because a relatively high proportion of the insured workers in the area was attached to the selected industries in 1923; and similarly an area that had a low proportion of its workers in the particular industries in 1923 may have had less than its fair share (in the second sense) even if the percentage rate of increase in the selected industries has been as high as, or higher than, in the country as a whole.

The more rapidly expanding areas have, in general, provided a greater attraction, in the second sense, for the expanding industries than have the less rapidly expanding areas. We might expect to find that this has also been true in the first sense, i.e. that the expanding industries have expanded at a higher percentage rate in the more prosperous than in the less prosperous areas. Two reasons might be advanced. First, the development of electrical power together with the great and still growing attraction of the London market might be expected to have caused the expanding basic industries to grow more quickly in London and the Home Counties than elsewhere. Secondly, we might expect to find that local industries have expanded at a greater proportionate rate in the rapidly expanding, prosperous areas,

since their size must depend largely on the size of the population and
on its purchasing power.

It does not, however, follow inevitably from the fact that the total
numbers of insured persons in certain areas have expanded relatively
quickly, that the expanding industries in those areas have also
expanded relatively quickly. Let us suppose that a community
consists of two distinct areas A and B, that in A one half of the
occupied population are employed in declining industries and the
other half in a miscellaneous group of expanding industries, and that
in B all the occupied population are employed in the same miscellaneous group of expanding industries. Let us further assume that the
population of the community as a whole is stationary. It is clear that
the miscellaneous group may expand at the same rate in both A and
B, and that if they are to expand at all it can only be by drawing
upon the unemployed workers in the declining industries of A; that
is to say, there will be migration both from A to B and from the
depressed industries to the expanding industries within A. The same
statement will be true if the population of the community is
increasing but the rate of expansion of the expanding industries is
higher than the rate of growth of the population. For this reason it
does not necessarily follow that because the growth of population in
London and the Home Counties has been accelerated by immigration
from other parts of the country the expanding industries of that area
have expanded at a higher rate than in the areas from which the
immigrants have been drawn. It is conceivable that in London and
the Home Counties the miscellaneous group of expanding industries
merely formed a much larger part of the industrial system than in
other areas.

Two facts may be mentioned at this stage which, while proving
nothing, do suggest that what actually happened corresponds closely
to the hypothetical case just described. The first is that, of the
twenty-three industries specified in the Ministry of Labour's evidence
as having shown a more rapid expansion (in Great Britain) than all
industries taken together, as many as eighteen were already heavily
weighted in London and the Home Counties in 1923, that is to say, a
higher proportion of the total insured population of the area was
attached to those eighteen industries than in the country as a whole.
The second fact is that only nine of the twenty-three rapidly
expanding industries expanded more quickly in London and the
Home Counties than elsewhere. These facts suggest at least that the
problem may justify further investigation.

LOCAL INDUSTRIES

We may first investigate the group known as local industries. From the forty-five industries distinguished by the Ministry of Labour it is possible to select seven that are mainly, though not wholly, local industries. These are (1) the distributive trades; (2) building; (3) gas, water and electricity supply; (4) tramway and omnibus service; (5) road transport (other than tramway and omnibus service); (6) laundries, job dyeing and dry cleaning, and (7) bread, biscuits, cakes, etc. The table overleaf[10] shows the percentage rates of change between 1923 and 1937 in the number of insured persons in each of these industries and in all seven taken together. Particulars are given for the country as a whole and for each of the seven areas under consideration. The last column shows the rate of growth (or decline) for all industries taken together.

The table calls for several comments. It will be observed that in every area the growth in the local industries was more rapid than that for all industries, but that there is no statistical connection between the two rates of growth. In London and the Home Counties the rate of growth in all industries was much higher and in local industries was lower than in the country as a whole. In West Riding, Notts. and Derby the rate of growth in all industries was lower and in local industries much higher than in the country as a whole. Again, it can be shown that in each of the five areas that expanded more slowly than the country as a whole the rate of growth, in relation to the total insured population, in each of the seven local industries, was higher than in London and the Home Counties. Moreover, the table shows, broadly, that, relatively to their size, the local industries in most other parts of the country expanded more rapidly than in London, where the growth in the number of insured workers and in economic activity has been popularly associated with the expansion of local services. (It is interesting to note that the least rapid rates of increase took place in London and the Home Counties, Mid-Scotland, and Lancashire, the three areas that were already best supplied with local industries in 1923, i.e. that had the highest proportions of their insured workers in the local industries.) Even when allowance is made for the difficulties involved in interpreting the statistics, it is evident that the relative growth of London and the Home Counties cannot be explained by the growth in the seven local industries specified in the table.

---

[10] Compiled from Ministry of Labour Tables IV – XII, p. 293 *et seq.*, of Evidence.

Percentage change in number of insured persons, 1923–37

	Distributive trades	Building	Gas, water and electricity supply	Road transport other than tram and bus service	Tramway and omnibus service	Laundries job-dyeing and dry cleaning	Bread, biscuits, cakes, etc.	Total seven "local" industries	Total all industries
London and Home Counties	+74.4	+41.6	+48.9	+24.9	+37.2	+58.5	–4.3	+54.2	+42.7
Midland Counties	+69.4	+74.7	–6.1	+89.5	+189.3	+136.7	+42.7	+67.2	+28.2
West Riding, Notts. and Derby	+75.0	+57.5	+23.4	+102.1	+149.1	+108.2	+16.8	+68.8	+15.0
Mid-Scotland	+44.5	+51.2	+15.1	+10.6	+92.3	+51.7	+25.1	+42.8	+9.5
Lancashire	+50.2	+42.8	+34.9	+19.7	+142.8	+79.8	+21.1	+47.4	+7.6
Northumberland and Durham	+59.6	+62.7	+41.9	+56.3	+258.4	+56.9	+16.7	+62.8	+4.7
Glamorgan and Monmouth	+74.5	+19.8	+80.7	+96.4	+196.1	+51.6	+9.5	+58.8	–4.3
Great Britain	+66.3	+51.4	+32.6	+43.1	+91.7	+66.6	+12.4	+56.8	+22.3

Note—Italics show a rate of increase equal to, or greater than, the corresponding rate in London and the Home Counties.

RAPIDLY EXPANDING BASIC INDUSTRIES

We may next examine the expanding basic industries. Of the 45 industries distinguished by the Ministry of Labour, 23 expanded more rapidly in Great Britain than all industries together, and of this total six were local industries. The following table shows, for each area, the percentage rates of growth in the remaining rapidly expanding industries (excluding public works contracting) taken together, and the percentage rates of growth in all industries are also shown for comparison. Again there is no obvious relation between the rates of growth in the 16 rapidly expanding basic industries and in all industries. In London and the Home Counties, for example, the rate of growth of the 16 industries was lower than in the Lancashire and the West Riding, Notts. and Derby areas, and not much higher than in Northumberland and Durham, while the rate of growth was only slightly higher in the Midland counties than in Glamorgan and Monmouth.

	Great Britain	London and Home Counties	Midland Counties	W. Riding, Notts. and Derby	Mid-Scotland	Lancs.	Northumberland and Durham	Glamorgan and Monmouth
Total, 16 industries	66	69	51	75	46	86	63	49
Total, all industries	22	43	28	15	10	8	5	−4

The details for the individual industries show that in only one case (brick, tile, pipe, etc.) was the rate of growth higher in London and the Home Counties than in any of the other areas. Rates of growth are, of course, misleading; an increase from 10 to 20 represents a rate twice as high as an increase from 100 to 150. In the case of motor vehicles, cycles and aircraft the rate of growth in London and the Home Counties, where the industry is very large, is only (and there only slightly) exceeded in Glamorgan and Monmouth where the industry is very small. Nevertheless the details show that in the case of most industries the rate of growth in London and the Home Counties is exceeded in one or more areas in which the industries are comparable in size.

We have seen that there is no clearly marked tendency for the expanding basic industries, or for the local industries, to expand more quickly in the more rapidly expanding areas, i.e., that those areas have not, in one important sense, provided a greater attraction for the expanding industries than that provided by the relatively declining areas. This suggests, although it does not prove, that in individual industries in general the rate of expansion was, on balance, no greater in the more prosperous than in the more depressed areas, or in other words that the divergence between the rates of growth in the various areas may be almost completely accounted for by the difference, in 1923, in their industrial structures. This possibility is strengthened by the fact that both in London and the Home Counties and in the Midland Counties only 25 of the 45 industries distinguished in the Ministry of Labour's evidence expanded more quickly than in the country as a whole, and that in every other area, except Mid-Scotland, at least 23 of the 45 industries expanded more quickly than in the country as a whole.[11] In some cases, however, an industry in an area is very small, in other cases very large. Moreover, some of the industries in an area, counted as having expanded more rapidly than in the country as a whole, have only just accomplished this feat, while others have done it by a wide margin. It is therefore not yet possible to say that the divergence in the rates of growth of the various areas can be entirely accounted for by the differences, in 1923, in their industrial structures.

A further calculation has therefore been made, and the results are shown in the following table. The first column shows the percentage rate of change in the insured population that actually occurred in each area. The second column shows the rate of change that would have occurred if the numbers insured in each industry had changed in each area at the same rate as in the country as a whole, i.e., if each area had had its 'fair share' (in the first sense described in an earlier paragraph) in the absolute expansion or contraction of each industry.[12] The third column is obtained by subtracting the figures in the second column from those in the first column. It gives some idea of the gain (+) or loss (−) accruing on balance to each area, as a result of the proportionate rates of change in the various industries being different from the national rates − as a result, in other words, of what may be called 'shifts' of particular industries towards or away from the areas. (A 'shift' may be defined as the actual change in the

[11] The details are: W. Riding, Notts. and Derby, 28; Mid-Scotland, 11; Lancashire, 25; Northumberland and Durham; 23; Glamorgan and Monmouth, 24.

[12] For the purpose of this table, the industries and services that come under the heading 'all other industries and services' in the Ministry of Labour's evidence have been counted as one industry. This group includes about 17 per cent of the total number of insured persons in Great Britain in 1937, and the proportion varied between 12 per cent and 19 per cent in the various areas. The rate of increase between 1923 and 1937 was 18.5 per cent in Great Britain, and this rate varied between 11 per cent and 19 per cent in the various areas. It must also be remembered that many of the industries in the Ministry of Labour's evidence are in reality groups of industries, the composition of which may vary from one area to another.

number attached to a particular industry in an area *minus* the change that would have taken place if the industry had expanded or contracted at the same rate in the area as in the country as a whole. A 'shift', in other words, is the amount by which the actual expansion in an industry in an area exceeds or falls short of the 'fair' share of the area in the national expansion of the industry.)

Change in number insured, 1923-37, as per cent. of number insured in 1923.

	I	II	I–II
London and Home Counties	+42.7	+40.2	+2.5
Midland Counties	+28.2	+29.2	−1.0
W. Riding, Notts. and Derby	+15.0	+ 8.9	+6.1
Mid-Scotland	+ 9.5	+18.1	−8.6
Lancashire	+ 7.6	+11.0	−3.4
Northumberland and Durham	+ 4.7	+ 3.6	+1.1
Glamorgan and Monmouth	− 4.3	+ 0.5	−4.8
Great Britain	+22.3	+22.3	−

I. Actual change.
II. Change that would have occurred if number insured in each industry had changed at same proportionate rate in each area as in the whole of Great Britain.

The table confirms what the earlier analysis suggested. The gains or losses due to the 'shifting' of industries are, on balance, unimportant, the most marked exceptions occurring in the Mid-Scotland, and in the West Riding, Notts. and Derby areas. There is no clearly marked tendency for the rates of expansion to be greater in the rapidly expanding areas, and smaller in the other areas, than they would have been if each industry had expanded at the same rate in each area. The divergence between the rates of growth in the various areas may be largely explained by the varying patterns of industry in 1923.[13]

Certain shifts have, of course, taken place. General engineering, for example, expanded in London and the Home Counties and in the

[13] It should be remembered that the whole analysis refers to insured persons, whether employed or unemployed, and that, for example, the proportion unemployed fell, between 1923 and 1937, in London and the Home Counties and in the Midland Counties, and rose markedly in Glamorgan and Monmouth. This does not however necessarily mean that, if the same analysis were carried out in terms of employment, the more prosperous areas would show marked inward shifts and the less prosperous marked outward shifts. Thus, for example, although the figure for Glamorgan and Monmouth in column I of the table would be greatly reduced from −4.3 per cent to −20.5 per cent, the figure in column II would also in all probability be greatly reduced, since in the coal mining industry in the country as a whole the number of insured persons in employment showed a much more marked proportionate fall between 1923 and 1937 (−40.6 per cent) than did the total number of insured persons attached to the industry (−28.0 per cent).

Midland counties, but declined in every other area; the coal-mining industry suffered more severely in South Wales and Lancashire than in the West Riding, Notts and Derby area; while the hotel and allied industries showed a much higher rate of increase in the 'Rest of Great Britain' than elsewhere.

As an example of the way in which the shifts into and out of particular areas have, in general, roughly cancelled each other out, we may give the figures for the most important shifts into and out of London and the Home Counties. The industries showing the largest inward shifts were: the distributive trades (31,000); general engineering, etc. (29,000); dress-making and millinery (19,000); miscellaneous metal goods industries (15,000); motor vehicles, cycles and aircraft (14,000); chemicals (including explosives, oil, paint, soap, ink, etc.) (9,000). The industries showing the largest outward shifts were: tramway and omnibus service (25,000); building (22,000); hotel, boarding house, etc., service (16,000); road transport (other than tramway and omnibus service) (10,000); printing, publishing and bookbinding (9,000).[14] On balance there was a net shift of only 60,000 into London and the Home Counties, representing 2.5 per cent of the number insured in that area in 1923. It should not, however, be forgotten that the statistics refer only to insured persons and do not include non-insured workers employed in the business professions, in the central offices of national organisations, in central administration, etc. Although complete statistics for this group are not available there appears to be little doubt that the rate of increase of the group has been higher than in the country as a whole.

It may be noted in passing that the heavy and intermediate basic industries have shown marked inward shifts, while among the light basic industries the net total of inward shifts was relatively small. This is evident from a study of the following table, the exact meaning of which is described in the explanatory notes. The net inward shift in the light industries was small, both absolutely and in relation to the total number of insured persons in the industries.[15]

We may now bring together the results that have already been obtained. These are shown in the table on pp. 94–5, in which some additional figures are also given.

Four groups of industries are distinguished, the 7 local industries, the 16 rapidly expanding basic industries, the 5 rapidly declining basic industries (all of which have already been mentioned) and a fourth group of 18 other industries, the composition of which is explained in the note below the table.

---

[14] There was also an outward shift of 19,000 in public works contracting.
[15] This statement remains true even if hotel, etc., service is excluded from the light industries.

	1923	Insured persons, aged 16-64, in London and the Home Counties, (excluding agriculture). (Thousands)	
		Increase 1923-37.	Net total of shifts, 1923-37.
7 Local Industries	840	+ 456	−28
11 Heavy Basic Industries	278	+ 103	+58
7 Intermediate Basic Industries	142	+ 81	+31
19 Light Basic Industries	588	+ 261	+12
Public Works Contracting	30	+ 24	−19
All other Industries and Services	542	+ 107	+ 7
Total	2,421	+1,032.5	+60

Notes:
(1) The third column represents the difference between the actual increase in each group and the increase that would have taken place if the number of insured persons in each industry taken separately had changed at the same rate as in Great Britain.

(2) The 'heavy' basic industries are those basic industries in which the number of insured females was less than one-tenth of the total number of insured persons at July, 1937. In the 'intermediate' basic industries the proportion of females exceeds one-tenth but is less than one-third; and in the 'light' basic industries the proportion of females exceeds one-third.

(3) Hotel, etc., service is included among the light industries. In this industry there was an outward shift of 16,000, the number insured in 1923 being 117,000.

The table may best be appreciated if we first consider Section II. It is seen that, if each group of industries is taken separately, there is little connexion between the rates of increase, in an area, of the group and of all industries taken together. The group does not necessarily increase more rapidly in a prosperous, than in a declining, area.[16] (The relatively small rate of decline in the five rapidly

[16] It may be noted that this statement is not true in the case of the '18 other industries' if public works contracting be excluded. (See note§ below table). The remaining seventeen industries as a whole definitely expanded more rapidly in the prosperous, than in the depressed areas. There were in fact exceedingly high rates of increase in public works contracting in Glamorgan and Monmouth and in Northumberland and Durham. This may reflect one or more of three things:—
(i) It may mean that there were much larger increases in public expenditure in the two areas than in the country as a whole, and that this was mainly responsible for the prevention of large net 'shifts' out of those areas.
(ii) It may mean that there was a big move from the use of direct, to the use of indirect, labour, by local authorities in those areas. This would raise the figures for 'public works contracting' in the areas at the expense of those for 'local government service.' If this has been the case, then it is better to include 'public works contracting' with the other seventeen industries in the group, since one of those industries, called 'all other industries and services,' included 'local government service.'
(iii) It may represent merely a big increase in unemployment in the two areas. The unemployment percentage for public works contracting in the whole country rose from about 20 per cent in June, 1923 to about 35 per cent in June, 1937, and it is possible that many of those in the two areas classified under 'public works contracting' are simply unemployed persons whose last job was an odd one in 'public works contracting' and would have obtained other jobs in other industries had they lived in a more prosperous area.

	Great Britain	London and Home Counties	Midland Counties	West Riding, Notts and Derby	Mid-Scotland	Lancs.	Northumberland and Durham	Glamorgan and Monmouth
I. Per cent insured in 1923 in:								
7 'local' industries	24	35	16	14	25	19	16	13
16 rapidly expanding 'basic' industries	14	21	26	9	10	9	6	4
5 rapidly declining 'basic' industries (see table on page 83)	23	1	12	43	24	36	49	59
18 other industries‡	39	43	46	33	40	36	28	24
All industries	100	100	100	100	100	100	100	100
II. Per cent increase (+) or decrease (−) 1923–37:								
7 'local' industries	+57	+54	+67	+69	+43	+47	+63	+59
16 rapidly expanding 'basic' industries	+66	+69	+51	+75	+46	+86	+63	+49
5 rapidly declining 'basic' industries	−25	−4	−28	−15	−31	−28	−29	−34
18 other industries‡	+14	+21	+17	+15	+5	+2	+18§	+26§
All industries	+22	+43	+28	+15	+10	+8	+5	−4

	+22	+40	+29	+9	+18	+11	+4	+1
III. 'Hypothetical' increase† 1923–37, per cent.								
IV. Per cent insured in 1937 in:								
7 'local' industries	30	38	20	21	33	26	25	22
16 rapidly expanding 'basic' industries	19	25	30	14	13	16	9	6
5 rapidly declining 'basic' industries	14	1	7	32	15	24	33	41
18 other industries‡	37	36	42	33	39	35	32	31
All industries	100	100	100	100	100	100	100	100

‡ This group includes (a) all those separately distinguished basic industries, other than the '5 rapidly declining basic industries,' that declined, or expanded at less than the national rate (+22.3 per cent) in Great Britain; (b) public works contracting; (c) a large group of industries which were included, in the Ministry of Labour evidence, under the heading 'all other industries and services' and which includes both 'basic' industries (some rapidly expanding) and also some industries, such as 'local government service,' which should probably be called 'local.'

† i.e, the rate at which the number of insured persons in an area would have increased if each industry had expanded (or contracted) in the area at the same rate as in Great Britain.

§ The high rates of increase in the '18 other industries' in Northumberland and Durham and in Glamorgan and Monmouth may be accounted for by high rates of increase in those areas in 'public works contracting' (+377 per cent and +833 per cent as compared with +142 per cent in Great Britain). If this industry be excluded, the expansion in the remaining seventeen is seen to have been considerably lower in the two areas than in Great Britain.

declining industries in London and the Home Counties is of little significance, since the proportion of insured persons in those industries was almost negligible.)

Section II therefore offers no explanation of the disparities in the rates of growth of the various areas. This must be looked for in Section I, which shows the proportion of the insured population in each area that was attached to each of the groups of industries in 1923.[17] We see that London and the Home Counties had much more than their 'fair' share in the local industries and in the rapidly expanding industries. (35 per cent and 21 per cent respectively of the total insured population of the area were insured in these two groups of industries as compared with only 24 per cent and 14 per cent in Great Britain as a whole.) On the other hand, the area had an insignificant proportion in the rapidly declining industries.

The Midland counties had less than their 'fair' share in the local industries, but much more in the rapidly expanding industries (26 per cent as compared with 14 per cent in Great Britain) and much less in the rapidly declining industries.

All the other areas (except Mid-Scotland) had far more than their 'fair' share in the rapidly declining industries and far less in the local and rapidly expanding groups. In Mid-Scotland, on the other hand, the pattern was very similar to the national pattern.

Section I thus explains (except in the case of Mid-Scotland) what Section II does not. It explains why the two most rapidly expanding areas did in fact expand more rapidly, and the other areas less rapidly, than the country as a whole. The case of Mid-Scotland remains to be explained by Section II. The figures given in Section I suggest that that area should have expanded at roughly the national rate.

We may now return to Sections II and III and consider the figures by areas rather than by groups of industries. It is fairly easy to explain the relation between the actual rate of expansion in each area and what is called the 'hypothetical' rate, i.e., the rate at which the area would have expanded if each industry had grown in the area at the national rate. In London and the Home Counties, for example, both the group of 'other industries', and, to a less extent, the rapidly expanding industries expanded more rapidly, while the local industries expanded less rapidly, than in Great Britain as a whole. The relatively small decline in the rapidly declining industries is of little significance, and on balance we find, as we might have expected, that

---

[17] The proportion attached to each industry within the groups is also, of course, important in explaining the divergences between the rates of growth in the various areas.

the actual rate of increase in the area was rather higher, but not much higher, than the hypothetical rate.

In all other areas except the West Riding, Notts. and Derby, and the Mid-Scotland, areas, the fairly close approximation of the actual to the hypothetical rates can be explained in a similar manner. In every case at least one group expanded more quickly, and at least one group less quickly, than in the country as a whole. On the other hand, we find that in the West Riding, Notts. and Derby area each group fared better than in the whole of Great Britain, while in Mid-Scotland the reverse was the case. As we might expect, the actual rate of increase was considerably higher than the hypothetical rate in the former area and considerably lower in the latter.[18]

It can be easily shown from the figures in the table how very difficult it would have been for the number of insured persons in the least rapidly expanding areas to have grown as quickly as in the country as a whole. Given the decline in the five rapidly declining industries, Glamorgan and Monmouth and Northumberland and Durham could have expanded at the national rate only if, for example, each of the remaining three groups of industries had grown at three times the national rates in the former area and at twice the national rates in the latter.

Section IV, which shows how the insured population of each area was distributed among the four groups in 1937, may be of some use in estimating future trends, although it is hard to tell which industries will expand and which will decline in the future. It shows how much less the national economy, and in particular the economy of certain areas, is now dependent upon the five important industries that have declined rapidly since 1923. Even now, however, two-fifths of the insured population is attached to those industries in Glamorgan and Monmouth, one-third in Northumberland and Durham and in the West Riding, Notts. and Derby area, and one-quarter in Lancashire. A second point that is clearly brought out by the table is the great importance of what we have called the local industries. Thirty per cent of the insured population is now attached to those industries in Great Britain as a whole, and at least one-fifth in each of the areas.

CONCLUSION

The present chapter has been devoted to a broad statement of the trends of industry and population and a discussion of the immediate

[18] The 'explanation' given in this paragraph, and in the one preceding it, of the relation between the actual and the hypothetical rates in the various areas, is of course extremely rough and ready. A full explanation can only be provided by a study of the relevant figures for each of the individual industries specified in the Ministry of Labour evidence.

causes of those trends. It has been shown that the occupied
population of Great Britain between the ages of sixteen and sixty-
four has increased more rapidly than the total population, and that
the number of insured persons has increased more rapidly than the
occupied population. It has also been shown that the increase, in
population and in insured persons, during the periods for which
information was available, has been more marked in London and the
Home Counties than in the country as a whole and that in most
other areas the increase has been less marked. The fact that migration
on a relatively large scale has taken place may therefore be accepted.[19] It has also been shown that the migration from other areas
into London and the Home Counties has been due to a combination
of two circumstances.

In the first place migration would have taken place even if the
expanding industries had not expanded more rapidly in London and
the Home Counties than in other parts of the country provided that
the contracting industries were located (as indeed they were) in those
other parts; for the rate of expansion of London and the Home
Counties would have been determined by the rate of expansion of
the expanding industries, which was higher than the rate of expansion of industry in the country as a whole and higher than the rate of
growth of the population of the country as a whole. On the other
side the rate of expansion of all industries in other areas was
determined by the combined rate of expansion (or contraction) of
both expanding industries and contracting industries. This was lower
than the rate of natural increase of the population of those areas
(other than the Midlands) for which reason (even though, as was
actually the case, the rate of increase of the expanding industries was
not lower than the national rate) there was a surplus population
available for migration. Thus it should not be assumed that the other
areas failed to enjoy the same relative expansion in the expanding
industries as London and the Home Counties enjoyed.

In the second place it has been shown that, over and above the
increase in insured population that would have taken place upon the
assumption that the expanding industries did not increase at a higher
rate than in the country as a whole, there was in the London and
Home Counties area an inward shift of only about 60,000 insured
persons, to which number there should be added an unknown

[19] A considerable volume of migration was of a long distance character; a sample
investigation by the Ministry of Labour suggested that approximately one half of the
persons insured at July, 1937, who had left the Wales, Scotland and Northern Divisions as
insured persons, had migrated to the London and South Eastern Divisions.

number representing the shift into non-insured occupations. This inward shift was shown to be due to the tendency for certain specified industries, such as general engineering, to grow in London and the Home Counties more rapidly (in the relative sense) than in other parts of the country.

The broad conclusions suggested by the statistical analysis in this chapter may be summarised as follows. In the main, and ignoring that large group of activities of a financial, social and administrative character associated with a capital city, the relative growth of the London and Home Counties area is due not to an increase in London industries at a higher rate than that of similar industries in Great Britain as a whole but to the fact that (*a*) the area is composed almost entirely of expanding industries (and largely of those industries that were growing more rapidly than population in the country as a whole) and (*b*) such industries form a much smaller proportion of the total in other areas in which the contracting industries form a larger, or much larger, proportion of the total. The apparent attraction of London thus means little more than the normal growth of a prosperous area which is able to foster its prosperity by immigration. It does not appear to mean a change in the competitive power of London that may not be capable of explanation by the fact that prosperity breeds prosperity.

3 Interwar Population Changes in Town and Country[1]

1. INTRODUCTION

It is well known that Britain is a nation of town-dwellers. Four-fifths of the population live in administrative areas classified as urban, over one-half in 'conurbations' of over 100,000 inhabitants, and two-fifths in the seven 'million-cities,' or conurbations with over a million inhabitants. In this paper an attempt will be made to discover to what extent, and in what senses, we have become even more 'urbanized' since the end of the war of 1914–18. No attempt is made to discuss the effects of the recent evacuation from large towns.

The difficulties before us are of two types. Some concern the meaning of growing or diminishing urbanization, some are statistical. It may perhaps be a useful introduction to the main discussion to give a few illustrations of the problems involved.

There are, first, the problems connected with the question 'When is a man living in a town?' There are many possible answers, but for our present purpose we may perhaps use Professor Fawcett's definition of a 'conurbation' as 'an area occupied by a continuous series of dwellings, factories, and other buildings, harbours and docks, urban parks and playing fields, etc., which are not separated from each other by rural land; though in many cases in this country such an urban area includes enclaves of rural land which is still in agricultural occupation.'[2] Such an area can be fairly clearly identified at any particular time, although it is, of course, continually changing. It very seldom, however, corresponds exactly

---

[1] *Journal of the Royal Statistical Society* part I, 1940. This paper is, with minor alterations, a copy of a memorandum prepared for the Royal Commission on the Geographical Distribution of the Industrial Population. It was based partly on evidence that had been submitted to the Commission, not all of which was published, and I am grateful to the Chairman for his permission to publish it.

[2] *Geographical Journal*, February 1932, p. 100.

to any one urban administrative area, or even to any collection of urban administrative areas. A man may be living within an urban administrative area, and yet not within a conurbation, as defined, decause the administrative area may include rural land. Similarly a man may be living in a rural adminstrative area, and yet in a conurbation, possibly a very large one.

Secondly, there is the question 'When is a man living in a large town?' Given our definition of 'conurbation,' we may say that a town is a large one when it covers a large area or has a large population, and it is clear, for example, that a man may be living in a small administrative area (in terms of population or acreage) and yet in a large conurbation, since conurbations may include many administrative areas.

Thirdly, it follows from what has just been said that a town may grow or decline in two different ways: in population or in area. If the population of a town has grown without spreading over the neighbouring country, the inhabitants have become more closely packed together. If the population of a town has simply spread itself out, without growing in number, so that any increase through the excess of births over deaths or through the incorporation or rural inhabitants has been lost by migration, then the centre of the town is farther from the open country, although the inhabitants are presumably living in less crowded conditions. In practice, over a period of time, changes in the population and in the area of a town may occur in an infinite variety of combinations. These changes open up many possible avenues of investigation. One with which we are particularly concerned is the attempt to measure changes in the population of towns, within changing boundaries determined by inspection of the areas concerned. In practice, we are able to measure population changes within unchanged boundaries, whether they be those of administrative areas or of 'conurbations ' determined, as far as practicable, in a scientific manner. No comprehensive data are, however, available by which we can measure population changes within changing boundaries, scientifically determined, although such data could in principle be obtained through laborious investigation. The nearest approach to the kind of changing boundaries we should like to have consists of administrative boundaries which, in the case of urban areas, are commonly extended as the population spreads into the neighbouring country. The extensions are, however, made at irregular intervals, so that the growth of the population of a town between two dates, especially when these are not far apart, may often be as well, or better, measured by using figures for an unchanged area (preferably a more extensive rather than a less extensive one) than by using the administrative areas as they were constituted at each date.

Fourthly, there is the distinction between a man's residence and his place of work. This distinction is roughly the same as that between a night and a day population. We may find, for example, that the population working in a town has increased more quickly than the population living there, one possible reason being that the people who previously lived near their work in a town have moved into the country, and now travel in to their work.

We are now in a position to clear up a rather important difficulty. It is quite possible for a country to become more 'urbanized' in the sense that a larger proportion of its population is living in large towns than before, without there being any movement of the population from the country and from small towns to large lowns. There may even be movement in the opposite direction. This is simply because, as the population of the country grows, small towns will normally become bigger ones, even if they do not attract any immigrants. The urban population will grow both by the excess of births over deaths and by a process of spreading which will 'urbanize' previously rural inhabitants. Thus the towns will grow both in area and in population. Provided the national population is increasing, the proportion living in towns with more than a certain population can, indeed, only be prevented from rising if the population of large towns grows more slowly than that of the rest of the country — that is to say, in general, if there is a net migration out of large towns. It will be argued in this paper that what increase there has been in urbanization in this country since the war of 1914—18 has taken the form more of the natural development of towns than of migration into them from the rest of the country.

Finally, there are many purely statistical difficulties. Some of the available figures cover the sixteen-year period 1921—37, some the fourteen-year period 1923—37, and some only the intercensal period 1921—31. Some of the figures are for Great Britain, others for England and Wales only. There is the important distinction to be borne in mind between the population usually resident in an area and the population enumerated in the area on the night of the Census. This distinction is particularly important in studying changes during the intercensal period 1921—31. As a final example it may be mentioned that the areas covered by the Ministry of Labour's figures of insured persons in large towns are neither easily defined nor strictly comparable with the areas used in the discussion of changes in total population.

In Section 2 we shall consider the distribution of the whole population according to place of residence, and in Section 3 the working population according to place of work.

2. DISTRIBUTION OF THE WHOLE POPULATION ACCORDING TO PLACE OF RESIDENCE

A. THE GROWTH AND SPREAD OF TOWNS

The population statistics furnished to the Royal Commission on the Geographical Distribution of the Industrial Population by the Registrars General contained a table on the 'distribution of total population by size of towns'. From this the following information, relating to the post-war period, has been extracted.

The table is based on administrative areas as constituted at each date. It will be seen that the number of people in each of the first four groups (large towns) has increased, while the number in each of the remaining four groups (small towns and rural areas) has fallen.

TABLE I

Urban and rural distribution of population and distribution by size of towns. Great Britain

	Number of areas			Population of areas (thousands)			Population per 1,000 total population		
	1921	1931	1937	1921	1931	1937	1921	1931	1937
Towns									
Over 250,000	14	15	17	11,129	11,675	11,938	260.4	260.7	259.5
100,000–250,000	36	40	44	5,493	6,083	6,403	128.4	135.8	139.2
50,000–100,000	58	65	80	4,089	4,586	5,611	95.6	102.4	121.9
20,000– 50,000	173	199	239	5,475	6,178	7,506	128.0	137.9	163.1
10,000– 20,000	264	260	237	3,803	3,693	3,416	88.9	82.4	74.3
5,000– 10,000	304	279	224	2,166	1,989	1,611	50.6	44.4	35.0
Under 5,000	595	600	484	1,652	1,628	1,329	38.6	36.3	28.9
Total Towns	1,444	1,458	1,325	33,807	35,831	37,814	790.5	799.9	821.9
Rural Areas	–	–	–	8,962	8,963	8,193	209.5	200.1	178.1
Total	–	–	–	42,769	44,795	46,008	1,000.0	1,000.0	1,000.0

Notes:

(1) A town is defined as a Borough or Urban District.

(2) For the purpose of this table the Administrative County of London is reckoned as one district. If the County of London (in which the population declined) is excluded, the proportion in towns with over 250,000 inhabitants shows a continuous increase between 1921 and 1937 (1921, 155 per thousand; 1931, 162; 1937, 170).

(3) The figures for 1921 and 1931 are based on Census-enumerated populations, those for 1937 on estimates of resident mid-year populations.

The rise in the number in middle-sized towns (20,000 – 100,000) is particularly noticeable. The number of people in urban administrative areas containing 20,000 or more persons has increased by 19 per cent between 1921 and 1937, while the number living in other areas has fallen by 12 per cent, and, as a result, the proportion living in the former type of area has increased from 61 per cent to 68 per cent. It is important, however, not to read too much into the table. The results do not necessarily mean that the number (and the proportion) in what were at some given date small towns and rural areas has declined, while that in larger towns has increased. First, changes of the nature, though not necessarily of the magnitude, indicated in the table might have taken place simply because small towns had grown into larger ones. Some towns that in 1921 were in one size group would have moved into the one above even if the population of all areas had expanded at the same proportionate rate and there had been no change in boundaries. Secondly, small town and rural areas have been in many cases absorbed by large towns through an extension of the boundaries of the latter, and this would also have contributed to the results shown in the table.[3] As a result of changes of both types, the number of areas is seen to have increased in each of the first four groups, and to have fallen in each of the next three. The number of rural areas has also fallen. The picture of people migrating from the country and from small towns into larger towns, which the table suggests at first sight, may thus be misleading. It is certainly not definitely proved by the table, which is quite consistent with the hypothesis that there was no migration at all.

The table is not, however, without value. It does suggest that we are now even more a nation living in large towns that we were in 1921. A man living in an urban area the population of which has increased since 1921 without change of boundary is more of a town-dweller than he was in 1921, in the sense that he is living in a

[3] There are other partial explanations of a wholly statistical nature. (a) The relative increase in the population in larger towns between 1921 and 1931 may be partly explained by the fact that the figures for the two years are based on the populations enumerated at the two Censuses, which were taken at different times of the year (see footnotes 6 and 7 of this Study). (b) The relative increase between 1931 and 1937 in the population in large towns may be partly explained by the fact that the 1937 figures are based on estimates of mid-year resident populations which tend to be bigger than Census-enumerated populations in the case of large towns and smaller in the case of small towns and rural areas. (Table 9A of the General Tables of the 1931 *Census of England and Wales* shows that the enumerated population was smaller than the resident population in Greater London and the County Boroughs outside Greater London, and greater in the other urban areas and rural districts outside Greater London. Table 16 of Volume II of the *Report of the 1931 Census of Scotland* shows that the enumerated population was smaller than the resident population in the Large Burghs and greater in the rest of the country.)

more crowded area – which may, of course, have its advantages as well as its disadvantages. A man living in an administrative area the population of which has expanded through the uniting of two or more previously separate administrative areas, whether he lives in the centre of a town or on the outskirts, is more of a town-dweller in so far as the extension of boundaries represents a real spreading of one or more of the areas so that they merge into each other. (This will normally be approximately true, although with many qualifications.) He is now living in a more extensive area of a more or less continuous urban nature. It is clear, however, that the figures shown in the table are the net result of changes of so many different types that it is impossible to obtain more than a tentative and very general impression.

The table, as already stated, certainly does not prove that there was a movement of population from the country and from small towns into larger towns. Table II suggests, on the contrary, that such a movement did not take place. In this table, which is for England and Wales only, urban areas are classified according to the size of their populations in 1931. The populations *of the same areas* in 1921 are also shown, together with the corresponding rates of increase in each class. Similar details are shown for rural areas as a whole. In this way the effects of changes in administrative boundaries are eliminated, while the table also differs from the previous one in that particular areas do not appear in one group in 1921 and in another in 1931.

Column 5 shows in the first place that in the areas that remained 'rural' in an administrative sense in 1931 the population had grown since 1921 actually more quickly than in the areas that were urban in 1931. 'The recently noticeable tendency for new industries to take advantage of the relatively cheaper sites in the country for their works and factories may account in part for this, but it is probably due also to urban development in peripheral areas which have not yet been brought within the sphere of urban administration' (*Census of England and Wales, 1931, Preliminary Report*, p. xvi). It seems, therefore, that there was no migration from rural areas as constituted in 1931 into urban areas as constituted in 1931. There might, however, have been migration from rural areas far from towns into those rural areas on the fringes of towns that were mentioned in the quotation. This would constitute a real movement from country to town. The Registrar General for England and Wales has, however, expressed the opinion that 'the character of the most recent advance [in urbanization] . . . as indeed of the whole of the advance during the present century is essentially different from that of periods prior

TABLE II

Population changes in urban and rural areas and in towns of various sizes
England and Wales, 1921–31

Enumerated population of area, 1931	No. of areas	Enumerated population, 1931 (thousands)	Enumerated population of same areas, 1921 (thousands)	Mean percentage of increase (+) or decrease (−) of population, 1921–31	Same as (5) but excluding urban areas within Greater London†
(1)	(2)	(3)	(4)	(5)	(6)
Urban Areas					
Over 1,000,000*	2	5,399	5,407	−0.1	+8.7‡
500,000 and under 1,000,000	3	2,134	2,053	+4.0	+4.0
250,000 and under 500,000	8	2,614	2.528	+3.4	+4.2
150,000 and under 250,000	13	2,590	2,474	+4.7	+2.3
100,000 and under 150,000	25	3,150	2,965	+6.3	+3.3
75,000 and under 100,000	21	1,832	1,667	+9.9	+2.6
50,000 and under 75,000	41	2,523	2,344	+7.6	+4.3
40,000 and under 50,000	34	1,498	1,370	+9.3	+2.8
30,000 and under 40,000	54	1,835	1,741	+5.4	+3.1
20,000 and under 30,000	95	2,324	2,121	+9.6	+5.4
15,000 and under 20,000	90	1,566	1,435	+9.2	+7.2
10,000 and under 15,000	143	1,761	1,685	+4.5	+4.0
5,000 and under 10,000	232	1,658	1,605	+3.3	+3.1
4,000 and under 5,000	89	395	391	+1.0	+1.0
3,000 and under 4,000	92	320	320	−0.0	−0.0
2,000 and under 3,000	93	233	240	−2.6	−2.9
Under 2,000	83	116	119	−2.7	−2.7
Total Urban Areas	1,120	31,948	30,463	+4.9	+3.8
Rural Areas	638	8,000	7,424	+7.8	+7.8
England and Wales	1,758	39,948	37,887	+5.5	+5.5

Compiled from *Census of England and Wales*, 1931, *Preliminary Report*, Tables E, G, and VI. The figures, being those of the preliminary report, differ slightly from the final figures, and, being those of enumerated populations, are subject to the difficulty discussed in footnote 6 of this study.

*Administrative County of London here reckoned as one district.

†In the compilation of this column, urban districts which are partly inside and partly outside the Greater London boundary have been treated as being wholly within the boundary. The population of all the urban areas of Greater London taken together increased by 8.1 per cent.

‡Birmingham only.

to 1901 when the labour demands of newly developed industries were drawing masses of people from the countryside to the towns. The comparatively small increases in urbanization now being registered represent little more than the natural development of the urban areas themselves. . . . Organized town planning and the more generous scale of housing now demanded by the population have destroyed the rural character of many areas adjacent to towns; but apart from the incorporation of the few old inhabitants of the rural areas annexed, the population movement involved has been largely the spreading or the decentralization of the towns themselves' (*Census of England and Wales, 1931, Preliminary Report*, p. xv). It will be noted that the relative decline of the rural areas shown in Table I is almost certainly fully accounted for by the incorporation of rural into urban administrative areas.

In the second place, column 5 shows that the population of towns with between 5,000 and 20,000 inhabitants increased whereas, according to the previous table, the population living in towns of those sizes fell. The very small towns declined, and the middle sized towns showed the greatest expansion. Many of the middle-sized towns that expanded most rapidly are, however, in Greater London and if these are excluded, as is done in column 6, the rates of increase in the various classes appear to be merely irregular. There is no clear tendency for the populations of large towns to increase more quickly than those of small towns, if we exclude towns with very small populations.

Further evidence[4] for the whole of Great Britain shows that, over the longer period 1921—37, there has been only a very slight increase in the proportion of the population living in Greater London and in the 46 largest urban administrative areas outside Greater London (those with populations of over 100,000 in 1937); and this slight increase can probably be wholly explained by extensions of administrative boundaries. Apart from Greater London and a number of seaside and midland towns, a net gain by migration has definitely been the exception rather than the rule.

We have seen that the proportion of the population in the larger urban administrative areas has increased, while the proportion in the smaller urban and rural administrative areas has fallen. On the other hand, we have seen that, if we take unchanging boundaries, the larger urban administrative areas have in general increased no more quickly than the smaller urban and rural administrative areas. These facts may seem to suggest that towns have merely grown and spread outwards, while there has been on balance little migration from the smaller towns and from the country to the larger towns. It may, however, be legitimately argued that our 'smaller towns' are often not separate units surrounded by open country, but rather parts of large conurbations, and that such large conurbations may well have contained those administrative areas, both urban and rural and of all

---

[4] Contained in the statistics furnished to the Commission by the Registrars General.

sizes, the populations of which increased most rapidly. (We have already seen that many of the middle-sized 'towns' that expanded most rapidly are in fact parts of one great conurbation, that of London.) If this has been so, the population of those large conurbations will have increased more rapidly than that of the rest of the country and attracted immigrants, so that the proportion of the population in them will have become larger. This possibility is neither proved nor disproved by the figures so far examined. It must be considered as a separate problem.

On examination it appears that we need not greatly modify our provisional conclusions. There has indeed been considerable net migration into the Greater London conurbation. Between 1921 and 1931 this amounted to nearly a quarter of a million, while between 1931 and 1937 there was a further immigration of a quarter of a million. In other large conurbations, however, the position was in general the reverse. Between 1921 and 1931 each of the fifteen largest conurbations[5] outside Greater London (those with populations in excess of 250,000 in 1931) lost population by migration, while the same is true of the majority of the smaller conurbations. The loss by migration between 1921 and 1931 of the 15 largest conurbations outside Greater London amounted to about 450,000 (the 6 'million cities' outside Greater London alone lost about one third of a million), while Greater London, as we have seen, gained less than a quarter of a million. The 16 largest conurbations, including Greater London, thus lost nearly a quarter of a million by migration, or about 1 per cent of their 1921 population. In the whole of Great Britain, however, the rate of loss by migration was rather higher, and the rate of natural increase rather lower, so that the population of the largest conurbations increased rather more rapidly than that of the country as a whole (5.2 per cent as against 4.8 per cent). The divergence becomes a little greater if we compare the 16 conurbations with the rest of the country, in which the population increased by 4.5 per cent.[6] Moreover, if rather larger

[5] As defined by Professor Fawcett in the *Geographical Journal*, February 1932.
[6] According to the figures given by Professor Fawcett (*Geographical Journal*, February 1932), the population of the 16 largest conurbations increased between 1921 and 1931 by 6.2 per cent as against 4.7 per cent in the whole of Great Britain, and 3.5 per cent in Great Britain excluding the 16 conurbations. The divergence thus appears to be much more marked. It was necessary, however, at the date of writing, to use the Preliminary Census Report, which does not give figures for resident populations. Professor Fawcett points out that 'the 1921 Census was taken on June 19—20 and that of 1931 on April 26—27, so that the population of many holiday resorts was unduly swollen in 1921, and that of some of the industrial areas was correspondingly reduced. Thus the figures tend to exaggerate the real increase in such industrial areas, and to diminish that in holiday resorts.' It is this fact that explains the discrepancies between the results obtained by Professor Fawcett and those reached in the text, which are based on mid-year resident populations.

areas had been taken for the conurbations, it is possible that they would have shown a somewhat higher rate of increase. (This is certainly true of the London, Birmingham and Tyneside conurbations, for which statistics were prepared for the Commission by the Registrar General for England and Wales, taking (a) areas defined by Professor Fawcett, and (b) those areas together with all contiguous urban areas.) Nevertheless it can hardly be said that the relative growth of the conurbations was very important, and there is no

TABLE III
Growth of the largest conurbations 1921–31

| | Mid-year resident population | | |
Conurbation*	1931 (thousands)	Increase (+) or decrease (−) 1921–31, as per cent. of 1921 population	Gain (+) or loss (−) by migration, 1921–31, as per cent. of 1921 population
London	8,238	+9.3	+3.2
Manchester	2,398	+0.5	−2.9
Birmingham	1,893	+6.7	−1.8
West Yorkshire	1,434	+0.9	−1.5
Merseyside	1,288	+4.2	−4.6
Glasgow†	1,253	+1.6	‡
Tyneside	1,105	+0.8	−8.5
Sheffield	513	−1.3	−7.1
Edinburgh	443	+3.1	−0.1
Bristol	424	+4.6	−0.6
Stoke-on-Trent	340	+2.1	−6.9
Nottingham	340	+5.3	−1.2
Hull	326	+6.7	−2.2
Teesmouth	297	+8.8	−2.4
Portsmouth	296	+1.8	−5.6
Leicester	260	+2.8	−2.4
16 *Conurbations*	20,849	+5.2	‡
Rest of Great Britain	23,982	+4.5	‡
Great Britain	44,831	+4.8	−1.3

Calculated from *Census of England and Wales*, 1931, General Tables, Table 9B, and from statistics furnished by the Registrars General of England and Wales and of Scotland.

*As defined by Professor Fawcett, *Geographical Journal*, February 1932.

†The Glasgow conurbation for which figures are given is that defined by the Registrar General for Scotland in a memorandum prepared for the Commission. This memorandum contained estimates of the *resident* population of the conurbation, while particulars of enumerated population only are available for the conurbation as defined by Professor Fawcett. The populations contained in the two areas, however, differ by only about 5 per cent., that defined by Professor Fawcett containing the larger population.

‡No figures for migration are available for the Glasgow conurbation, but there was an estimated net loss by migration of 73,000 (6.9 per cent.) from the City of Glasgow, which contains nearly nine-tenths of the population of the whole conurbation (*Census of Scotland*, 1931, Vol. II, Table 2). The rate of net migration out of the 16 conurbations was about 1.0 or 1.1 per cent., and out of the Rest of Great Britain about 1.4 per cent.

reason to believe that it would appear to be more important if the whole inter-war period were taken. Moreover, if the London conurbation is excluded, we find that the remaining conurbations with more than a quarter of a million inhabitants expanded by only about 2.7 per cent.[7]

It may be, of course, that the population of the areas just outside the conurbations expanded rapidly, but such areas were not, according to Professor Fawcett, part of the conurbations in 1931. If this has happened there may have been a significant migration towards, if not into, the large conurbations. No statistics relating to this question are readily available. Also it is very likely that, by taking unchanged boundaries, we are under-stating the increase in the population living in conurbations, in so far as the urbanization, through the spreading towns, of people previously living in the country is not counted. We need not, however, modify the general conclusion that there has been no great measure of migration into the large conurbations as a whole. It is also unlikely that, even after allowing for the incorporation of rural inhabitants, the 15 large conurbations outside London would show an increase as great as that in the rest of the country (excluding Greater London).

We may now briefly examine the problem on a regional, rather than on a national basis. Our results so far certainly suggest that in the regions that lost population by net emigration the large towns lost in general as much as the smaller towns and rural areas, and that in the regions that gained by net immigration the smaller towns and rural areas gained as much as the larger towns.

One source of information consists of population estimates for 46 large towns outside Greater London, furnished to the Commission by the Registrars General. The 46 towns are those urban administrative areas (mostly County Boroughs) that had resident populations of more than 100,000 persons in 1937. 35 of those towns extended their boundaries appreciably between 1921 and 1937, and in none of the others was there any appreciable net reduction in area. We may

---

[7] In the 21 conurbations with between 100,000 and 250,000 inhabitants the rate of increase was about 5.2 per cent, but it may be noted that if we exclude three seaside resorts, Blackpool, Bournemouth and Southend-on-Sea, each of which expanded by about 30 per cent, the rate of increase in the remaining 18 conurbations is reduced to only about 1.9 per cent. In the 38 smaller conurbations with populations of between 50,000 and 100,000 the rate of increase was 2.8 per cent. The population of all the conurbations with over 50,000 taken together increased by 5 per cent, and the rest of the country, which contains 40 per cent of the population, by 4.6 per cent. Thus, if we exclude London and the three seaside resorts, we find that outside all the conurbations the population expanded more quickly than in any of the three groups of conurbations (50,000 − 100,000; 100,000 − 250,000; over 250,000).

compare the rates of growth between 1921 and 1937 of the population of those towns and of the 15 Regions into which Great Britain is divided by the Registrars General. We find that in only 21 of the towns did the population increase more rapidly than in the regions in which they are situated, and in perhaps 4 of these[8] this was entirely due to an extension of boundaries. If we take the 1921 boundaries, we thus find that nearly two-thirds of the towns expanded less rapidly than the surrounding regions, while, even if we make no allowance for the boundary changes, we still find that well over one-half of the towns expanded less quickly than the surrounding regions.

The population has in many cases, however, increased relatively rapidly on the outskirts of large towns, and it may be that the areas in which this has happened have been outside the boundaries (even where these have been extended) of the large towns we have considered. We must therefore enquire whether these rapid increases have been sufficient to make large towns, in a wider sense, expand more rapidly than the surrounding regions. Some relevant figures are shown in Table IV for the seven largest conurbations, explanatory details being given below the table. Some of the figures are for the period 1921–37, others for the shorter period 1921–31 only. Where figures are readily available for a conurbation according to more than one definition, that area has been chosen that shows the greatest proportionate increase. No general tendency is apparent for the population of the conurbations to increase more quickly than that of the surrounding country.

The London conurbation expanded less quickly between 1921 and 1937 than the rest of the South-east Region. Between 1921 and 1931 the Manchester conurbation expanded less quickly than the remainder of the North IV Region (Lancashire and Chesire), excluding the Liverpool conurbation, and the West Yorkshire conurbation expanded less quickly than the rest of the North III Region (West Riding and York County Borough). In the other four cases the growth of the conurbations in relation to the surrounding regions is not very striking. During the periods considered, the population of no conurbation rose by as much as 5 per cent in relation to the surrounding region. The relative growth naturally becomes even less marked if we compare the conurbations with the whole of the regions in which they are situated.

---

[8] Owing to the nature of the statistics furnished to the Commission by the Registrars General it is not possible to be more precise than this.

TABLE IV
Increase (+) or decrease (−) in mid-year resident
population (per cent.)

Conurbation				Whole region
(1) London, 1921−37	+17.7	Rest of South-East Region	+18.5	+17.9
(2) Birmingham, 1921−37	+12.2	Rest of Midland I Region	+ 7.1	+ 9.3
(3) Tyneside, 1921−37	− 0.4	Rest of North I Region	− 3.0	− 1.4
(4) Glasgow, 1921−31	+ 1.6	Rest of West Central Scotland Region	− 2.2	− 0.2
(5) Merseyside, 1921−31	+ 4.2	Rest of North IV Region*	+ 2.5	+ 2.1
(6) Manchester, 1921−31	+ 0.5			
(7) West Yorkshire, 1921−31	+ 1.0	Rest of North III Region	+ 6.6	+ 4.2

(1) Area falling approximately within a circle of 25 miles radius from Charing Cross.

(5), (6) and (7) As defined by Professor Fawcett.

(2) and (3) As defined by Professor Fawcett plus all other contiguous urban areas.

(4) As defined by the Registrar General for Scotland.

(1), (2), (3) and (4) Calculated from statistics furnished by the Registrars General.

(5), (6) and (7) Calculated from Table 9B of General Tables, *Census of England and Wales*, 1931.

*A very small part of the Manchester conurbation is outside the North IV Region, but it seems fitting to compare it with that region. If figures for surrounding regions were also used, the relatively slow growth of the Manchester conurbation would appear to be even more marked.

B. THE GROWTH ON THE FRINGES OF TOWNS

The growth on the fringes of towns in relation to the central areas seems to have been both marked and general. This fact has already been mentioned, and it may now be examined in more detail. Table V, for the London conurbation, shows the changes that have taken place between 1921 and 1937 in the resident populations of the central area and of successive rings, each with a lower density of population than those it encircles. In the smaller innermost area, covering only 10,000 acres, the resident population fell by 19½ per cent. In the London administrative county, excluding this central area, the population fell by 6½ per cent. In the next ring it rose by 39 per cent, and in the next ring, lying between two circles of approximately 10 and 15 miles radius from Charing Cross, the resident population rose by as much as 154 per cent. This was the area in which the resident population increased most rapidly. Farther out the rise was less rapid, 56½ per cent in the next ring, and 28 per cent in the outermost one.

TABLE V

London conurbation

	Acre-age (thou-sands)	Estimated resident population (thousands). (Density in persons per acre in italics)		Increase (+) or decrease (−) in resident population, 1921−37	
		1921	1937	Thousands	Per cent.
A. Nucleus consisting of 8 inner Metropolitan Boroughs and City of London.	10	1,059 *105.9*	853 *84.5*	−206	−19½
B. London Administrative County, except A.	65	3,465 *53.4*	3,241 *50.0*	−224	−6½
C. Area recommended by Royal Commission on Local Government, 1923 (equivalent to circle of 10 miles radius)−except A and B.	180	2,681 *14.9*	3,721 *20.7*	+1,040	+39
D. Greater London (equivalent to circle of 15 miles radius) except A, B and C.	189	331 *1.8*	840 *4.4*	+509	+154
E. Circle of 20 miles radius from Charing Cross except A, B, C and D.	360	453 *1.3*	709 *2.0*	+256	+56½
F. Circle of 25 miles radius from Charing Cross, except A, B, C, D and E.	454	349 *0.8*	447 *1.0*	+98	+28
Total	1,258	8,337 *6.6*	9,811 *7.8*	+1,474	+17½

Calculated from statistics furnished to the Commission by the Registrars General.

In the other conurbations it is less easy to draw rings. Instead, we may compare population changes in administrative areas with relatively great, and in administrative areas with relatively small, population densities. The less densely populated areas correspond more or less to the fringes of the conurbations. Table VI shows the changes that have taken place between 1921 and 1937 in the Birmingham and Tyneside areas. In both the area includes the conurbation as defined by Professor Fawcett, together with all contiguous urban administrative areas.

In the Birmingham conurbation, in 10 out of the 11 areas in which the density of population was greater than 10 persons per acre, the

Studies in Political Economy

TABLE VI

Areas as constituted in 1937	Resident population (thousands)		Increase (+) or decrease (−), 1921–37		Number of areas in which population	
					In- creased	De- creased
	1921	1937	Thou- sands	Per cent.	relatively to pop- ulation of whole conurbation	
Birmingham conurbation						
11 administrative areas with more than 10 persons per acre in 1921	1,536	1,669	+133	+8½	1	10
16 administrative areas with less than 10 persons per acre in 1921	341	437	+96	+28	12	4
All areas	1,877	2,106	+229	+12	13	14
Tyneside conurbation						
8 administrative areas with more than 10 persons per acre in 1921	884	867	−18	−2	3	5
22 administrative areas with less than 10 persons per acre in 1921	531	543	+12	+2	13	9
All areas	1,416	1,409	−6	−½	16	14

Calculated from statistics furnished to the Commission by the Registrars General.

population either fell or rose less quickly than that of the whole conurbation. In all those areas together the resident population rose by only 8½ per cent, while in all the other less densely populated areas it rose by as much as 28 per cent. On Tyneside, the population of the 8 areas with high densities fell by 2 per cent, while the population of all the other areas rose by 2 per cent.

The figures for the Glasgow conurbation are available only for the period 1921–31, but they show the same tendency. The population of the two most densely populated areas, the parishes of Glasgow (including Barony) and Govan (including Gorbals), fell by 3½ per cent, while that of all the other areas in the conurbation (as defined by the Registrar General for Scotland) rose by as much as 26½ per cent. The figures for the Manchester and Merseyside conurbations show a similar tendency. The West Yorkshire conurbation, although showing no such tendency when an analysis is made by administrative areas (*i.e.*, local government areas), does show it quite clearly when the figures for Wards and Civil Parishes are studied. An analysis of this type is, indeed, necessary when dealing with the smaller conurbations that do not contain a sufficient number of administrative areas for any conclusions to be drawn. An examination of the population changes between 1921 and 1931 in the Wards and Civil Parishes of the larger urban administrative areas[9] shows an unmistakable tendency towards the relative growth of the less densely populated areas at the expense of those most densely populated. (The very densely populated Wards and Civil Parishes, with densities of, say, 50 persons per acre or more, very often show a decline in population.) This it true of large urban administrative areas in general, whether they form part of the seven largest conurbations or not.

It seems safe to say that a relatively large growth on the fringes of towns has been general.[10] The inner areas, on the other hand, seem in many cases to have expanded less rapidly than the surrounding areas entirely outside the conurbations, and often, indeed, to have shown an absolute decline in population. On the question whether or not the population of the whole conurbations increased on balance more rapidly than that of the surrounding country, we have seen that this happened only in some cases and then not to any striking extent.

3. DISTRIBUTION OF THE WORKING POPULATION ACCORDING TO PLACE OF WORK

So far we have considered the whole population according to where they live. It may be that our conclusions will be different if we take only the working population according to where they work. First, it may be that the relative growth of large conurbations will appear to be greater if, for example, migration into them has been mainly of persons of working age, while migration out of them has been mainly of old persons, or if many of the additional workers in a town live right outside it and travel in to their work. Secondly, for similar reasons, the relative growth of the resident population on the fringes of towns may not mean a similar relative growth in the number of people working there.

[9] As shown in the County Volumes of the 1931 *Census of England and Wales*, and in the City Volumes of the 1931 *Census of Scotland.*
[10] The *P.E.P. Report on the Location of Industry,* analysing the 1921–31 period, states (p. 173) that 'a certain amount of rapid development probably occurred on the edges of most centres.'

The most important source of information consists of statistics of persons insured against unemployment submitted in evidence to the Commission by the Ministry of Labour.[11] The figures refer to a considerable number of large towns and to a small number of the largest conurbations. Although covering only a part of the occupied population, they give us a rough idea of where people work rather than of where they live. They must, however, be interpreted in the light of some very important considerations.[12]

Those in employment will normally appear in the statistics under the area in which they work, since their unemployment books will generally be exchanged by their employer each year at the employment exchange nearest to the firm's premises. Those out of work will, on the other hand, usually appear in the statistics under the area in which they live, since they will themselves normally register at the employment exchange nearest to their home, which may not also be the one nearest to their work. Therefore if there is, for example, an increase in the proportion unemployed between two dates, a relative growth in the number of insured persons returned in the more residential areas (inside or outside the conurbations), as compared with the more industrial areas, may not represent a true shift of industry and trade in the direction apparently indicated.

The figures relating to those in employment may also appear to show shifts from one area to another which have no real basis. In the first place, 'changes have occurred from time to time in the number of Employment Exchanges and, consequently, in the areas served by particular Exchanges.'[13] Secondly, an employer will sometimes 'change the local office at which his books are exchanged, and this happens most frequently in large industrial areas where a firm's premises may be situated at a more or less equal distance from two local offices.'[14] Thirdly, 'it is also not unusual for firms who have works, branches or depots in different towns, governed by a central organisation, to keep the Unemployment Books of their work-people at their Headquarters and exchange them at the Employment Exchange nearest thereto.'[14] As a result of the growing integration of industry, the figures may therefore show a relative growth, both in large towns as compared with the surrounding country and in the centres of towns as compared with the outer areas, that has no real foundation.

[11] Some useful statistics for the Manchester conurbation were submitted in evidence by Manchester Corporation.
[12] See the evidence submitted to the Commission by the Ministry of Labour, Appendix I, paragraphs 1–6 (especially 5 and 6), for a full discussion.
[13] *Loc. cit.*, paragraph 5.
[14] *Loc. cit.*, paragraph 6.

Finally, the exclusion of agricultural workers from the figures will tend to raise artificially the rate of growth in the less urbanized areas. If agricultural workers, whose numbers have fallen notably, were included, the rate of growth would be reduced more in the rural than in the urban areas.[15]

The statistics must therefore be interpreted with great caution. Certain factors may tend to raise artificially the rate of growth in the central as compared with the outer areas of towns, or in conurbations as compared with the rest of the country, while other factors may have an opposite tendency. Since it is difficult to evaluate the relative importance of the different factors, it is obvious that no very definite conclusions can be drawn.

A. THE GROWTH OF TOWNS

Let us consider the first possibility. Has the number of persons working in large towns increased more quickly than the number working in the rest of the country? The figures for large towns given by the Ministry of Labour refer to the number of insured persons returned by Employment Exchanges within large administrative areas, although it must be remembered that the area covered by the Exchange or Exchanges in a town almost invariably extends beyond the administrative boundaries.[16] These figures certainly suggest at first sight that there has been a relative increase in the number of persons working in large towns. The total number of insured persons in towns with populations of over 150,000[17] in 1931 (including Greater London) increased between 1923 and 1937 by 28 per cent, while in the rest of the country the increase was only 18 per cent. The rapid growth of Greater London played, of course, a very important part in raising the rate of growth of the towns as a whole (although it does not entirely account for it), and in as many as one half of the towns the rate of increase was lower than in the whole of Great Britain. Nevertheless, if we take the figures on a regional basis, we find that in most cases the towns expanded considerably more quickly than the industrial areas in which they are situated. Some details are given in Table VII.

---

[15] It may also be mentioned that the figures for 1923 include, while those for 1937 exclude, insured persons in the banking industry. This might perhaps be expected to reduce the rate of increase in the number of insured persons more heavily in towns, and especially in the centres of towns, than in the rest of the country, but this possibility is of only slight importance, and does not materially affect the general conclusions reached in the text.

[16] Appendix I, paragraph 5, of Ministry of Labour's evidence.

[17] This refers to the administrative areas of towns, not necessarily to the areas covered by the Employment Exchanges.

Studies in Political Economy

TABLE VII
Increase (+) or decrease (−) in numbers insured against
unemployment. 1923–37. Per cent

London and Home Counties*	+42.7
Greater London	+36.1
Midland Counties†	+28.2
Birmingham	+40.4
Stoke-on-Trent	+21.2
Leicester	+23.0
Coventry	+79.0
West Riding, Notts, and Derby	+15.0
Leeds	+28.0
Sheffield	+24.3
Nottingham	+24.5
Bradford	+ 4.1
Mid-Scotland‡	+ 9.5
Glasgow	+14.2
Edinburgh, Leith and Portobello	+19.6
Lancashire	+ 7.6
Manchester and Salford	+19.1
Liverpool	+18.2
Bolton	+ 8.3
Northumberland and Durham	+ 4.7
Newcastle-on-Tyne	+23.4
Sunderland	+14.7
Glamorgan and Monmouth	− 4.3
Cardiff	+17.8
Swansea	+19.2
Rest of Great Britain§	+27.8
Great Britain	+22.3

Compiled from statistics given in the evidence (including supplementary evidence) of the Ministry of Labour.

*London, Middlesex, Bucks., Surrey, Kent, Essex, Herts., Beds.

†Staffs., Warwickshire, Worcestershire, Leicestershire, Northants.

‡Counties of Lanark, Renfrew, Dumbarton, Midlothian, West Lothian.

§The percentage rates of increase in the large towns in the 'Rest of Great Britain' were as follows: Bristol, 19.2; Hull, 20.6; Portsmouth, 35.0; Dundee, 1.1; Southampton, 28.4; Aberdeen, 23.6; Plymouth and Devonport, 23.7.

What is the significance of the figures? Has the number working in large towns really shown so large a relative increase, both in the country as a whole and within regions? We have seen that the statistical difficulties involved are considerable, but that some of the errors introduced are biased in one direction, some in the other. There is, however, another important consideration. It will be shown in the next section that, except in London, the number of insured persons has increased much less rapidly in the outer rings of conurbations than in the central areas, and it may be that if we had comprehensive figures for a large number of conurbations, the relative growth in the large towns as a whole would be greatly diminished, or perhaps disappear. Thus, for example, while Table VII shows that the number of insured persons returned by Exchanges within Birmingham County Borough increased by 40.4 per cent between 1923 and 1937, the figures for the whole Birmingham conurbation show an increase of only 31.6 per cent, or little more than in the whole of the Midland Counties. Newcastle and Sunderland show increases of 23.4 per cent and 14.7 per cent respectively, while in the whole of the Tyneside conurbation the rate of increase was only 3.2 per cent, or less than that for the whole of Northumberland and Durham. Glasgow shows an increase of 14.2 per cent, the Glasgow conurbation one of only 11.8 per cent. Manchester 'Inner City'[18] shows an increase, between 1927 and 1937, of 9.9 per cent, the whole conurbation one of 0.7 per cent only. In some of the smaller conurbations, where the main town forms a larger proportion of the whole, the difference might of course be less marked.

Table VII shows, also, that in Greater London the rate of increase was lower than in the rest of the Home Counties.[19] Finally, it will be seen that in the 'Rest of Great Britain' (i.e., the area outside the seven main industrial areas distinguished by the Ministry of Labour), which contains none of the seven largest conurbations excepting parts of Cheshire, the number of insured persons increased more quickly than in Great Britain as a whole.

In view of these considerations, and of the statistical difficulties involved, it does not seem at all safe to say that there has been any relative growth in the number of people working in large urban centres, either in the country as a whole or within regions. There is, moreover, some evidence that many smaller towns have expanded as quickly as, or more quickly than, the large ones. Dr. Brinley Thomas has remarked on the surprising extent to which certain 'country towns' in the South-east, such as Bedford, Luton, Welwyn, Aylesbury and Letchworth, have received immigrant labour, especially during the period of recovery from the great depression.[20] In the Midlands, also, he has found that 'considerable absorbing power has been shown by a number of independent centres scattered over the Division, e.g. Rugby, Corby and Newark, which is a reminder of the result obtained for the 'country towns' in the analysis of the South-east. There seems to be a decentralization of industry going on: sometimes old towns acquire a new lease of life, and in other

[18] For definition, see footnote to Table VIII.
[19] If a larger area than Greater London were taken to represent the London conurbation, the rate of increase would probably be higher than 36.1 per cent, but it is unlikely that it would be higher than that for London and the Home Counties.
[20] *Economica*, August 1937.

cases, such as Corby, a completely new community springs into being. The population, under the influence of new forces, is redistributing itself in a manner which promises less congestion in a few areas than in the past.'[2][1]

B. INNER AREAS AND OUTER RINGS OF TOWNS

We may now consider the second question. Has the relative growth of the resident population on the fringes also meant a similar growth in industry and trade in those areas, or has it merely meant that people are now living farther out from their work? In the case of London, industry and trade certainly seem to have grown more quickly in the outer regions than in the centre. The number of insured persons increased, between 1923 and 1937, by only 24 per cent in the County of London, while in the outer ring that comprises the rest of Greater London the increase was 78 per cent. In the rest of the Home Counties, excluding Greater London, the increase was 70 per cent. The figures are shown below.

Persons insured against unemployment (aged 16–64)

	1923 (thousands)	1937 (thousands)	Increase 1923–37	
			(thousands)	(per cent)
County of London	1,507	1,863	356	24
Greater London, excluding County of London	443	790	347	78
Home Counties,* excluding Greater London	470	799	329	70

Compiled from statistics given in the evidence, including supplementary evidence, of the Ministry of Labour.
*See Table VII for definition.

This happened despite the probable tendency for unemployment books to be exchanged more and more by the headquarters of firms in the centre of London. Some evidence is also provided by figures given in the Board of Trade's *Survey of Industrial Development.* Only 193 factories were opened in London Administrative County in 1936 and 1937, while 250 were closed. Of the latter, 81 were transferred to the fringe or to a nearby town.

In the case of the other four conurbations for which information is available, the figures given below in Table VIII suggest that

2 1 Ibid., November 1938.

TABLE VIII
Persons insured against unemployment (aged 16—64)

	1923 (thousands)	1937 (thousands)	Increase (+) or decrease (−), 1923—37	
			(thousands)	(per cent.)
Birmingham conurbation *				
Birmingham†	321	451	+130	+40
Rest of conurbation	270	327	+ 57	+21
Glasgow conurbation *				
Glasgow†	372	425	+ 53	+14
Rest of conurbation	86	87	+ 1	+ 1
Tyneside conurbation *				
Newcastle-on-Tyne†	103	127	+ 24	+23
Sunderland†	55	63	+ 8	+15
Rest of conurbation	178	157	− 21	−12
Manchester conurbation *				
Inner City‡	429§	472	+ 42§	+10§
Outer Ring	500§	465	− 36§	− 7§

Calculated from statistics given in the evidence (including supplementary evidence) of the Ministry of Labour, and in the evidence of the Corporation of Manchester.

*The areas covered are as far as possible those defined by Prof. Fawcett.

†*I.e.*, areas covered by employment exchanges within Birmingham, Newcastle-on-Tyne and Sunderland County Boroughs, and Glasgow Large Burgh.

‡Area covered by following Exchanges: Manchester, Eccles, Levenshulme, Newton Heath, Openshaw, Pendlebury, Prestwich, Salford, Stretford, Withington.

§The figures for the Manchester conurbation refer to the years 1927 (not 1923) and 1937.

industry and trade have grown not only as quickly in the central areas as in the outer regions, but actually considerably more quickly. This result may, of course, be to some extent unreal, if some unemployment books which were previously exchanged near out-lying places of work are now exchanged instead near central headquarters. On the other hand, in those towns in which the proportion unemployed has increased, we should expect the outer areas to have shown a 'false' expansion, for the reasons given in a previous paragraph. Moreover, the relative growth of the inner areas is so marked in each case that it must surely have some significance. We may therefore fairly safely say that the relative growth in the number of people living in the outer areas has at least not been accompanied by a similar relative growth in the number working there, while there may easily have been a relative growth in the number working in the inner areas.[22]

[22] The *P.E.P. Report on the Location of Industry* suggests, however (p. 47), that an outward movement of industry has been fairly general, but gives no supporting statistics.

4. CONCLUSION

We have shown how difficult it is to decide exactly what is meant by a growth of urbanization, and we have discussed some of the statistical problems involved in measuring it. It is not easy to draw general conclusions, but some attempt may perhaps be made briefly to summarize our results.

We seem to have become more urbanized since the war of 1914–18, in the sense that the proportion of the population living in large urban centres has increased. This can be explained, however, largely by the growth of towns through the processes of natural increase and spreading; smaller towns have simply become larger towns. There has not in addition been any considerable migration into the larger towns from the rest of the country. There has been some relative growth in the population of the largest conurbations as a whole, even within unchanged boundaries, but this has not been at all large, and can be wholly explained by the relative growth of London. Outside London, probably the only 'million city' that has grown relatively has been Birmingham, while only one or two of the other conurbations with more than 100,000 inhabitants, such as those of Hull and Teesmouth, have shown a relative growth. Outside London, it is in fact unlikely that the largest conurbations as a whole have grown as quickly as the rest of the country, even if we include as part of their growth those people who have become town-dwellers as a result of the spreading of towns. Thus, while we now find a considerably larger proportion of the population living in London, by far the greatest conurbation in the country, the proportion living in the other large conurbations as a whole may be actually smaller.

We have also seen that, within regions, there has been no clear tendency for the large conurbations to gain immigrants more quickly, or to lose emigrants more slowly, than the surrounding country.

It is not unlikely that the above general conclusions apply to places of work as well as to places of residence. There seems to be no convincing evidence to show that there has been any marked relative growth in the population working in the large towns, either in the country as a whole or within regions.

There has been a relative growth in the number of people living in the outer, less densely populated, areas of large towns, the number living in the most densely populated parts having in many cases declined absolutely. In London there has been a similar outward movement, at least in a relative sense, of industry and trade, but in the other largest conurbations the movement seems to have been, if anything, in the opposite direction.

Part Two: The War

4 The Prime Minister's Statistical Section[1]

ORIGINS AND DUTIES

Soon after the outbreak of war in September Mr. Winston Churchill, then First Lord of the Admiralty, appointed Professor Lindemann, the Oxford physicist, as his personal adviser. At first he was intended to advise mainly on scientific matters, but in October the First Lord asked him to form a statistical branch as well, and within a month or so some half a dozen economists, nearly all in their twenties, had been collected from the universities. 'S Branch', as it was called, was to collect and co-ordinate Admiralty and cognate statistics for the First Lord and also to advise him on wider matters with which he was concerned as a member of the War Cabinet. When Mr. Churchill became Prime Minister in May 1940 the Branch was transformed into the Prime Minister's Statistical Section and the scope of its work greatly enlarged. It remained in being until the change of Government in July 1945. In December 1942 Professor Lindemann (now Lord Cherwell) was appointed Paymaster-General, and the Section was sometimes known thereafter as the Office of the Paymaster-General. An important part of its work was now to advise Lord Cherwell in his personal capacity as a member of the House of Lords, a Minister, an attender at meetings of the War Cabinet and a member of several Cabinet committees. Individual member of the Section also undertook work from time to time, on interdepartmental committees or otherwise, that had only an indirect bearing on their work for the Prime Minister. But the Section continued to be primarily the Prime Minister's personal section, acting through Lord Cherwell as his personal adviser, and it is with this aspect of its work that the present chapter deals.

The total establishment was in the neighbourhood of twenty. On the average there were perhaps half a dozen economists; one scientific officer; one established civil servant (with economic training) to help keep the amateurs on the rails; some half a dozen

[1] Chapter in *Lessons of the British War Economy*, 1951, ed. D. N. Chester.

computers; two or three typists and clerks; and last, but not least, a number of what were called 'chartists'—about four were fully employed in the early period when there was much drawing of new charts and diagrams.

The staff had contacts with nearly every Ministry, most of all with the Service and supply departments, the Ministries of War Transport, Fuel and Power, Food, Labour and Economic Warfare, the Treasury and the Board of Trade. They dealt with departmental officers at all levels, and Lord Cherwell had much conversation and correspondence with various Ministers. Work was informal and intimate, and Lord Cherwell spent much of his time in discussion with his staff.

The main method of communication with the Prime Minister, apart from tables and charts submitted regularly, was through minutes from Lord Cherwell supplemented by his frequent discussions with the Prime Minister. There was a steady flow of these minutes, which totalled some 2,000 over the whole period of nearly six years, or an average of roughly one per day.

One of their main characteristics was brevity, a quality on which the Prime Minister insisted. This at times meant some sacrifice of accuracy and perhaps undue emphasis of one side of the case. But to members of his staff who had delved deeply in the problem and whose inclination, both as academics and as temporary civil servants, was to tell the whole story, Lord Cherwell's reply was always, 'l'art d'être ennuyeux c'est tout dire'. Brevity was an essential quality of minutes addressed to so burdened a man as the Prime Minister, and I believe that the minutes, while less complete, were often more readable than official reports composed to please every member of an interdepartmental committee or all the interested parties within a Ministry.

Some of the minutes were comments on official papers circulated to the Cabinet or Cabinet committees; some commented on minutes sent by other Ministers to the Prime Minister; many were written in response to requests by the Prime Minister for information and an opinion on specific topics; many raised matters which Lord Cherwell, on his own initiative, wished to bring to the Prime Minister's attention.

The Section was thus much more than a purely statistical one. It was concerned not merely with the collection and presentation of statistics but with the conclusions to be drawn from them, and it also made frequent recommendations on general economic policy. Except at the Prime Minister's request minutes were seldom submitted unless they recommended action. Lord Cherwell was loth to add minutes that were only for information to the pile of papers always in the Prime Minister's box.

A minute from Lord Cherwell recommending action might occasionally form the basis of a directive by the Prime Minister, after consultation with the Ministers concerned. More often the Prime Minister would address an inquiry to the appropriate departmental Minister or Ministers, or ask a Minister without departmental responsibility to conduct an inquiry and report. The Ministerial reply would normally be passed to Lord Cherwell for comment. When a new line of policy was settled the Prime Minister would sometimes ask for periodic progress reports which would in turn be examined by the Section. As these were normally of a statistical nature the obligation to make returns might occasionally encourage action, undesirable in itself, simply to boost the figures, but this was unusual. The progress report was in general a useful method of ensuring that decisions were implemented or at least, when this was impracticable, not forgotten.

CHARACTER OF THE WORK

Part of Lord Cherwell's work was in the scientific field and concerned with the technical details of instruments of war, their development, production and use. An analysis of the minutes he submitted to Mr. Churchill shows that nearly one-third were mainly on such scientific matters. It is impossible, however, to draw a hard and fast line between minutes on 'scientific', and minutes on statistical and economic, matters, and it would be a mistake to think that these two aspects of Lord Cherwell's work were in wholly watertight compartments. In the development of new weapons, for example, questions of manpower and materials were often as important as more technical details. When weapons reached the stage of production and use there was obvious scope for statistical treatment to test their effectiveness, the adequacy or superfluity of stocks, and the like. The technical details of the war at sea had an obvious bearing on the shipping and import position. We are concerned here with the statistical and economic side of the work, but the fact that Lord Cherwell was also deeply concerned with 'scientific' matters is a characteristic of the Section that must be emphasized.

On what may be called the non-scientific side of the work the range of subjects covered was wide. Of the 'non-scientific' minutes sent to the Prime Minister perhaps 30 per cent were mainly concerned with the armed forces, 20 per cent mainly with shipping,

15 per cent with food, agriculture and raw materials, about 10 per cent with postwar problems, and the remaining 25 per cent with miscellaneous topics ranging widely from the building programme to the shortage of matches, from economic warfare to the supply of doctors, from Russia and India to export policy, rationing, inflation and austerity. These proportions varied, of course, from time to time. The emphasis on postwar problems naturally increased during the last few years, and the proportion of minutes dealing with the armed forces tended to decline. The proportions are rough and ready, since many of the minutes covered a number of fields. A characteristic of the Section was indeed the breadth of its interests. I think it fair to say that this facilitated a breadth of vision as well, although an excessive range of interests may also lead to amateurish dabbling. The Section cannot be wholly acquitted of this, at least in the early period, but as time went on it gained much from its continuity and from the comparative freedom of its members from routine administrative duties. This enabled them to acquire some expert knowledge in a fair number of subjects and to gain in the end the confidence of most departments concerned.

It will be seen that much of the work related to the armed forces, of which the Section kept copious records. This interest, together with Lord Cherwell's work on more technical matters, differentiated the Section in an important respect from the Economic Section of the War Cabinet secretariat. The latter body was more concerned with the maximization of the war effort as a whole than with the use made of resources once they had been set aside for war purposes. The maximization of the total war effort may be a problem that can be considered from the civilian side alone. We know that, after a point, cuts in civilian transport, medical services, food, or consumer goods in general will affect the ability and willingness of the civilian population to produce warlike goods. The problem is to transfer resources from civilian to warlike uses up to the point where a further transfer will bring no *net* gain to the war effort. But in practice, where particular adjustments at the margin are under consideration, it may be useful to have some idea of what would happen to resoures if they were transferred to the military sector. The total effect of the transfer might be to increase a less urgent, at the expense of a more urgent, part of the war effort. For example, to cut bus services in order to release oil tankers for military use might, where the extra oil demanded by the armed forces was not 'really necessary', add little to their effectiveness while it held up production of essential weapons through the indirect effect on the workers involved. Then again some knowledge of the state of the armed forces is required when advising on the allocation of, say, manpower between the various Services, their respective production departments, and the building programme.

USE OF STATISTICS

We have seen that the Section was much more than a purely statistical one, but a considerable part of the work was, of course, of a statistical nature. In the early days of the war many government statistics were extremely confusing, conflicting and incomplete. It was extraordinarily difficult to get a simple, overall picture of what was happening. The Section devoted much energy to the collection of statistics, to the reconciliation of apparent discrepancies, and to the simple presentation of the facts, especially in the form of charts. Such simple presentation was required for the use of the Section itself, for the information of the Prime Minister, and also, on occasion, for the information, through the Prime Minister, of President Roosevelt and other Americans. The development of the Central Statistical Office, and of central statistical departments in the various Ministries, reduced the burden of collection and reconciliation as time went on; and as the general statistical picture, and the more important orders of magnitude, became better known, the need for simple tables, charts and exposition was diminished. But the Section continued to keep many detailed statistical records in the form required for its particular purposes, and until the end it provided Mr. Churchill with statistical summaries for use at his conferences with allied leaders.

The Section was also statistical in that it was interested primarily in the quantitative aspect of problems. Few of Lord Cherwell's minutes to the Prime Minister were free from figures. An argument was hardly considered respectable unless backed by statistics. An attempt to establish a prima facie case for action by the Prime Minister had at least to be illustrated by appropriate orders of magnitude.

The establishment of such orders of magnitude sometimes involved much work, especially when a major change in Government policy was being recommended. Before proposing to the Prime Minister that, say, the building programme should be curtailed, it would be necessary to show, by some simple quantitative measures, that further building on the current scale was relatively unnecessary, and that the saving of imports and manpower to be achieved was large. A proposal that military vehicles should be dismantled before shipment, despite the inconvenience involved, would have to be backed by a demonstration that the shipping to be saved was substantial. The Section would also have to examine carefully many of the detailed technical problems involved and if possible to secure the support and agreement of departmental officers. All this meant that weeks of work might lie behind a half-page minute to the Prime Minister.

The collection and clarification of statistics relating to the past was a necessary preliminary to work on estimates of the future. Much of the Section's time was devoted to such work. Being responsible for warning the Prime Minister of impending shortages, it had to make independent forecasts of its own; and it often had to make critical analyses of forecasts and requirements submitted by departments. In the early years especially, a finding of undue pessimism was as common as one of excessive optimism. The Section often reached the conclusion that departments were exaggerating the demands likely to be placed upon them and underestimating what could be done with the resources at their disposal. The detection in this way of excessive 'requirements' can often be as important in avoiding waste and maldistribution of resources as the forecasting of a shortage that will cause a bottleneck. The rather rudimentary statistical organization of some departments in the earlier part of the war, coupled with a natural desire to be 'on the safe side', provided scope for a non-departmental body prepared both to examine critically the details of departmental calculations and to apply broad, common-sense tests to the conclusions reached. As statistical departments were strengthened throughout the government service, and as more and more experience was gained of war conditions, estimates of the future improved greatly; and with the formation of bodies like the Ministry of Production the need for scrutiny by the Section was diminished. But the natural tendency of departments to take a departmental rather than a national view continued, and the criticism of departmental estimates remained an important part of the Section's work until the end.

When it comes to forecasting shortages the ability of an organization like the Prime Minister's Statistical Section is limited. It may be able to give an opinion on, for example, the likelihood of a coal shortage, or a general appraisal of the shipping or manpower position in the near or distant future. It may possibly, by keeping detailed statistics of weapons of war, be able to forcast a likely lack of balance. But it will seldom, except by accident or by personal contact with those immediately responsible, be able to foresee a bottleneck in, for example, drop-forgings, alloy steel or some aircraft component, unless it is large enough to duplicate much of the detailed work of production departments.

It was necessary on occasion to call the Prime Minister's attention to impending shortages that were clear for all to see, but on which sufficiently urgent action was not being taken. The Section would then also propose what it considered to be the least harmful methods of adequately meeting the shortage. This might involve quite disproportionate cuts in some sectors — a drastic reduction in military shipments to theatres overseas, but little or no cut in imports; a drastic cut in raw materials imports, but little reduction in imports of food. Such proposals were at times different from those that might have emerged from normal interdepartmental negotiations. An acceptable compromise is then normally the object. The measures agreed may sometimes, too, be inadequate to meet the case, leaving the final incidence of the shortage unsettled, with possibly disastrous effects on some sector of the economy. Whether or not such compromises and half-measures would have been better policy, it is necessary to record that the Prime Minister did on occasion make proposals, or issue directives, based on the apparently less 'reasonable' recommendations of Lord Cherwell and his staff.

When reviewing the various possible methods of meeting a shortage the Section always attempted to evaluate their relative importance. This helped to concentrate attention on those that really mattered and to avoid useless discussions of the trivial. It was desired to increase imports or balance the coal budget; this measure might contribute several million tons, that several hundred thousand, another a mere hundred or so. Such indications, however rough and ready, may be invaluable to the Prime Minister when conducting a meeting. They serve as a useful reminder that success in dealing with a problem is not to be gauged by the *number* of measures taken. As Lord Cherwell, with his flair for orders of magnitude, never tired of insisting, a small change in a big thing may often be more effective, and is usually more desirable, than a lot of big changes in a lot of small things.

SOME LESSONS

The foregoing pages have described in very general terms what the Prime Minister's Statistical Section was, how it worked and what it did. It is hard to assess its accomplishments or to strike a balance between its merits and defects. One who was a member of the Section from its first day till its last is hardly qualified to deliver judgment.

Whatever the verdict the success or failure of Mr. Churchill's Statistical Section under Lord Cherwell during these six years would neither establish nor disprove the case for a Prime Minister's statistical or economic section in general. The character of the

Section depended greatly on these two personalities, on the nature of the problems that arose during the second world war, and on the general organization of the government service during the period. It may nevertheless be useful to outline some considerations that will be relevant if the establishment of such a body is ever again considered.

Much will depend on the personality of the Prime Minister. In the first place, some Prime Ministers may not be greatly interested in the quantitative aspect of problems. They may prefer, in making a decision, to rely on personal discussion with the Ministers concerned. They may not, in addition, feel the need for a simple, independent, overall appraisal in quantitative terms. Such Prime Ministers will have little need of a statistical section of any kind.

In the second place, an organization of this type can easily arouse the opposition of departmental officers and of their Ministers. Some Prime Ministers may not be prepared to risk this opposition. Even if they are, it may be hard for members of the section to co-operate successfully with departmental officers if they lack the backing of a strong Prime Minister. This difficulty applies to most organizations without a departmental minister. Except in cases of collusion between the section and departmental officers, the latter may often be reluctant, and very naturally so, to divulge information that may be used to criticize their Ministry, or to spare the time needed to provide information in the form requested. They may fear that figures given will be misinterpreted. They may be reluctant to confirm calculations of a type to which they are unaccustomed in their departmental work, but which are essential for a section which has to paint with a broad brush. Averages, they will argue, are misleading because of the dispersion about them. How can you possibly say what tonnage of imports is sacrificed for every extra soldier sent to the Middle East? And so on.

The experience of the Section during the war showed, however, that these difficulties are not insuperable. Given understanding on both sides good relations can be built up. It is an advantage to have in the section some members who have worked in a department. The fundamental remedy is for the section to become sufficiently expert to gain the confidence of departmental officers. For this purpose the staff must be large enough to make some specialization possible, and the turnover must not be too rapid. The section must be absolutely confident of any facts and figures supplied by it that are likely to be quoted outside. In framing estimates and making calculations even more care is required than is expended by departmental experts who are, after all, the recognized authorities. Whenever possible the agreement of the latter should be secured in advance. A sense of proportion must, of course, be preserved. A large collection of unduly cautious specialists of long standing might be of even less value than a few careless, tactless amateurs. A little irresponsibility is desirable in a section intended partly as an irritant.

A possible criticism of an organization like the Prime Minister's Statistical Section in the recent war is that it may give undue influence to people who develop prejudices. It is inevitable that such a section, and its head, will come to take a certain line on a number of matters — it could hardly fail to do so and avoid inconsistency. The question is whether these lines are sound or otherwise, a matter on which opinion will not always be unaminous. There is no doubt that the Section did develop views — or prejudices, if you will. Lord Cherwell held views on the correct distribution of our war effort between land, air and sea; on the importance of feeding the people; on postwar problems; and on many other matters. But such views were not inflexible. Opinions based on continuous study of the relevant facts and figures naturally changed from time to time as circumstances altered. The opinion of the Section that the coal shortage in the earlier years of the war was not quite so disturbing as sometimes supposed had changed, long before the end, to an equally firm conviction that the outlook was more serious than commonly imagined. Both views, I believe, were right. Despite a general emphasis on the vital need to maintain imports at a minimum level, even at the expense of military shipping requirements, it was felt necessary to insist at various times that the estimates of import requirements were exaggerated, and that more shipping might be diverted to military use. A tendency, after about 1942, to stress the dangers of false economy in imposing austerity on the people followed an equally strong disposition, earlier in the war, to doubt whether our war-making plans were sufficiently ambitious.

Whether the views of the Prime Minister's advisers are right or wrong it is impossible to advise without them; and, as we have seen, advice can sometimes be too well-balanced.

A Prime Minister's statistical section could, of course, be a less ambitious affair. It could be relieved of the responsibility of giving advice. As a minimum it could act as little more than a post office for transmitting the Prime Minister's requests for statistical information to the appropriate departments. This would not be quite so pointless as it sounds. It may often be better to obtain information in this way than by a direct request from the Prime Minister concerned. The Prime Minister's statisticians, knowing what was in his mind, could help to frame the question in a precise statistical form that admitted of an answer. They might assist the departmental statisticians in any calculations required, if these were outside their normal line of country. They might also perhaps help to 'serve up' the reply in a form that would be readily understood by the Prime Minister and consistent with other statistics with which he was familiar.

Slightly more ambitious would be a section that collected and marshalled statistics from various sources when asked by the Prime Minister for general information on some fairly wide topic. The section might also keep its own records and prepare tables and charts for regular submission to the Prime Minister; it might draw his attention to the more important changes and tendencies from time to time; it might even give a balanced summary of the arguments for and against particular lines of action. All this was done by the Prime Minister's Statistical Section during the war. But if, as was the case, it goes further, if it recommends lines of action, either on its own initiative or at the Prime Minister's request, it becomes an advisory body with the advantages and disadvantages mentioned above.

A Prime Minister's statistical section might thus take various forms, so that even if a body of the 1939—45 variety were ruled out there would be other possibilities.

It may be thought that other bodies, such as the Central Statistical Office and the Economic Section of the Cabinet secretariat, could perform many of these duties. This may be so, but it is worth recording that during the last war, while there was close and cordial co-operation between these bodies and the Prime Minister's Statistical Section, there was little overlapping. Nor, I think, did members of the three bodies have any feeling that effort was being duplicated in a wasteful manner.

The function of the Economic Section was to advise the War Cabinet, and the Lord President in particular, on economic matters. That of the Central Statistical Office was to serve Ministers and departments generally by the collection, reconciliation and presentation of statistics. When the Central Statistical Office was established in January 1941, and separated from what then became the Economic Section of the War Cabinet secretariat, one of the main objects was to provide at least one source of authoritative statistical information which was entirely divorced from the business of advising, and so free from any suspicion of tendentious bias.

The Prime Minister's Section differed from the Central Statistical Office in being an advisory body; it was established, moreover, some time before the services of the Central Statistical Office became available; and the range of interests of the two bodies did not wholly coincide. It differed from the Economic Section, as has been said, in its much more detailed work on the military side; it also laid greater emphasis on quantitative studies and on the keeping of statistical records. Most important of all, it was essentially personal to the Prime Minister; it worked continuously for him; it had some idea of what was in his mind; it knew the sort of thing he wanted to know and how he liked to have it presented; its loyalty was to him and to no one else. This is the crux of the matter. The desirability or otherwise of a staff of this sort depends largely on how strongly the Prime Minister of the day feels the need for such a staff — a staff entirely his own. Some of the possible dangers have already been mentioned. It may be that the Prime Minister should be advised by the responsible Ministers and by no one else; that once Ministers have been appointed they should be allowed to get on with the job. On the other hand, the Prime Minister must see that they do get on with the job. He must decide, too, what job they are to get on with, both when there is a clash of departmental interests and also when a fundamental change is required in the policy of the Government. How far should the Prime Minister be assisted in these duties by personal advisers? The question is really one of degree. All Prime Ministers have a personal staff. They have private secretaries and a Parliamentary Private Secretary; they are assisted by the Secretary to the Cabinet; if Minister of Defence, they have military advisers; and so on. The question at issue here is whether, since so many of the problems with which Prime Ministers must deal have economic and quantitative aspects, their staff should also include economists and statisticians. Is it right that, when Ministers meet to discuss such matters, the Prime Minister alone should be largely unsupported by expert advice?

Part Three: The Early Postwar Years

5 Britain's foreign trade problem[1]

INTRODUCTION

It is universally agreed that unless we can export much more than before the war we shall have to import much less.

But what we should do in the circumstances is a matter of hot dispute.

Much of the debate revolves round general propositions that can be proved or disproved only by studying the facts, and the importance of such a study is the main excuse for this article and for its numerous figures and footnotes.

A minority believe that we could easily dispense with a large part of our imports, and would therefore have us retreat into our shell; but it is argued in Section 1 that this would entail extreme austerity.

In Section 2 we see that our export problem, while greatly aggravated by the war, is of long standing, and bound up with the industrialisation of overseas countries; certain morals for our economic policy are suggested.

From Section 3 it appears that a large increase in our exports will be impossible without an expansion of world trade as a whole, and that this would result from a general reduction of trade barriers; while Section 4 demonstrates the vital importance to Britain of multilateral trade.

But it will also be necessary to expand our share in world trade, and the prospects are examined in Sections 5 and 6. In Section 5 (a) we see that the capture of German and Japanese markets will be of value only if we do not have to subsidise our late enemies correspondingly; and the wisdom of reaching agreement with the United States, our main competitor, on rules for the fair conduct of export trade, is emphasised in Section 5 (b).

Section 6 is a reminder that the quantity of exports we sell is by no means independent of their price; and that this can be greatly influenced by changes in the value of sterling. But the manipulation

[1] *Economic Journal,* March 1947.

of our currency will not always achieve equilibrium in our balance of payments, and we must therefore reserve the right to restrict imports by more direct measures. How this can be reconciled with a widespread reduction of trade barriers is discussed in Section 7, which examines briefly, in the light of the morals emerging from our study, the rival merits of international agreements on the lines of Bretton Woods and I.T.O., and of a policy that would preserve our full economic sovereignty.

1. THE EXPORT TARGET

A large expansion in British exports is generally accepted as indispensable to our economic well-being. The Government target is a volume of exports 75% in excess of the pre-war level,[2] and there has been little tendency, in informed public discussion, to regard this figure as excessive[3]; if anything, the criticism has been that it is too low.

The main reasons for such a high export target are well known. They are briefly recapitulated below, together with some rough indications of their respective orders of importance.[4]

(i) To finance the war and its aftermath, we have been obliged to live on our overseas capital. This does not mean that we have sold all our foreign investments. Before the war the nominal value of these was estimated at £3,700 million,[5] and up to June 1945 we had realised from their sale only about £1,100 million;[6] although the two figures are not directly comparable, it is clear that a large part of our overseas wealth remains intact. Even in 1945 our gross receipts from foreign investments totalled £170 million,[6] compared with rather more than £200 million before the war (when, however, the general price level was lower). But a large part of our remaining receipts will be offset by interest and amortisation payments on the huge sums we

---

[2] Cmd. 7018.
[3] See, for example, F. W. Paish, in *Royal Economic Society Memorandum* No. 105, F. A. Friday, in the *Bulletin of the Oxford University Institute of Statistics* for June, 1946, and Dr. E. C. Snow, in *The Times*, January 23rd, 1947.
[4] This task is complicated by the rise in prices that has taken place since before the war. The proportions of the required increase in exports attributed to the various causes will vary according to the way in which the calculation is set out. This is one important reason why the figures in the text differ from those in Friday, *op. cit.* It is believed, however, that they give a correct general impression.
[5] Kindersley, *Economic Journal*, December, 1939. This is believed to be an under-estimate of the value of our overseas investments. See *Bulletin of the Oxford University Institute of Statistics*, January, 1946, p. 27.
[6] Cmd. 6707.

have been forced to borrow.[7] In 1945 we paid out £73 million in interest, dividends, etc.,[8] and this figure will be augmented by, among other things, the £45 million payable annually on our American and Canadian loans, and by large amortisation payments, measured in scores of millions, on our sterling balances. The net result will depend greatly on the arrangements made for scaling down and funding these balances, and it is to be hoped that a fair bargain will be struck which recognises that these are mainly debts incurred between allies fighting a common war. But it is probably safe to assume that our exports will have to be increased in volume by, say, 40% to make good our loss of income on overseas investments and to pay the charges on the debts we have incurred.

(ii) We can hardly contemplate, in present circumstances, an indefinite continuation of the pre-war deficit in our balance of payments, which amounted in 1938 to £70 million.[9] To make this good would have required, before the war, an increase of about 15% in our exports.

(iii) In the past our imports have usually increased with the national income; and in normal circumstances the growth of our population since 1938, the maintenance of full employment and the general increase of productivity, would have led to a considerable increase in the demand for imported food and materials. It would be by no means excessive to add, say, a further 15% of the pre-war level of exports on to our target on this count. This would allow for an increase of only 8% in our imports, to take care of an increase of some 5% in our population (by the early 'fifties) and an increase in the real national income which even the most pessimistic agree is likely to take place, and which the optimists believe may be as high as 25%.

In addition to these three main factors there are a number of imponderables that may tend to increase the exports required. Overseas expenditure by the Government for political and military reasons may well be higher than before the war,[10] and the terms at

---

[7] Our present external liabilities, together with our prospective debts to the United States and Canada, are around £5,000 million. It is interesting to compare this with the sum of approximately £6,500 million (at £1 = 20 gold marks) fixed for German reparations in 1921.

[8] Cmd. 6707. Both the figure of £73 million and that of £170 million mentioned earlier include certain collections of interest on external securities remitted to overseas holders.

[9] Cmd. 6623.

[10] In 1946, net Government expenditure overseas was about £300 million, compared with only £13 million in 1938. For 1947 it has been estimated at £175 million (Cmd. 7046). Continuing expenditure of this order would involve a substantial increase in the export target.

which we exchange our exports for our imports may deteriorate. For a time, too, our merchant fleet — which makes an important contribution to our balance of payments — will be smaller than before the war. It fell from 16½ million gross tons in 1939 to little more than 11½ in 1943.[11] But it has already recovered, at the time of writing, to over 13 million tons, and our shipyards should easily be able to restore our fleet to the pre-war size by 1950.

Taking everything into account, an increase of exports by 75% seems a reasonable target; and whether the correct figure is 50%, 75% or 100% will not greatly affect the general nature of the problem now confronting us.

What will happen if we do not achieve our target? We might, of course, default on our debt payments or cut down those of our military and political commitments that cost foreign exchange; both courses are clearly undesirable, although government expenditure overseas will have to be more carefully scrutinised than hitherto. We might attempt to borrow more money or to sell our remaining foreign assets. Such expedients are likewise undesirable for many reasons, nor could they continue indefinitely. Their practicability, too, is by no means certain; loans to a country with a chronic deficit are hardly good business, and many of our remaining overseas assets are not readily marketable. A failure to achieve our export target must therefore, by and large, result in a corresponding reduction in our imports. A small part of this reduction might fall on our 'invisible' imports, such as films, tourist expenditure and remittances abroad; but as these three items amounted to little more than 5% of our 'visible' imports, we shall not be far out if we assume that the whole cut would fall on the latter.

To illustrate the implications of not achieving our export target, let us see what would happen if our exports failed, in the long run, to exceed the 1938 volume. They had already recovered to this level by the middle of 1946, and to 11% above by the last quarter, and are likely to increase still further in the present sellers' market, given an adequate supply of coal for the export industries, but when immediate shortages overseas are made good they might well fall back to the 1938 level. With exports permanently at this level our imports would have to be cut to something like two-thirds of the 1938 volume.[12]

[11] Vessels of 1,600 gross tons and over.
[12] The calculation, in round figures and at 1938 prices, is as follows. Our retained imports in 1938 were £860 million. It is assumed, as in the text, that the export target of 175% of pre-war allows for an increase in imports of 8% — *i.e.*, to £930 million. Our exports in 1938 were £470 million, and if the target were achieved they would be £820 million — an increase of £350 million. If they failed to exceed the 1938 level, our imports would therefore fall

As will be seen from Table I, this would be lower than at any time during the war. From 1942 until the end of the war the volume of our imports was, on the average, about three-quarters of the 1938 level.[13]

TABLE I

*Volume of Retained Imports**

(1938 = 100)

1938	100
1939	97
1940	94
1941	82
1942	70
1943	77
1944	80
July 1944–June 1945†	74
July 1945–Dec. 1946‡	65

*The figures are substantially comparable throughout, those for 1942–45 being exclusive of munitions imported by Government Departments; the indices for 1940 and 1941 would, however, be several points lower if munitions had been excluded in those years.
†Broadly last year of war.
‡Broadly first eighteen months of peace.

This does not necessarily imply that a permanent fall in imports to two-thirds of the pre-war level would mean a standard of living lower than we enjoyed during the war. Much of our war-time austerity was caused by the diversion of resources to war purposes.[14] In addition, we were forced during the war to save shipping rather than foreign exchange; this governed our choice of imports and led us, for example, to import expensive steel rather than cheap iron ore. For

---

from the target of £930 million to £580 million, or 67% of the 1938 level. The true figure might well turn out to be nearer one-half than two-thirds, if the assumptions implied in the 75% export target prove optimistic; this may well be true of, for example, Government expenditure overseas, invisible exports and the terms of trade.
[13] The fall in *tonnage* was, of course, considerably greater than the fall in volume (*i.e.*, value corrected for price changes); our efforts to save shipping involved a shift to imports with a high value per ton, *e.g.*, steel instead of iron ore, dried eggs instead of maize.
[14] In particular, a large part of the war-time petroleum imports were used directly by the Services.

both these reasons our war-time standards were lower than would be necessitated in peace-time by a cut of one-quarter in our imports.

But in other ways our war-time standards were maintained by expedients that cannot be continued indefinitely. We postponed maintenance of our capital equipment; we stopped building houses; we made a drastic cut in our exports, which consume imported materials; we cut down our forests; and some hold that we exhausted our land.

It is not easy to strike a balance between these two sets of countervailing considerations; and our war-time experience is thus a poor guide to peace-time conditions. It is of rather more significance, perhaps, that a permanent cut in our imports by one-third below the pre-war level would mean restricting them to approximately the level achieved in the first, austere, eighteen months of peace, especially when we remember that during this latter period our stocks of many important raw materials and foodstuffs were falling.

But even the last eighteen months have been an abnormal period of reconversion from war to peace, and the only way to get a true picture of what import economies would mean in the long run is to start off with our pre-war imports. In 1938 these were made up as follows.[15]

	£ million
Food	410
Raw materials	225
Manufacturers	216
Other	7
	858

Economies might be made in two ways: (a) by replacing imports by home production, and (b) by reducing overall consumption of goods which are, in part at least, imported. Against these economies we must set (c) the greater needs of a higher population and of an increasing industrial production. Consider in the first place (a) and (c).

The savings to be achieved in *food* imports by greater home production are smaller than is often imagined. Before the war, in very round figures, we imported £400 million of food and feeding-stuffs, and home agriculture produced £200 million, after deducting

---

[15] 'Food' corresponds to Class I of the Trade Returns, plus oilseeds and nuts, less tobacco; 'raw materials' to Class II, plus tobacco, less oilseeds and nuts; 'manufactures' to Class III; and 'other' to Classes IV and V (parcel post and animals, not for food).

the value of imported feeding-stuffs, etc.[16] During the war our output increased, it is true, by more than 70% in terms of calories and of protein,[17] and by 120% in units of shipping space; but we did this largely by concentrating on cheap foods like potatoes. Measured in money value, which is the relevant yardstick here, the increase in the volume of home output was only 30–35%,[18] or about £60–70 million at pre-war prices. It may be that, in peace-time, if we aimed wholly at saving foreign exchange rather than shipping, we could increase our output by more than one-third above the pre-war level; on the other hand, it is often argued that we achieved the war-time increase only by exhausting the land. It may be that in due course 'Britain can feed herself,'[19] but even if practicable, this revolution could hardly be achieved overnight. The possibilities of increasing agricultural production deserve urgent attention, but for the next decade, let us say, it would be imprudent to count on an output much larger than we achieved during the war: an increase of, say, 40% on the pre-war output would save about £80 million of imported food at pre-war prices. But against this must be set an extra requirement of some £30 million to feed the additional population, which is expected, by the early 'fifties, to be about 5% higher than in 1938. The net saving of food imports would thus be only £50 million at pre-war prices, a mere 6% of our total pre-war imports of all kinds; and even this small saving would soon be swallowed up by a modest improvement in our pre-war diet, which is generally regarded as desirable.

Our imports of *raw materials* consisted almost wholly of things that we cannot easily produce in significantly greater quantities at home, the main items being textile materials (£71 million), timber and paper-making materials (£59 million), tobacco (£23 million), non-ferrous ores (£15 million), hides and skins (£9 million) and rubber (£9 million). The few exceptions to this rule, such as iron ore, are of trivial importance. Timber production can be greatly increased as a temporary measure, but a large sustained increase is hardly possible in the foreseeable future.[20] The production of synthetic

---

[16] The total of rather more than £600 million represents the value at the farm and at the port; the retail value of our food supplies, which includes the cost of processing and distribution, was about twice as large.

[17] Cmd. 6564.

[18] In the *Journal of Proceedings of the Agricultural Economics Society*, Vol. VII, No. 1, Mr. Kirk, of the Ministry of Agriculture, estimates the increase at 30%; in Cmd. 7046 it is put at 35%.

[19] See book of that name by G. P. Pollitt.

[20] It is significant that timber production, which in 1943 reached a peak more than four times the rate at the outbreak of war (Cmd. 6564), had already dropped by 1946 to little more than twice that level, despite the severe world shortage.

materials offers important possibilities which should be fully explored, but this will often in turn entail imports of further materials, as with synthetic textiles, or the use of large quantities of coal, which is at present in short supply, or the loss of income from overseas investments in, for example, rubber plantations.

Our imports of raw materials have in the past varied closely with industrial production, and this is certain in future to be considerably higher than in 1938. The year 1938 was comparatively depressed; even in 1937, when we still had 11% unemployed, industrial production was 7% higher than in 1938. In addition, we must hope for a general increase in industrial productivity, and for a particularly high level of activity in the building and export industries, both large users of imported materials. Taking everything into account it would be surprising if we could get along with an increase of less than, say, 15% in our imports of materials. This would cost nearly £35 million at pre-war prices, and would offset a large part of the food savings estimated in the previous paragraph.

In principle a considerable part of our imports of *manufactures* could be replaced by home production. This would usually involve an increase in imports of crude materials, but the net saving would often be considerable. Instead, for example, of importing refined petroleum at an average pre-war cost of 3¾d. per gallon, we might import crude oil at a cost of 2¼d. a gallon and refine it at home; instead of importing iron and steel at an average cost of £11 a ton we might import pig iron at £6 a ton or iron ore at £2 10s. per ton of iron content (all pre-war prices). In the case of highly fabricated goods, such as machinery, electrical goods, vehicles, cutlery, hardware and instruments (on which we spent £34 million), the offsetting cost of imported materials would be negligible. An analysis of our pre-war imports of manufactures, totalling £216 million, suggests that a theoretical *net* saving of something approaching £100 million might be made in these ways. There would, however, be numerous practical difficulties and off-setting considerations. For example, the refining of oil at home might reduce the income from our overseas refineries; it might be a false economy to restrict imports of special new machinery which we could produce at home only after a long delay, or unduly to restrict marginal imports of any kind that stimulates our own manufacturers. In practice, it would probably be unwise to count on a net economy of more than, say, £50 million.

This brief review suggests that the total saving in imports from an increase in home production of all kinds, after allowing for the needs of a growing population and a growing industrial production, would be unlikely to exceed, say, £65 million, a mere 7½% of our pre-war imports.

A reduction of anything like one-third would therefore involve a heavy cut in the *consumption* of things that are, in whole or in part, imported. It is a mistake to think that much could be gained by keeping out obvious luxuries like champagne and caviare, flowers and the like. Even on a liberal interpretation, items such as these accounted for only a few per cent of our pre-war imports. Large reductions would have to be made in food and materials in general use. Even the restriction of our diet to the 1944 level would save less than 10% of our total pre-war imports,[21] leaving large cuts to be made in the consumption of such items as paper, petrol, tyres, cigarettes and clothing, the raw materials for which are almost wholly imported, and necessitating the substitution wherever possible of home-produced materials such as cement for imported materials such as timber.

We have seen that a failure of our exports to exceed the 1938 level would involve a cut in our pre-war imports of perhaps one-third. While this would not mean starvation,[22] it would involve extreme austerity and inconvenience, and our full-employment policy would be constantly threatened by a shortage of materials. Even a failure to achieve our export target by a much smaller margin would mean substantial cuts in consumption that would materially affect our standard of living.

It may seem strange that a cut in imports of a few hundred million pounds, trivial in comparison with our pre-war national income of £4,600 million, should have such a marked effect on our prosperity. The reason is, of course, that such a cut would entail disproportionate reductions in the consumption of certain commodities that we cannot easily produce at home. Nearly half our imports were

[21] This statement is based on the following rough calculation. Pre-war food consumption (valued at the farm and at the port) was rather more than £600 million. Between 1938 and 1944 civilian food consumption per head (measured in retail value at constant prices) fell by 11% (*Impact of the War on Civilian Consumption in the United Kingdom, United States and Canada*, H.M.S.O., 1945). 11% of £600 million is £66 million, only 8% of our total 1938 imports of £858 million. (An alternative calculation shows an even smaller saving.)

[22] If, for example, to take an extreme case, we were forced to disregard the variety of our diet, and imported only cereals, we could get the same number of calories from our imports as before the war at a cost of less than £100 million, at pre-war prices, compared with the £400 million actually spent on food imports; if we also organised our agriculture so as to produce the maximum number of calories for human consumption, the import bill would be still further reduced. It is perhaps some consolation that, even with our total imports cut to a tenth of the pre-war volume, we could still avoid starvation!

food, of which we produced only one-third of our total requirements, and at least one-quarter were materials of which our home
production formed less than 10% of the total.

Provided we can *sell* our exports in the required quantities, the
effort of *producing* a few hundred millions more than pre-war will, it
is true, not greatly affect our standard of living; it will require only,
say, 1¼ million extra workers,[23] out of a total labour force of some
20 millions. The really serious effect on our standard of living will
arise if we cannot sell our exports, and have to cut our imports
substantially. The main problem, in the long run, is thus one of
selling, not of production; although the opposite is, of course, the
case to-day.

From this brief analysis it is clear that a very large increase in our
exports is essential to our economic well-being. The possibilities of
replacing imports by home production of food, synthetic materials
and the like should certainly be explored as a matter of urgency, so
that we may be ready to mitigate the consequences of a severe
import cut, should this be necessary when the sellers' market is over
and the American loan exhausted. But such possibilities are limited,
and it remains true that an increase of 75% in our exports is by no
means an excessive target. In the rest of this article we shall examine
the prospects of achieving such an increase; and as we proceed draw
certain morals for our international economic policy.

2. LONG-TERM TRENDS

First let us look at the course of our exports and imports over the
last century, as portrayed (on a logarithmic scale) in Diagram I. The
figures show the quantum (or volume) of our exports and imports
(*i.e.*, after allowing for changes in prices[24]) in each year as a
percentage of the quantum in 1913.

The export line fluctuates considerably, mainly as a result of wars
and trade cycles, but if we concentrate attention on the main peaks
of the curve, the general impression is that exports were rising at an
ever-decreasing rate up to 1913, and falling at an ever-increasing rate
thereafter, up to the outbreak of the recent war. This trend would
not necessarily be a cause for disquiet were it not that our imports,
which rose more or less in line with our exports during the sixty or
seventy years before World War I, continued to rise after 1913
(roughly in line with the real national income as hitherto), while our

[23] Direct and indirect.
[24] The correction for price changes necessarily involves difficulties to which most index
numbers are subject, and no great reliance can be placed on the final result, especially when
long-term changes are concerned; but the general impression given by the diagram is
probably correct.

DIAGRAM I

A Century of British Trade 1847–1946

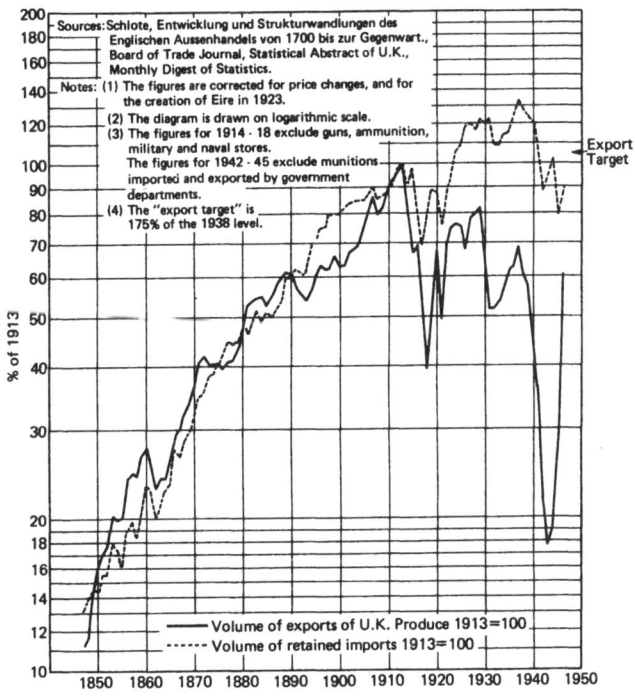

Sources: Schlote, Entwicklung und Strukturwandlungen des
Englischen Aussenhandels von 1700 bis zur Gegenwart.,
Board of Trade Journal, Statistical Abstract of U.K.,
Monthly Digest of Statistics.

Notes: (1) The figures are corrected for price changes, and for
the creation of Eire in 1923.

(2) The diagram is drawn on logarithmic scale.
(3) The figures for 1914 - 18 exclude guns, ammunition,
military and naval stores.
The figures for 1942 - 45 exclude munitions
imported and exported by government
departments.
(4) The "export target" is
175% of the 1938 level.

Export Target

——— Volume of exports of U.K. Produce 1913=100
------ Volume of retained imports 1913=100

exports were falling steeply. Between 1913 and 1938 the quantum of
our imports rose by a quarter, while the quantum of our exports fell
by two-fifths.[25]

How, then, were we able to pay for such greatly increased
imports? The answer is twofold. First, we have been exchanging
exports for imports at an increasingly advantageous rate. While the
average sterling price of our imports was no higher in 1938 than in

---

[25] This may exaggerate the fall in our exports in so far as the index numbers fail to take
account of improvements in quality.

1913, the prices fetched by our exports rose by about two-fifths.[26] Secondly, we gave up investing abroad, and began, in fact, to live on our overseas capital. In 1913 our visible and invisible exports not only paid for our imports, but exceeded them by some 30%; the margin — about £200 million — was added to our capital abroad. In the years 1923—29 the favourable margin was only 7%; between 1930 and 1937 our visible and invisible exports paid for 97% of our imports; and in 1938 for only 92%. To pay for the remainder we were drawing on our overseas capital.

These two developments tended to mask the fact that we were importing more and more and exporting less and less. But even if there had been no war this would sooner or later have been forced on our attention. Clearly we could not have continued indefinitely to live on our overseas capital at an ever-increasing rate. Moreover, the consequent need to reverse the decline in our exports would have forced us to offer them at a lower price, by depreciating sterling or otherwise; and the growth of restriction schemes among primary producers, the creation of 'dust-bowls,' and the gradual movement of the depressed agricultural populations of the world to more lucrative openings in industry, might well have arrested the long-term relative decline in the price of our imports.

Even before the war, then, the trend of our exports in relation to imports gave cause for concern. We shall see that two important causes of the decline in our exports after 1913 were the growth of tariffs and other trade barriers which limited the total world trade in manufactures, and the over-valuation of sterling which reduced our share of that trade. Both these developments could in principle have been reversed by a better international policy. But there may also be something more fundamental that is making it more and more difficult to sell our exports — namely, the steady industrialisation of overseas countries that used to be good customers.

It is often held that such industrialisation will always be to our advantage, but this generalisation hardly stands up to investigation. Imagine a country with a virtual monopoly in the production of, say, oranges, which is not very good at producing anything else. Such a country may be able to build up a very respectable standard of living by exporting its oranges, at a good price, in return for the other goods it requires. If now other countries learn to produce cheap oranges for themselves, it is likely that our original orange country

---

[26]This may partly reflect improvements in quality. The index numbers on which the statement is based refer, strictly, to 'average values' rather than to prices.

will suffer. In rather the same way we built up during the last century a large population on a small island which can produce only a fraction of the food and raw materials we require. We did this by being the world's manufacturer. Even as late as 1870, with little more than 2% of the world's population, we still produced one-third of the world's manufactures, and two-fifths of the world's exports of manufactures came from this country. We sold our manufactures abroad, at a good price, to countries that could not produce them for themselves, and obtained in return the food and raw materials we could not produce in Britain. If now all other countries learn to produce all kinds of manufactures, it is surely at least possible that this country may suffer. The process is, of course, continuing apace. Our share of the world's manufacturing production had dropped to less than one-tenth at the outbreak of the war, and our share in world exports of manufactures to less than one-fifth.

We may look at the matter in another way, and consider the effects of industrialisation overseas on the demand for our exports. It is true that we stand to gain orders for capital goods while the overseas countries are industrialising, and that when their standard of living has increased they will be able to buy more of everything, including goods from this country. But, unfortunately, they will also reduce their purchases from us of goods, such as cotton goods, which they can now produce for themselves. One cannot say *a priori* what the net effect of these favourable and unfavourable influences is likely to be. It is at least *possible* that on balance the demand for our exports will fall.

But is it *likely* that we shall suffer? The evidence from the past is hardly reassuring. Nearly the whole fall in the volume of our exports between 1913 and 1937 can be accounted for by the halving of our trade to the industrialised and industrialising countries of the world – industrial Europe, the U.S.A., Japan, Russia and India. These countries, together with ourselves, made nine-tenths of the world's manufactures. Our exports to the other countries of the world, which are predominantly primary producers, hardly fell at all. Exports to three rapidly industrialising countries – India, Japan and Russia – actually fell by two-thirds, hardly a good omen for the future. Nor was this a new tendency. In the forty years before the First World War, the value of our exports to industrial Europe and the U.S.A. rose by little more than one-quarter, while exports to other countries increased two-and-a-half times. Seven-eighths of the rise in our exports during this period went to these predominantly unindustrialised countries. The figures are as in the table.

(£ millions)

	Value of U.K. exports		
	1871–73	1911–13	
Industrial Europe and U.S.A.	113	145	+ 32
Other countries	132	345	+213
Total	245	490	+245

It is sometimes held that, as the world industrialises, world trade will increase, particularly in industrial specialities, and with it the trade of Britain. This again is scarcely borne out by the facts. Between 1913 and 1937 the world's output of manufactures doubled, but world trade in manufactures failed to rise, and the volume of trade between the nine main industrial countries of the world[27] fell by about one-fifth. Trade and production in primary products, on the other hand, increased much more nearly in line, the former by about 25%, the latter by about 45%. It is true that the failure of trade in manufactures to expand was partly the result of tariffs and the like, but high and greatly increased tariffs were also placed on primary products,[28] and the fact that self-sufficiency can be fostered more easily in manufacturing than in primary production suggests that the mutual advantage of international trade in manufactures may not be so great.

Even, then, had there been no war, the industrialisation of the world might have made it more and more difficult for us to sell our exports abroad and to maintain and increase the standard of living of our large population on this small island. (It may be argued that for many years we have in fact been exchanging our manufactures for imported food and raw materials at a steadily improving rate, but we have seen that this may well have been the result of temporary phenomena masking more fundamental changes.)

If this analysis is correct, if the industrialisation of overseas countries is likely to be disadvantageous to us on balance, certain morals can be drawn for our international economic policy. Clearly nothing we do will stop this industrialisation, nor should we, as world citizens, wish to stop it where it is the best way of removing poverty from the world. But we can legitimately urge, through the

---

[27] United Kingdom, United States, Russia, Germany, France, Japan, Italy, Canada, India.
[28] See H. Liepmann, *Tariff Levels*.

International Bank for Reconstruction and Development or otherwise, that in the development of backward countries due emphasis should be laid on primary production. This will certainly be in our interest as a large importer of primary products; and it will often be in the interest of backward countries themselves, for whom food is often the most pressing need, to begin with agricultural development, rather than to rush into industrialisation for its own sake, often behind high tariff walls, the effect of which may be to depress rather than to raise the standard of living. For the same reasons, we stand to gain from any international agreement which limits, in time and in degree, the protection given to 'infant' industries. Finally, since much of the industrialisation of backward countries will be financed by international lending, and since our power to make foreign loans will be limited for many years to come, we should welcome any provision, such as will apply to loans guaranteed by the International Bank, that foreign loans shall not be tied to exports from the lending countries. In this way we may at least gain orders for capital goods, even when they are financed by loans from other countries, such as America; we shall have something to set against the decline in demand for British goods which the industrialising countries are enabled to produce for themselves.

We have seen that the war has not suddenly created an export problem. It has rather intensified — in enormous degree — a problem that has been with us for many years. In the first place, we must now not only arrest the decline in our exports, but expand them by 75% in the space of a few years. We have to go back almost exactly a century to find such an achievement in the course of five years.[29] Secondly, the problem has been intensified by the war-time stimulus to industrialisation in certain overseas countries, such as Canada, Australia, India and Brazil.[30] Thirdly, we have lost contact with many overseas markets during the war, when our exports were perforce cut to 30% of the pre-war level.

3. THE WORLD MARKET FOR MANUFACTURES

Let us now examine the market in which we may hope to sell our exports. This is, for the most part, the world market for manufactured goods. Before the war, manufactures, other than of food and drink, represented rather more than three-quarters of our total

[29] There was, of course, a very rapid recovery after 1918, but this has been more than matched by that of 1945—46, and our required increase of 75% has to be superimposed on the level reached by mid-1946, when exports were running at roughly the 1938 rate.
[30] For an interesting survey of some of these developments, see *World Economic Survey, 1942—44*, Chapter II, and the Cotton Working Party Report.

exports. The remainder consisted mainly of coal, food, drink and certain waste products of industry. It is unlikely that coal exports will recover even to the pre-war level for a good many years to come, and this decline may well offset any expansion in such items as whisky. In this case there will have to be an increase of nearly 100% in exports of manufactures, if our exports as a whole are to be raised by 75% above the pre-war level.

Our exports of manufactures before the war represented only about 2% of the total world consumption of manufactured goods. (This is true even if we interpret manufactures in a narrow sense so as to exclude baking, brewing and other food industries, building, electric power and the like, which have for the most part a local market, and so confine our attention largely to goods which can be transported fairly easily from country to country.) In this sense our exports formed only a very small proportion of the 'world market' for manufactures, and it might seem at first sight a comparatively easy task to double them. The world's consumption of manufactured goods increased during the sixty years before 1939 at a rate of about $3\frac{1}{2}$% per annum[31] (only one-fifth of this expansion being accounted for by the increase of population), so that if only seven months' normal increase were directed to British exports, our problem would be solved! Alternatively, all we need do is to capture an extra 2% of the total world market.

Unfortunately, however, our task is not quite so simple as these figures suggest. Only about one-tenth of the world's manufacturing production entered into international trade in 1937, so that although the share of our exports in the world's *consumption* of manufactures was only 2%, our share of the world's *exports* of manufactures was about 20%. The position was somewhat as shown in Table II.

If the 'world market' is interpreted in this narrower sense, the task of doubling our exports of manufactures appears much more formidable. It is far more difficult to capture 20% than to capture 2% of the 'world market.' If world trade in manufactures remained the same as before the war, we should have to win from our competitors as much as one-quarter of their pre-war markets.

But it is important always to bear in mind the size of the world market in the wider sense, for it reminds us of another possibility of great importance — that of increasing the proportion of the world's output of manufactures that enters into international trade. This has not always been a mere 10%. In the late 'twenties it was about 15%, and in 1913 about 20% (in 1880 it was probably more than 25%);

---

[31] *Industrialisation and Foreign Trade* (League of Nations, 1945), p. 14.

TABLE II

World Output and Exports of Manufactures Other than of Foodstuffs, 1937*

(Billions of dollars)

	Output of manufactures	Exports of manufactures
U.K.	9	2
Other countries	91	8
World	100	10

*These rough estimates are calculated mainly from figures given in *Industrialisation and Foreign Trade*; use was also made of the *Review of World Trade* and of various British production and price statistics.

The definition of manufactures is intended to be that used in the Brussels International Classification for foreign trade statistics. It excludes building, electric power and certain coarse industrial products such as unworked metals, sawn wood, pulp, coke, cement and fertilisers.

The figure for world output is arrived at after eliminating 'double counting' of products entering more than once into recorded industrial output *within one country*; it will include a certain amount of double counting of goods produced in one country and further processed in another, but this seems correct for a comparison with exports.

but between 1913 and 1937, as we have seen, world manufacturing output doubled, while international trade in manufactures failed to rise. Now, one reason for this, as has been suggested, may be that, as more and more countries learn to produce manufactures, the mutual advantage of international trade in manufactures becomes smaller. But there can be little doubt than an important contributory cause was the growth of tariffs, quotas and other restrictions of international trade. In continental Europe, for example, the tariff level on manufactured goods nearly doubled between 1913 and 1931,[32] and there was a general growth of other restrictions. There can be equally little doubt that a widespread removal of these barriers would considerably increase the proportion of manufacturing output entering into international trade. If only we could return to the proportion of, say, the late 'twenties, world trade in manufactures would be increased by 50% above the pre-war level (even assuming world manufacturing output to be no greater than before the war).

[32] Based on figures in H. Liepmann, *op. cit.*

Our export task would then be vastly easier; a doubling of our exports of manufactures would be consistent with an increase of nearly two-fifths in our competitors' exports,[33] a far cry from forcing them to reduce their exports by a quarter.

In the absence of compelling reasons to the contrary, it is therefore greatly in our interest to support any general international agreement to break down barriers to international trade.

4. MULTILATERAL TRADE

Apart from tariffs and the like, an important factor tending to reduce international trade in the inter-war years was the spread of bilateralism. Many countries, especially when faced with balance of payments difficulties, restricted their imports from countries with which they had 'unfavourable' balances, and so tended to equalise payments and receipts, not only between each country and the rest of the world, but between each pair of countries. In the 'twenties something like one-quarter of all international trade was multi-lateral[34] — *i.e.*, the sum of all the 'unfavourable' balances between pairs of countries represented one-quarter of international trade. If bilateralism had been pursued to its logical conclusion, entirely by cutting off imports equal to those 'unfavourable' balances between pairs of countries, world trade would clearly have become one-quarter smaller. In fact there would have been some offset, in so far as nations expanded their imports from countries with which they had 'favourable' balances, to replace imports from countries with which their balance was 'unfavourable'; but even so the volume of trade would certainly have been reduced for the same reasons that bilateral barter between individuals does not permit of anything like the same volume of trade as the multilateral exchange which is a characteristic of all advanced communities.[35]

---

[33] Putting pre-war world exports of manufactures at 100, the position would be roughly as follows:

	Pre-war	Post-war
U.K.	20	40
Others	80	110
	100	150

[34] *The Network of World Trade* (League of Nations, 1942), *q.v.* for a good description of the trend to bilateralism in the 'thirties.
[35] It is true that bilateral agreements between pairs of countries to take each others' goods may enable some trade to be done that would not otherwise take place. But it by no means follows that the general adoption of bilateral practices would, on balance, increase world trade as a whole; for we have seen that bilateralism has also a strong tendency to reduce international exchange.

Since, then, our interest lies in expanding world trade, we should clearly discourage a practice that may reduce it by anything up to one-quarter.

There is often a very natural reluctance to admit the advantages of multilateral trade. Attention was continuously drawn before the war to the fact that our imports from this or that country were much greater than our exports to it. Why, it was asked, should we tolerate this? A first answer is, of course, that we often had important 'invisible' exports to the country in question – in the form of shipping services, income on investments and so on – so that the 'unfavourable' balance was not so great as appeared from the figures of physical exports and imports to which most publicity is directed. But even so there were many countries that paid far less to us on account of the various international transactions than we paid to them. Why should we tolerate this? The answer is that many other countries were in turn paying us more than we paid them. So long, indeed, as our payments as a whole are covered by our receipts as a whole – as they must be in the long run – any 'unfavourable' balances with one set of countries must necessarily be offset by 'favourable' balances with others. This other side of the medal is often forgotten. If we go in for cutting down 'unfavourable' balances – that is to say, for bilateralism – other countries, with whom we have 'favourable' balances, will do the same, and we shall lose a part of our export trade with them.

The quantitative importance of this for the United Kingdom has never, so far as I am aware, been evaluated. Only our balance of payments with the rest of the world as a whole has hitherto been estimated, not the balance with each individual country. The material available is admittedly unsatisfactory, but the importance of the problem seems to justify an attempt to make an estimate, however rough. This has been done for the year 1930. The year was chosen partly for its statistical convenience, partly because our international payments and receipts on current account were roughly in balance in that year, and partly because it was just before the widespread growth of bilateralism in the 'thirties.

Our balance of payments on current account in 1930 is summarised in round figures in Table III.[36]

[36] The method of presentation differs somewhat from that normally adopted; in particular, imports are entered f.o.b. rather than c.i.f., and the shipping items are treated differently. (Sources used in estimating the necessary corrections include Isserlis, 'Tramp Shipping, Cargoes and Freights,' in *Journal of the Royal Statistical Society*, 1938; and *Board of Trade Journal* February 23, 1933.) According to the Board of Trade estimate, there was a small favourable balance in 1930 of £28 million (2½%), but in order to simplify the discussion this balance has been eliminated by an appropriate adjustment of the figures.

TABLE III

Estimated U.K. Balance of Payments on Current Account, 1930

(Adjusted so that the final balance is nil)

	£ millions
1. Payments on current account (*imports f.o.b.; payments to foreigners for carrying our imports; payments by U.K. ships in overseas ports*)	1050
2. Receipts on current account:	
(*a*) Exports of U.K. produce	570
(*b*) Other receipts (*exports of imported merchandise; income from overseas investments; gross earnings of British ships carrying exports and trading between overseas ports; payments by foreign ships in U.K. ports; government transactions, commissions, and miscellaneous (net)*)	480 } 1050
3. Balance (*receipts less payments*)	—

The next task is to work out the balance of payments with each of the countries (some 100 in all) with which we trade, and to separate those with which we had favourable and unfavourable balances respectively.[37] This is a difficult calculation, involving a good many rather arbitrary assumptions. The final result, which is set out in Table IV, must therefore be subject to a fairly wide margin of error, but it is unlikely to give a false general impression.

It will be seen that, of our international transactions on current account of rather more than £1,000 million, about one-quarter was multilateral. On our transactions with countries in Group A we earned a surplus of £250 million, which we used to finance a deficit of £250 million with countries in Group B. In other words, £250 million of our receipts depended on the willingness of countries in Group A to run up 'unfavourable' balances with us.

[37] The greatest difficulties arise with 'invisible' exports and imports. The largest of these is income on overseas investments, and this was distributed between countries mainly on the basis of Lord Kindersley's estimate of the geographical distribution of our overseas investments in 1930 (*Economic Journal*, June, 1933; and see also *The Problem of International Investment*, published by the Royal Institute of International Affairs). The various shipping items were distributed between countries largely on the basis of the Navigation Accounts, which give details of shipping movements at United Kingdom ports, distinguishing the nationality of vessels, and the areas from which ships have come, and to which they are proceeding; Isserlis, *op. cit.*, was also used.

There is insufficient space to set out the calculations in further detail, but the foregoing will give some idea of the types of method employed.

The small favourable balance on current account of £28 millions has been eliminated partly by scaling down proportionately the total receipts of the two groups of countries, and partly by rounding.

TABLE IV

Estimated U.K. Balance of Payments on Current Account, 1930

(Adjusted so that the final balance is nil)

(£ millions)

	Group A. Countries with which we had a favourable balance	Group B. Countries with which we had an unfavourable balance	All countries
1. Payments	460	590	1050
2. Receipts:			
(a) Exports of U.K. produce	380 } 710	190 } 340	570 } 1050
(b) Other receipts	330	150	480
3. Balance (receipts less payments)	+250	−250	−

If they had decided to eliminate these balances, we should have lost £250 million worth of exports, equal to more than two-fifths of our total visible exports of £570 million — a sobering thought when we tend to be carried away by the iniquity of countries in Group B, which spent less with us than we spent with them. It is true that, with a tendency to bilateralism all round, we should have switched some of our purchases from Group B to Group A, thus mitigating the cut imposed on our exports by Group A, but we could hardly have switched as much as £250 million. This would have meant a cut of over two-fifths in purchases from Group B, and an increase of more than one-half in purchases from Group A. It is doubtful whether Group A could have supplied such a large part of the goods formerly bought from Group B. Even if this had been possible, the cost to us would have been much greater; the reason, after all, why we had such a large import surplus from Group B countries was that they could supply us with many commodities more cheaply than could Group A.

The dependence of our 'visible' exports on multilateral trade is even more strikingly illustrated in Table V. This is merely a re-arrangement of the items in Table IV.

Group A countries spent nearly three times as much on our exports as was necessary to balance their receipts from us; in other words, no less than two-thirds of our exports to them depended on their willingness to run 'unfavourable' balances with us.

Since in future we shall have such great difficulty in paying for our

TABLE V

(£ millions)

	Group A countries	Group B countries	All countries
I. Exports of U.K. produce *required* to balance accounts with each country (1 minus 2(*b*) in previous table)	130	440	570
II. *Actual* exports of U.K. produce (2(*a*) in previous table)	380	190	570
Balance (II less I)	+250	−250	—

imports, it may at first sight seem reasonable to say to other countries: 'We are very sorry we cannot afford to buy from you more than you buy from us.' But before embarking on such a policy we should do well to consider carefully the implications of its widespread adoption — and any general agreement to forswear such a policy would be impossible without our co-operation. It would, in fact, mean the deliberate sacrifice of many profitable openings for our exports. If countries of the A type allowed us to spend the currency we earned by our exports to them only on imports from them, and refused to allow us to convert it into other currencies, there would be no object, after a point, in any further expansion of our exports to them, even though their inhabitants were keen to buy more of our goods, and even though we were very short of goods that were, however, only obtainable in countries of the B type.

Our present situation, with an export surplus to Europe and an import surplus from America, is a good illustration. It has been used as an argument for bilateralism — and there is no doubt a need to redirect our trade while so many currencies are inconvertible; but it is also a very strong argument for the earliest possible *general* convertibility of currencies and for multilateralism.[38]

In the conditions of 1930 a general policy of bilateralism would have meant the sacrifice of profitable openings for anything up to two-fifths of our exports. Conditions are now, of course, very different, but there is no obvious reason why the general profitability of multilateral trade should have become any smaller, and we can certainly not afford to sacrifice openings for two-fifths, or even for

[38]The strength of this argument is by no means diminished by the fact that we are committed, under the Anglo-American Financial Agreement, to make sterling convertible at an early date, while other countries, according to the Bretton Woods agreement, are given three to five years' grace.

one-fifth, of our exports. We must sell our exports wherever we can find a market, and we must be able to convert the proceeds into any other currency, so that we can buy our imports where they are obtainable, and where they are cheapest; for we cannot afford to squander foreign exchange on imports from expensive sources.

5. OUR COMPETITORS

We have seen that our export target will be very hard to achieve unless total world trade in manufactures is expanded, and that we should therefore do everything we can to encourage the breaking down of import barriers and the promotion of multilateral trade. But unless world trade in manufactures can be doubled, which is a very optimistic assumption, we shall also have to increase our share of that trade if we are to double our exports of manufactures.

Let us therefore look at the position of our main competitors. Diagram II shows the value of manufactures exported by each of the main industrial countries in 1937. Out of a total of 10 billion dollars,[39] we find that Germany exported 2 billion dollars worth, Japan nearly 1, the United Kingdom nearly 2, the United States rather more than 1½, and other countries, mainly in Europe, 3½.

GERMANY AND JAPAN

The first striking fact is that Germany and Japan, our two major enemies in World War II, exported nearly three-tenths of the world total. If, as a result of the peace terms, the exporting power of these countries is diminished, the gain to our exports may be substantial. If, for example, their exports were cut to one-half of pre-war, but world trade in manufactures stayed the same, the remaining countries would gain markets totalling 1½ billion dollars, at pre-war prices. If, further, this gain were shared in proportion to pre-war exports, ours would increase by about 400 million dollars — an increase of one-fifth on pre-war. While this would by no means solve our problem, it would be an important contribution.

It is true that, as a result of Germany's and Japan's reduced *importing* power, we might lose, say, half of our pre-war exports to them; but this would be a mere 60 million dollars. It may also be argued that the other pre-war suppliers of Germany and Japan, having less to spend, would reduce their imports of manufactures; but a large part (probably half at least) of their import economies would be in primary products rather than in manufactures, so that the world market for manufactures would not be reduced by nearly

[39] Total world exports of all kinds were about 25 billion dollars, including 5½ billion of foodstuffs and 9½ billion of raw materials and semi-manufactures.

DIAGRAM II
World Exports of Manufactures in 1937
Figures in billions of dollars

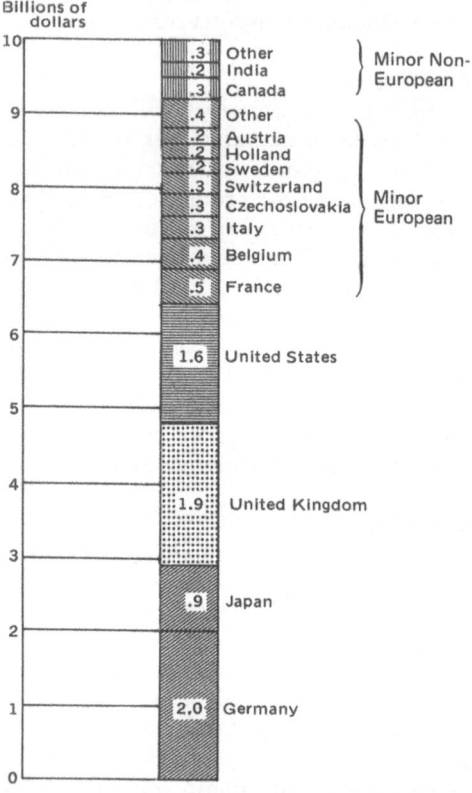

Source: Statistisches Jahrbuch für das Deutsche Reich

as much as German and Japanese exports were curtailed. Just as the sudden death of 30% of, say, the engineering workers in this country would greatly increase the demand for the services of the remaining 70%, despite the disappearance of the purchasing power of the 30%, so a large reduction in the manufactured exports of countries which supplied nearly 30% of the world's total will undoubtedly benefit the remaining industrial countries. It must also be remembered that overseas countries' losses of foreign exchange as a result of reduced exports to Germany and Japan will be largely offset by reduced interest payments to Britain, together with large annual receipts from Britain on account of the debts we have incurred.[40]

Will the power of Germany and Japan to export manufactures be severely curtailed? In the case of Germany this seems likely. About 7% of her industrial capacity was in the eastern area which is likely to be ceded to Poland;[41] roughly 33% was in the Russian zone of occupation, and much of this — probably more than one-half[42] — has been removed by the occupying power; a considerable part of the remaining 60% in the Western zones of occupation was destroyed by air and land warfare. There has already, therefore, been a big reduction, of perhaps 30% or 40%, in Germany's industrial capacity. In addition, a reparations plan has been published[43] which involves the removal of further industrial plant from the western zones. The plan envisages a reduction in Germany's industrial capacity to little more than half the 1938 level, and a particularly severe contraction in her metal, metal-using and chemical industries,[44] which supplied at least 70% of Germany's pre-war exports of manufactures.[45] The contraction of the capital goods industries will, moreover, make it very difficult to expand exporting capacity in other, more peaceful industries, such as textiles and paper.

In these circumstances it is unlikely that Germany will have sufficient industrial capacity, after meeting her minimum internal needs, to export nearly as many manufactures as before the war. This line of argument must not, of course, be pressed too far. Before the war probably 15–20% of Germany's manufacturing output (other than of foodstuffs) was exported, and 80–85% used at home. If both manufacturing capacity and manufactured exports are halved, internal consumption of manufactures will be halved also; while if manufactured exports are maintained at the pre-war level, internal

---

[40] Overseas countries will have anything up to £200 million more of foreign exchange per annum as a result of our heavy overseas disinvestment. Germany's post-war imports have been estimated by the Control Council for Germany at about £100 million (at 1936 prices) less than in 1936. Even after allowing for the general rise in prices, for other items in Germany's balance of payments, and for a reduction in Japanese imports, it is therefore likely that overseas countries as a whole, though not necessarily individual countries, will have gained nearly as much foreign exchange from us as they will have lost through reduced sales to Germany and Japan.

[41] Including the northern part of East Prussia, which goes to Russia.

[42] *The Times*, September 27th, 1946.

[43] This was approved by the Control Council and published on March 27th, 1946.

[44] Mechanical engineering capacity, for example, is to be reduced to 38%, electrical engineering to 50% of the 1938 level, steel to 39%, motor vehicles to 26% and basic chemicals to 40% of the 1936 level.

[45] The cut is not, however, to be so severe in some of the lighter branches of these industries, such as pharmaceuticals, dyestuffs and precision instruments, which accounted for a substantial fraction of Germany's exports.

consumption will be further depressed, but only to about two-fifths of pre-war. A small difference in internal consumption, in other words, will make a big difference in the manufactures available for export, and this makes it particularly difficult to estimate Germany's export possibilities. As she will be extremely short of the means of paying for vital imports, she may be willing to maintain exports at a higher level than might be expected, at the expense of a small further cut in internal consumption of manufactures.

Taking everything into account, however, it seems certain that Germany's exports of manufactures will be well below the pre-war level for a good many years to come. The Control Council's estimate, which implies a cut of more than one-half in Germany's 1937 exports of manufactures,[46] may well err, if anything, on the generous side.

This will undoubtedly, as we saw, be of substantial benefit to our exports. Will it also assist our balance of payments? The danger here is that Germany's exports may be insufficient to pay for imports large enough to give her what we should regard as a tolerable standard of living, and that we shall find ourselves, as one of the major occupying powers, subsidising her imports — as we are doing at present — which means a loss of foreign exchange.

But surely, it may be argued, Germany can survive quite comfortably on imports very much lower than before the war. After all, she produced 85% of her food supplies, so that a small cut in consumption would effect a great saving in food imports (which accounted for about 35% of her total imports); imports of textiles, oil and rubber (a further 25%) could be largely replaced by synthetic production; her need for imports of ores (a further 7%) will be greatly reduced by the contraction of her heavy industries; and a higher rate of felling in her forests would make timber and pulpwood imports (a further 5%) unnecessary.

All this would be perfectly true if it did not ignore certain developments of the last year or so.   ,

In the first place, Germany is likely to lose to Poland and Russia one-quarter of her agricultural land, while the number of mouths to be fed will be nearly as great as before the war,[47] owing to the

---

[46] The Control Council's estimate of total exports is 3 billion Rm. at 1936 prices. This is rather less than 55% of the 1937 volume of exports; and assuming that exports of primary products, particularly coal and potash, will recover to at least the pre-war level, this means a cut of more than 50% in manufactured exports.

[47] In the reparations plan, the post-war population of Germany is estimated at 66½ million, compared with 68 million in 1936. The Census taken in October 1946 showed a total population, west of the Oder–Neisse line, of nearly 66 millions. This includes a 'special' population of about 1 million, who may or may not remain in Germany, but excludes several million Germans who were still prisoners of war abroad.

transfer of population from the East. If the pre-war diet were maintained, this would mean food imports nearly 2½ times as great as before the war.[48] Even with a cut in consumption and a marked change in the diet from expensive foods like meat and eggs to cheaper foods like grain and potatoes, the food import bill is now bound to be substantial, especially until Germany's herds can be rebuilt and her land can recover from the shortage of fertilisers. The reparations plan, in fact, appears to envisage food imports roughly as high as before the war.

Secondly, as measures of military security, German production of synthetic oil, rubber and ammonia, ball bearings, aluminium, magnesium and sea-going ships is to be prohibited. These prohibitions, and the possible need to import steel because of the drastic cut in steel capacity, will mean a greatly increased import bill; although production of the first four items mentioned may be retained until imports can be paid for.

One also hears of demands for payment by Germany of occupation costs and of interest on pre-war debts, and for the free delivery on reparation account of coal and other goods from current production.

All these place a heavy strain, or a potential strain, on Germany's balance of payments. Taken together with the large reduction in Germany's industrial capacity, they might well make a balance impossible, and entail a subsidy by us which we can ill afford. Unless, therefore, there are compelling non-economic reasons to the contrary, we should oppose any demands on Germany's balance of payments to which we are not already committed. In particular, we should exercise our right to retain a minimum production of such items as synthetic oil, rubber and ammonia, and ball bearings, unless, as seems unlikely, it becomes absolutely clear that imports of these can be paid for. We must oppose reparation deliveries of coal and the like to our allies; every ton of German coal exported free of charge is paid for, in part at least, by us, and there seems no reason why we should pay reparations to our allies. We should also probably oppose the exaction of payments on Germany's pre-war debts. Our share in such payments would be small,[49] our contribution to Germany's increased deficit large; and Germany could pay without incurring a deficit only by greatly increased competition in our export markets.[50]

[48] If pre-war food consumption be put at 100, home production at 85 and imports at 15, a fall of one quarter in home production, to 64, would raise the imports required to maintain the same total consumption to 36—*i.e.*, to 2.4 times the pre-war level.

[49] In 1935, only about 12% of Germany's foreign debt was owed to Britain.

[50] The payment of the foreign exchange costs of occupation, on the other hand, might not be to our disadvantage, since a large fraction of these would accrue to us.

We have seen that a contraction in Germany's exporting power
will be to our advantage, provided we do not have to subsidise
Germany. (The same will be true of Japan.) As a result, however, of
all the demands that have been placed, and may be placed, on
Germany's balance of payments, there is a danger, first, that
Germany will be forced to try to sell a large fraction of her pre-war
exports, in competition with our own, and, secondly, that she may
nevertheless fail to balance her payments, leaving us to pay a large
part of the difference. How things will in fact work out it is
impossible to forecast. The position in Germany is still obscure;
whether, for example, Germany will be treated as an economic whole
is, at the time of writing, uncertain. But it is to be hoped that our
policy will aim at ensuring that we do not, in the way described, get
the worst of both worlds.

THE UNITED STATES

After Germany, our largest pre-war competitor in the world market
for manufactures was the United States; and after the war she will
undoubtedly be our main competitor. United States exports of
manufactures had been steadily gaining on our own in the sixty or
seventy years before the war. In the early 1870's they were a mere
7% of the British, in 1913, 45%, and in 1937, 85%.[51]

Will this trend continue in the future? The United States certainly
began the peace-time race with a big start. During the war her
non-war exports fell by only one-third, ours by two-thirds.[52] Nor
must we forget Lend-Lease shipments, which made many countries
more familiar with American goods; if these are included, American
exports actually trebled in quantity during the war.[53] The current
shortage of man-power, moreover, which means severe competition
between home and overseas consumers, is far greater in this country
than in the United States. Even one year after the end of the
European war, American exports of manufactures were still more
than one and a half times our own.

The United States was thus better able than we were, during the
war and its aftermath, to maintain contact with her overseas

[51] The United States' *total* exports in 1937 were considerably greater than our own, on
account of her much larger exports of food, raw materials and semi-manufactures, which
made up half of her total exports. She was in fact by far the largest exporter of primary
products, and this, together with her substantial exports of finished manufactures, made her
the largest exporter in the world.
[52] *The Impact of the War on the Civilian Consumption of the United States, United
Kingdom and Canada,* p. 14.
[53] *Survey of Current Business,* February 1945, p. 19. 1943 and 1944 compared with
1936–38.

customers. But at least as important as contacts and goodwill is the question of price. Here we are not starting at a disadvantage. Our prices and wages rose rather more than the American during the war, but the dollar value of sterling is 17½ lower than in 1938. This depreciation of the pound had fully offset any relative increase in our wage and price structure, even before the relaxation of American price control in the middle of 1946, which considerably improved our competitive position.[54]

What will happen in the future is much more difficult to say. Our prices and wages are still affected by a host of controls, subsidies and taxes which, in part at least, may be regarded as abnormal. Much will depend on our ability to prevent a wage inflation while attempting to secure full employment; on the rate at which we can increase our industrial productivity; on the strength of American Trade Unions; and on innumerable other factors. Finally, of course, the present rate of exchange between pound and dollar is by no means sacrosanct.

For these reasons it is unprofitable to dwell at too great length on nice calculations of purchasing-power parity. More fundamental is the kind of export policy the United States is going to pursue, and the danger that this may be unduly aggressive. There is a great desire in America to export, and there may at times be a mistaken belief that an expansion in American exports will be of major help in preventing unemployment there. That this cannot be so is clear from a glance at the orders of magnitude involved. It is generally agreed by American experts that, to avoid heavy unemployment, American output will have to be some 60 billion dollars a year more than in 1937 (at 1937 prices), and 80–90 billion more than in the slump

[54]Two of the most relevant indices are set out below for what they are worth. The figures for the two countries are, of course, only very roughly comparable. The columns to be compared are numbers (1) and (3).

(1938 = 100)			
	U.S. dollars	U.K. sterling	U.K. dollars $(2) \times \frac{82\frac{1}{2}}{100}$	Month in 1946 used in comparison
	(1)	(2)	(3)	(4)
Average hourly earnings*	155	177†	146†	January
Wholesale prices of manufactured products	129	152	125	May

*October, 1938 = 100. The U.S. figure refers to factory employees only; the U.K. figure includes certain non-factory employees.
†If the number of workers in the various age and sex groups and in the various industries had remained in the same proportions as in 1938, these figures would be considerably lower, probably about 168 and 138. See *Ministry of Labour Gazette*, July 1946.

year of 1933.[55] Now, total American exports in 1937 were only 3¼ billion dollars, and of this little more than 1½ billion were finished manufactures — the main field for expansion.[56] Even on the most optimistic assumptions about the possibility of expanding world trade in manufactures above the level of 10 billion dollars achieved in 1937, and of expanding the U.S. share in that trade, and even allowing generously for the cumulative effect on American employment of an expansion in exports, it is clear that the latter could make only a minor contribution to solving an unemployment problem which may well be measured in scores of billions of dollars.

Strictly speaking, moreover, employment will be created only by an increase in the export *surplus* of goods and services, and this is limited by the various factors that limit international investment. There is, first of all, a maximum practicable rate at which the backward countries of the world can be developed. Even an enthusiast for such development, who recently examined the problem,[57] was unwilling to put the post-war 'investment outlet' for foreign capital in Asia, South-East Europe and Latin America at more than 3 billion dollars a year. In the second place, there is a limit to the amount of international trade that can be done on credit if an intolerable element of instability is to be avoided. Seldom before has international investment exceeded 2 billion dollars a year.[58] Even in the late 'twenties such investment represented only about 5% of total world international transactions on current account; and the drying up even of this small flow is commonly held to have been a major cause of the decline and dislocation of international trade in the 'thirties.

No conceivable expansion of American exports could therefore go far in providing the extra demand, compared with pre-war, required to prevent heavy unemployment. But this will not necessarily prevent a demand for Government assistance to exports if unemployment threatens, both from those who dislike the other measures necessary for a full-employment policy, and from those groups whose interest in export trade is substantial. Now, if America went in for a ruthless export drive, using export subsidies, tied loans, bilateral

---

[55] Based mainly on articles in the *Survey of Current Business.* See also article by R. D. G. Allen in *London and Cambridge Economic Service Memorandum*, No. 105, for a discussion and bibliography of the various estimates.

[56] This has certainly been true in the past. Between 1913 and 1937, for example, the volume of American exports of manufactures more than doubled, while exports of raw materials and semi-manufactures remained approximately the same, and exports of foodstuffs fell by more than two-fifths.

[57] Professor Staley, in *World Economic Development.*

[58] Staley, *op. cit.*, p. 80.

bargaining and every weapon in her armoury to the full, the effect on our exports might well be disastrous. It would mean that the United States was trying to get a larger share in the world market for manufactures by the use of practices whose repercussions might well reduce the total of world trade. This would be a tragedy indeed. American employment would not benefit appreciably, while we, dependent on imports equal to one-fifth of our national income compared with one-thirtieth in the United States, would suffer severely.

It is therefore of the utmost importance to us, first, that the United States should realise that unemployment can be avoided only if far more American goods can somehow be sold in America; and, secondly, that she should forswear as many as possible of the weapons she might use to push her export trade. We must never fail to bear this in mind when asked, as part of an international agreement to which the United States is a party, to forswear the use of these weapons ourselves. We may be tempted to think that, if it came to an export war, without rules, between the United States and ourselves, we might gain the day. But we must always remember, first, that the resulting dislocation might well reduce world trade below the level it might otherwise have reached, so that even if we increased our exports relatively to those of the United States they might still suffer on balance. We must remember, in the second place, that, contrary to popular belief, the United States' power to force other countries to take her exports will almost certainly be greater than our own. Quite apart from the ability of a country with gold reserves of some 20 billion dollars to offer credits on a generous scale, the dependence of overseas countries on the American market, and so their susceptibility to American pressure, is much greater than is commonly supposed.

It is a popular fallacy that the United States imports nothing; and the large flow of gold to America during the 'thirties is often adduced in evidence. But in fact American payments on current account to other countries during the years 1930—38 covered no less than 94% of her receipts from them; the large influx of gold was mainly due to the flight of foreign capital to America.

The United States was in fact the second largest importer in the world, after the United Kingdom, during the inter-war years.[59]

---

[59] This appears to be true of every year with the possible exception of 1934 and 1938, when Germany's recorded imports were slightly greater. Remembering, however, that United States imports are recorded f.o.b. and German imports c.i.f., it is doubtful whether the latter were appreciably, if at all, greater.

(During the 'twenties, she was even the largest importer of manufactures.) Even the bigger market in the United Kingdom is partly a statistical illusion. In 1937, for example, American retained imports, as recorded, were 3.0 billion dollars, while ours were 4.7 billion. But United States imports were recorded f.o.b.; ours c.i.f. If the latter were recorded f.o.b. they would have been only 4.1–4.2 billion dollars, reducing the difference to a little more than 1 billion. We must also remember the dependence of gold-producing countries on the United States. The 'gold scare' of 1937 reminds us of the influence America could exert on such countries. Pre-war gold production outside the United States, the profitable disposal of which depended greatly on American policy, exceeded 1 billion dollars a year. If this is added to her merchandise imports, the world depended on the United States market as much as on our own.[60]

This is a sobering thought. If ever we are tempted to use our bargaining power as a large importer to force other countries to take our exports, we would do well to remember that at least one-third of our exports went to countries which depended more on the United States market than on our own, and that those countries include important parts of the Empire, such as Canada, South Africa and Malaya.[61] In at least one-third of our markets the United States could beat us at our own game.

This was the position before the war; in future the American market will be even more important. In the past American imports have varied closely with industrial production,[62] and this will have to be at least twice as great as before the war to ensure full employment.[63] Even if America falls far short of her employment target, her imports are certain to be substantially higher than in the past. The same will be true of her tourist expenditure.[64]

[60] In addition, America spent some 300 million dollars a year more than we did on foreign travel, personal remittances abroad, and silver; but this was probably offset by the larger payments of our ships in overseas ports.

[61] See MacDougall, 'Britain's Bargaining Power,' in *Economic Journal,* March 1946, for details. The year chosen for analysis was 1938, a year of abnormally low American imports. If a different year had been chosen the pre-war influence of the United States in our overseas markets would have been even greater.

Mr. P. C. Armstrong, of Montreal, informs me that the British market for Canadian goods is more highly competitive than the American; we could more easily dispense with Canadian supplies than could the Americans. This would have to be set against the greater absolute size of Canada's American market in evaluating the respective bargaining powers of the United Kingdom and the United States.

[62] See *The United States in the World Economy,* p. 8.

[63] See R. D. G. Allen, *op. cit.*

[64] See Lord Keynes, 'The Balance of Payments of the United States,' in *Economic Journal,* June 1946.

Already, before the war, American imports of raw materials and of manufactures were not far short of our own. It was in food that she lagged behind, with imports only half as great as ours.[65] But American food imports have for many years been increasing by leaps and bounds. Table VI shows that they doubled in quantity in the twenty-five years before this war; ours increased by less than two-fifths.

TABLE VI

Volume of American Food Imports

(1923–25 = 100)

	Crude foodstuffs	Manufactured foodstuffs
1913	67	74
1921–25	98	96
1926–30	109	119
1931–35	110	112
1936–40	132	149

*Statistical Abstract of the United States 1941.

During the same period her food exports fell substantially. Table VII shows that the ratio of food exports to food imports fell steadily during the present century, apart from the war-time quinquennium 1915–20, when, as in the recent war, the trend was temporarily reversed.

At the turn of the century America's food exports were twice her food imports. By the outbreak of the recent war the position had been reversed. In 1898 she had a net export of farm products equal to 7% of her farm production. By 1937 she had a net import equal to 5% of her production.[66]

Nor must we forget that the population to be fed in the United States is still increasing quite rapidly; by 1960 it is likely to be some 20 million higher than at the outbreak of war.[67] When we remember

[65] See, e.g., *Network of World Trade*, p. 70.
[66] Clark, *The Economics of 1960*, p. 59, quoting Professor Pearson.
[67] The United States population in 1939 was about 131 million. According to *Estimates of Future Population of the United States, 1940–2000* (National Resources Planning Board, August 1943), it will have risen, by 1960, to 157 million on the most favourable assumptions, and to 148 million on the least favourable.

TABLE VII

American Food Exports as a Percentage of American Food Imports† ‡

1896—1900	212
1901—5	199
1906—10	154
1911—15	124
1915—20	181
1921—25	123
1926—30	84
1931—35	51
1936—40	41

†*Statistical Abstract of the United States*, 1941.
‡General imports through 1932, imports for consumption thereafter.

that our own food imports feed little more than 30 million people, it appears by no means impossible that they may, before long, be rivalled by the food imports of the United States.

All these facts, and many others, point to the United States as the leading purchaser of goods and services on the world market for many years to come. Her imports of raw materials and manufactures may well exceed our own; sooner or later she may even rival us as the world's largest food importer; in the absence of international agreement her policy will have a major influence on the gold-producing countries; her tourists will spend far more on foreign travel than those of any other country. When we add to this her ability to make loans and her general political power, can anyone deny the possibility that we might come off second best in economic warfare with the United States? It is true that her superior bargaining power as a large purchaser of goods and services is partially offset by the reputation of her market for instability. But this reputation is based largely on the experience of the 'thirties, and we can hardly assume that she will never learn to stabilise her economic activity. Her food imports, too, will become more stable as they form an ever growing proportion of American food consumption.

The United States will be by far our largest competitor in the world market for manufactures; between us we may account for half the world's exports. Any future threat of American depression might be the signal for a ruthless export war without rules, in which we might well come off second best. Ought we not to take advantage of the present American desire to formulate rules now?

6. THE PRICE OF EXPORTS AND THE VALUE OF THE POUND

We have now said something about our three main pre-war competitors in the world market for manufactures — the United States, Germany and Japan. These three, together with ourselves, accounted for two-thirds of the world total. There is no room for a separate discussion of our remaining competitors which, apart from Canada and India, were nearly all European countries whose trade has been even more severely dislocated than our own.

But before we leave the discussion of the need to expand our share of the world market for manufactures, one general point must be emphasised. Our share will depend greatly on the price at which we sell our goods, and this can be influenced by the exchange value of the pound. Our steadily declining share in the past must not be regarded as a tendency that can never be reversed; it was reversed, very sharply, by the depreciation of sterling in 1931, which for a time made our goods cheaper than those of our competitors.

Let us look at a few figures. Diagram III (*a*) compares our experience during the twenty-five years before this war with that of the United States. Line A shows that, between 1913 and 1922, our exports of manufactures fell by some 40% in relation to those of the United States (our exports fell to 67%, while American exports rose to 115%, of the 1913 volume); and this relative fall continued steadily during the rest of the 'twenties. In 1932 there was a sudden reversal of the trend, but after 1933 it continued as before. Now, there are doubtless many possible explanations of this, but surely an important cause of the relative decline in our exports between 1913 and 1930 may have been the high price of our manufactures during the 'twenties. Line B in the chart shows that we were attempting to sell our manufactures during that period at gold prices[68] one-third higher than those of the United States in comparison with 1913. It is also noteworthy that if we had stabilised the pound at the 1920 rate of exchange (about 75% of the 1913 parity — see line C) our export prices would have been approximately the same as those of the United States in comparison with 1913.

---

[68] Strictly, 'average values.' This correction also applies to the comparisons with Germany, Japan and France.

DIAGRAM III

Britain's Exports and Export Prices in relation to those of her Main Competitors

(Note: Figures for 1926, the year of the Coal and General Strikes, are excluded throughout)

U.K. and U.S.A. 1913 and 1922–38
1913 = 100

$A = \dfrac{\text{Volume of U.K. exports of manufactures}}{\text{Volume of U.S. exports of manufactures}}$

$B = \dfrac{\text{Gold price of U.K. exports of manufactures}}{\text{Gold price of U.S. exports of manufactures}}$

C = Dollar value of sterling (each year, 1913–38)

U.K. and Germany 1913 and 1925–37
1913 = 100

$A = \dfrac{\text{Volume of U.K. exports of manufactures}}{\text{Volume of German exports of manufactures}}$

$B = \dfrac{\text{Gold price of U.K. exports of manufactures}}{\text{Gold price of German exports of manufactures}}$

U.K. and Japan 1923–38
1927 = 100

$A = \dfrac{\text{Volume of total U.K. exports}}{\text{Volume of total Japanese exports}}$

$B = \dfrac{\text{Gold price of U.K. exports}}{\text{Gold price of Japanese exports}}$

U.K. and France 1924–38
1927 = 100

$A = \dfrac{\text{Volume of total U.K. exports}}{\text{Volume of total French exports}}$

$B = \dfrac{\text{Gold price of U.K. exports}}{\text{Gold price of French exports}}$

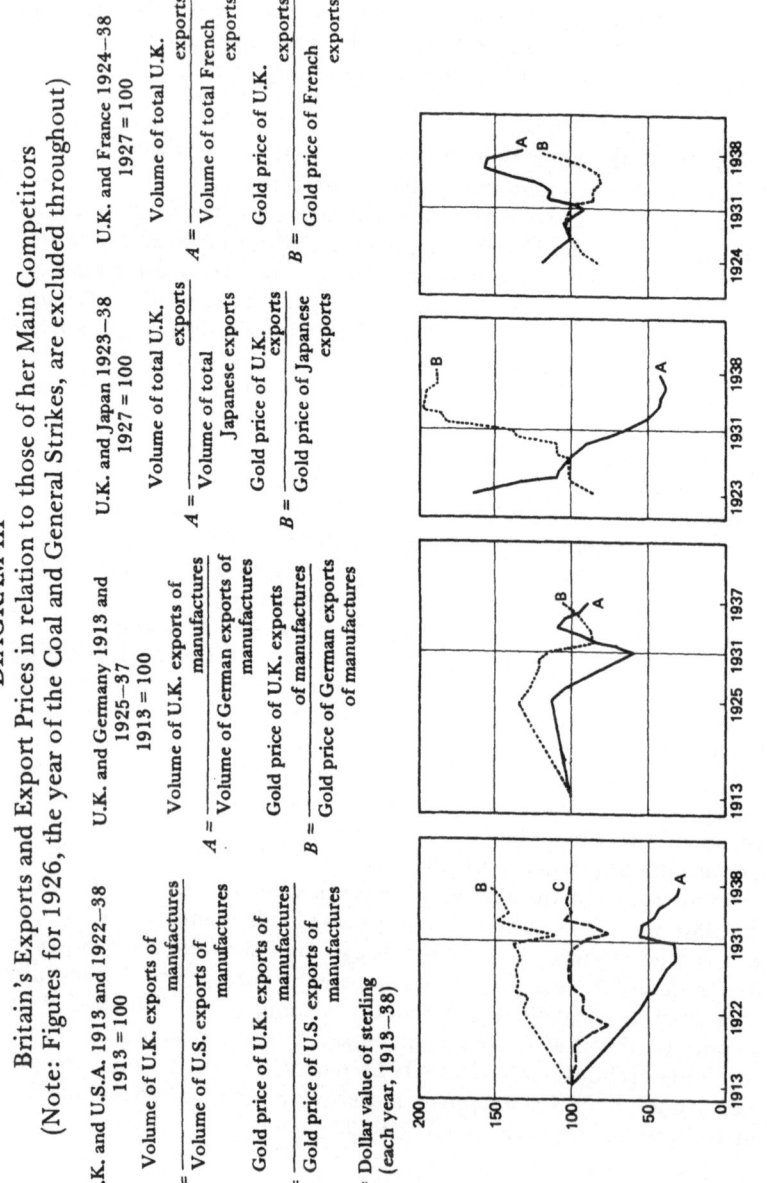

What effect such a decision would have had on the course of our exports it is impossible to say, but it is surely significant that the depreciation of sterling in 1931, and the corresponding fall in our relative export prices, was accompanied by a sharp relative rise in our exports of manufactures; and that when in 1933 the United States in turn depreciated the dollar, and our relative export prices rose again to a new high level, our exports fell steadily again, in relation to those of the United States, up to the outbreak of war.

Diagram III (*b*) gives a similar comparison with Germany. Here again, between 1925 and 1931, our gold prices were considerably higher than the German in comparison with 1913, and our exports of manufactures fell steadily in relation to German exports. (It is true that, despite our higher prices, British exports of manufactures in the year 1925 were greater, relatively, than the German, but Germany was still recovering from the war and the inflation.) After the depreciation of sterling in 1931 our exports rose very steeply for three years, in relation to the German. After 1934 they fell off again, when our relative prices began to rise.

Finally, Diagrams III (*c*) and III (*d*) compare our experience during the inter-war years with that of Japan and of France, our next largest competitors. The inverse relation between the volume and gold price of our exports compared with those of Japan and of France is fairly apparent. Japan, it will be remembered, depreciated her currency in the 'thirties much more than we did, and this partly accounts for the very large rise in our export prices in relation to those of Japan.

Statistics of this sort must, of course, be used with caution. The definition of 'manufactures' is not exactly the same in the United Kingdom, the United States and Germany; index-numbers of the type used are notoriously dangerous to interpret; they are not even all calculated on the same formulae; and there is always a danger of spurious correlation.[69] The charts will have fulfilled their purpose if they remind us of the obvious fact, which tends to be overlooked, that price is an extremely important factor in the selling of our exports, and that it can be affected by variations in the exchange value of sterling.

There is sometimes a tendency to regard our exports as rather

---

[69] For example, the bottom line of Diagram III (*a*) shows some tendency to vary inversely with general business activity, and this might possibly be explained by a higher proportion of capital and luxury goods in American than in British exports of manufactures. But 1930, 1931 and 1938 are important exceptions to this rule.

insensitive to such variations. It is argued that, despite a depreciation of sterling by 40% after 1931, our exports never recovered to the pre-depression level. But this argument ignores two facts: first, that there was a large increase in our *share* of world exports of manufactures; secondly, that while the pound depreciated by two-fifths in terms of gold, it never fell by much more than one-quarter compared with the currencies of our competitors. One after another these all depreciated in turn, in greater of less degree — Japan, Canada, India, Sweden and Austria in 1931, the United States in 1933, Czechoslovakia and Italy in 1934, Belgium in 1935, France, Holland and Switzerland in 1936. Germany retained the same nominal gold parity, but in practice the average value of the Reichsmark fell well below this level.

These developments are brought together in Table VIII and in Diagram IV. Line A in the diagram shows the value of sterling in terms of our competitors' currencies, and line B the reciprocal of this — *i.e.*, the value of our competitors' currencies in terms of sterling. Line C is an index of our share in the total quantity (not value) of world exports of manufactures.

It will be seen that after our depreciation in 1931 our share jumped by one-third, and remained at that high level for four years; this is all the more remarkable when we remember that our share had been falling steadily since 1913.[70] Similarly, when the exchange value of sterling (line A) began to rise, our share fell off again. The inverse relation between lines A and C, and the close direct relation between lines B and C, are indeed striking. This must be partly accidental — and the same relation does not hold in the years before 1931 — but it is worth recording that during the eight or nine years before this war a change of *X*% in the sterling value of our competitors' currencies was normally accompanied by a change of roughly *X*% in our quantitative share of the world's exports of manufactures. This is, of course, merely a statement of fact, and does not necessarily imply causal connexion.

Table VIII also shows that, by 1938, although sterling had depreciated by over 40% in terms of gold, it had fallen by only 15% in relation to our competitors' currencies. If we exclude the German Reichsmark, which is reckoned at the official rate, and so over-

---

[70]Our share in the *value* of world exports of manufactures was roughly as follows: 1913, 27%; 1925, 25%; 1927, 23%; 1929, 21%; 1931, 17%. (*Der Deutsche Aussenhandel unter der Einwirkung weltwirtschaftlicher Strukturwandlungen, Statistisches Jahrbuch für das deutsche Reich*, and *Industrialisation and Foreign Trade*.) Our share in the *quantity* of world exports of manufactures fell even more, because of the relative rise of our export prices.

DIAGRAM IV
The Value of Sterling and the British Share in World Exports
of Manufactures
Index numbers 1931 = 100

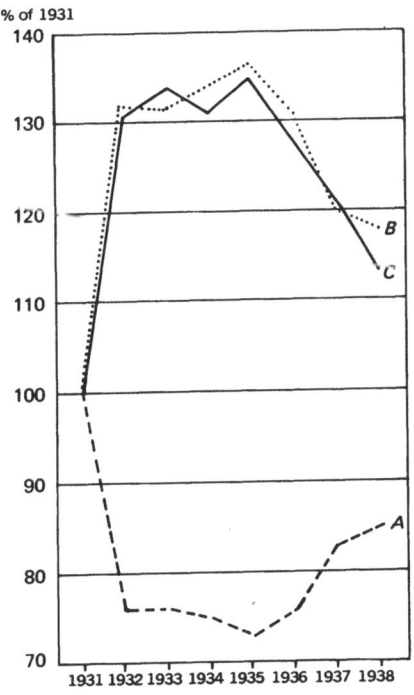

Line *A* = Value of sterling in terms of competitors' currencies
Line *B* = Value of competitors' currencies in terms of sterling (reciprocal of Line *A*)
Line *C* = U.K. share in quantity of world exports of manufactures
Note: See Table VIII for explanations

valued, the pound had in fact returned, on the average, to exactly its
1931 exchange value.

This brief analysis suggests three morals. First, the quantity of
exports we can sell will depend greatly on the price at which we sell
them. This reminds us of the danger of relying on bilateral bargains,
Empire sentiment and the like; unless we can sell at competitive
prices, our exports will sooner or later suffer. Secondly, the fact that
our exports are by no means unresponsive to changes in the value of
sterling points to the need of preserving our right to depreciate
sterling if this is likely, at any future time, to help restore our

TABLE VIII

The Value of Sterling and the British Share in World Exports of Manufactures

	1931	1932	1933	1934	1935	1936	1937	1938
(Index-numbers, 1931 = 100)								
1. Gold value of sterling	100*	72	68	62	60	60	60	59
2. Gold value of competitors' currencies†	100*	95	89	83	82	79	72	70
3. Value of sterling in terms of competitors' currencies (1 as % of 2)	100*	76	76	75	73	76	83	85
4. Volume of United Kingdom exports of manufactures	100	103	106	114	124	126	139	122
5. Volume of world exports of manufactures	100	78	79	87½	91	99	114½	108
6. Index of United Kingdom share in *quantity* of world exports of manufactures (4 as % of 5).	100	131	134	131	135	128	121	113

*June 1931.

†Average of twenty-six countries (which, together with the United Kingdom, accounted for 96% of world exports of manufactures in 1930), weighted according to value of exports of manufactures in 1930.

international equilibrium. Thirdly, however, we have seen that even a large depreciation will have no lasting value if other countries follow suit; hence the desirability of an international agreement, such as Bretton Woods, which will allow us to depreciate the pound if this is necessary to restore equilibrium, while prohibiting unwarranted competitive depreciation, such as that of the United States in 1933.

Our exports are not, of course, the only item in our balance of payments affected by a depreciation of sterling. The latter will, in particular, tend to raise the sterling price of our imports; and unless this reduces proportionately the quantity of our imports — which is unlikely in view of their essential nature — the total import bill, in terms of sterling, will increase. This will offset, in part or in whole, the higher sterling receipts from our exports. It is sometimes argued that the net effect will never in fact be favourable, but this generalisation seems to be just as unwarranted as the assumption that equilibrium can always be restored by a depreciation of the pound.

Let us illustrate this by an arithmetical example, using assumptions that are by no means unplausible. A recent article by Mr. F. W. Paish[71] set out a number of possible models of post-war equilibrium in our balance of payments. Let us start with one of these which put

[71] *Op. cit.*

imports at roughly £1,900 million, exports at £1,650 million, and other receipts less other payments (including re-payment of debt) at £250 million.[72] Now, suppose that at some future date imports are in fact coming in freely at a cost of £1,900 million, but that exports are only £1,500 million, leaving a deficit of £150 million after allowing for the other items. What now might be the effect of depreciating sterling by, say, 10%, assuming for simplicity's sake that the general level of British prices and employment, and world trade in manufactures, remain constant?

A depreciation of sterling by 10% would mean a rise of about 11% in the sterling value of foreign currencies. If our post-1931 experience were repeated, our exports would then increase by 11% — *i.e.*, by £165 million.[73] The sterling price of our imports would rise by a maximum of 11% if we make the pessimistic assumption that overseas suppliers would not reduce their prices in the face of a fall in British demand. On the basis of a recent study of our imports between the wars,[74] this rise in price might reduce the quantity of imports by about 6%. The sterling value of our imports would therefore rise by rather more than 4% — *i.e.*, by about £80 million The effect of depreciation on the other items in the balance of payments would be comparatively trivial,[75] so that the net improvement would be somewhere in the region of £85 million.

While this example is not intended to forecast what would happen if the pound were depreciated with imports and exports running at the levels assumed, it does show that depreciation *may* improve our balance of payments.[76] But it is equally obvious that, after a certain

[72] This assumed prices of imports and exports twice as high as in 1938, so that the volume of imports is 11% higher and of exports 75% higher.

[73] This assumes that our exports other than of manufactures would rise in proportion to our exports of manufactures. It also involves other assumptions that need not concern us here, as this is merely an example and not a forecast.

[74] Mr. Tse-Chun Chang, in the *Economic Journal* for June 1946, concludes that a 1% rise in import prices in relation to home prices, employment remaining the same, led to a fall of about 0.6% in the volume of imports.

[75] Payments on the American and Canadian loans would go up by about £5 million, and the cost of invisible imports (including government expenditure overseas) would also rise by a few million; but this might be offset, in part at least, by higher shipping earnings and other invisible exports. Payments on our sterling balances would be unaffected, provided these are fixed in terms of sterling. Income on our remaining investments overseas is to a large extent payable in sterling, but in so far as it is not, our balance of payments (in terms of sterling) would benefit.

[76] It might be argued than an improvement of £85 million in the balance of payments could have been better achieved, from the British point of view, without depreciation and without having to send more exports abroad, by a direct restriction of only 4½% in our imports, compared with 6% in the example. This raises important problems, both for economic theory and for the correct conduct of I.T.O. and of the Monetary Fund, but it must suffice to point out here (*a*) that, on slightly different (but equally plausible) assumptions from those used in the example, the problem would not arise, (*b*) that the danger of retaliatory import restrictions must be reckoned with.

point, it may not. The more our imports are reduced, and so confined to essentials, the less elastic is the demand for them likely to become; while the greater the share we obtain of the world market for manufactures, the smaller will be the elasticity of demand for our exports.[77]

It follows that circumstances may exist in which, even if the pound is depreciated to the optimum point (from the balance of payments point of view), yet there will still be a deficit. It is certainly true to-day that at no rate of exchange could our payments and receipts be balanced. This will continue to be true for some time yet, and perhaps even indefinitely. But this does not mean that the right to depreciate (or to appreciate) is worthless; on the contrary, it is hardly conceivable that the present exchange value of the pound will be the best possible for our balance of payments for all time. What it does mean is that we must also have the right to restrict our imports by methods more certain than exchange depreciation, if we cannot otherwise achieve a balance. How this right may be reconciled with a general breaking down of trade barriers is discussed in the concluding section.

7. CONCLUSION

The achievement of our export target, which may involve a doubling of our manufactured exports, will be a herculean task, but it is not entirely beyond the bounds of possibility. If for example, world trade in manufactures could be increased by one-quarter, and that of Germany and Japan were halved, the trade of the other exporting countries as a whole would increase by between 55% and 60%. To achieve her target, Britain would have in addition to increase her share in world exports of manufactures by rather more than one-quarter.

We shall clearly get nowhere near our target unless we can substantially increase both world trade in manufactures and our share of that trade. The Bretton Woods agreement and the proposals for an International Trade Organisation open up important possibilities in both directions. They aim at increasing world trade by lowering trade barriers and developing multilateral commerce. They also provide two essential pre-requisites for a successful attempt to increase our share in world trade. First, they give us the right to depreciate the pound, if this is necessary to restore our balance of payments, while denying the right of competitive depreciation where this is un-warranted; and the proposed limitations on import restrictions would

[77] See *International Economic Co-operation*, by Professor Tinbergen. On the basis of statistical studies he believes this to be true of exports in general.

also make our exports more sensitive to a depreciation of sterling. Secondly, they lay down a set of rules for the fair conduct of export trade, which is essential to us in view of the strong economic position of our main competitor, the United States. These rules are admittedly not ideal in every detail. It may be objected, for example, that they allow the United States to make tied loans, other than through the International Bank, while we are debarred, under the Loan Agreement, from releasing our sterling balances on similar terms. There is clearly room for further discussion on this, on Imperial Preference, and indeed on every other matter. But we must never lose sight of the great advantages offered by the general principles of Bretton Woods and I.T.O. to a country attempting to raise its exports by 75%.

We have also seen the necessity of preserving the right to restrict imports, so long as our international payments and receipts cannot be balanced by other means. Our need to insist on this right seems at first sight to rule out a general lowering of trade barriers. How can we expect other countries to break down their barriers and let in our exports if we preserve the right to exclude theirs by import restrictions? But it is precisely this apparent impossibility that I.T.O. would make possible, by allowing countries with an unfavourable balance of payments to impose import restrictions, while in general denying the right to others. The double advantage of this provision to ourselves is apparent, and being an eminently reasonable general proposition, it has also a good chance of widespread acceptance; which country, after all, can be sure that it will never again suffer from balance of payments difficulties?[7][8]

One promising general line for our commercial policy is thus to work, with the United States, for the widest possible acceptance of international agreements on the lines of Bretton Woods and I.T.O.; and when these agreements are satisfactorily concluded to collaborate wholeheartedly in their operation. But there are some to whom this course is anathema. Our foreign trade problem is so great, they argue, that we must forswear no weapon in our armoury. We must reserve the *unconditional* right to restrict imports; to vary the value of the pound; to buy from countries only if they will buy

---

[7][8] In this respect, I.T.O. is an advance on previous attempts to break down trade barriers. It recognises that countries cannot be expected never to restrict their imports; sometimes they have to, when they cannot export enough to pay for them. I.T.O. therefore provides that imports may be restricted if this is really necessary, but not otherwise. Rather in the same way, the Bretton Woods agreement does not expect countries never to alter the value of their currency; they may if it is necessary, but not otherwise. All this is a great advance in international co-operation. The two schemes are not a return to *laissez-faire*, as is sometimes claimed, but an attempt at conscious international planning and discipline.

from us; to exploit Empire sentiment to the full by maintaining and extending Imperial Preference; to use our bargaining power as a large importer; to subsidise our exports; and possibly to build up an economic bloc, centred on London, from which the United States would be excluded.

Much could be said for such a policy if we were sure that other countries would not follow suit. But this is rather too much to expect. Any hope of a widespread reduction in trade barriers and of reversing the trend to bilateralism would vanish, and with it would vanish any hope of increasing world trade. The spread of bilateral balancing of payments would rule out, as described earlier, a large field of expansion for British exports. The restriction of world trade as a whole would make necessary a much larger increase in the British share, if we were to achieve our export target; while at the same time this would be made more difficult by our inability to depreciate sterling without fear of unwarranted competitive depreciation and of offsetting tariffs and quotas against our exports.

Those who advocate a course that would have these results must therefore have great faith in our bargaining strength. But if, as we have tried to show, it is in fact smaller than that of the United States, this would hardly pull us through. A dollar bloc would undoubtedly be formed to counter the sterling bloc, and even the structure of Imperial Preference might crack under the strain. Many important countries of the Empire, including Canada, South Africa and Malaya, are, as we saw, more dependent on the United States than on Britain, and it would be unwise to rely on the imperial sentiment of countries like India; these four countries alone accounted for nearly half our export trade to the Empire.

The bargaining power of this country as a large importer is often exaggerated. It is easy to quote a few outstanding examples, such as New Zealand and Denmark, of countries which are greatly dependent on our market. We too often forget the large part of our trade done with countries that are not so dependent. As was shown in a previous article,[79] one-half of our pre-war trade was with countries which either depended on our market for one-fifth or less of their exports, or were even more dependent on some other market, usually that of the United States. Most of these countries could dispense with our market without great hardship if we tried to make them take our exports against their will; others would be driven into the rival dollar bloc. We might have more success with the remaining countries, which are more dependent on our market. But would it be wise,

[79] *Economic Journal*, March 1946.

when we have to expand our exports by 75%, to rely on trade with a bloc that has hitherto taken only half our exports (and supplied only half our imports), and which includes such countries as India, the Argentine and the pre-war Baltic states, where our political influence is uncertain?

A sterling bloc is sometimes advocated as a method of isolating ourselves from the possible effects of an American slump. The trouble is that it would also isolate us from a large part of the world's markets. It is true that a severe American slump, and the consequent fall in her imports, might set in train a cumulative downswing in world trade; but the remedy lies, not in an anti-American bloc, but in the scarce currency principle (proposed by the Americans themselves and embodied in the Bretton Woods agreement), which would enable the rest of the world to discriminate against United States exports, and so to isolate the disease.[80]

It is sometimes argued that if Germany – a smaller importer than ourselves – could make a success of bilateral bargaining, we could do even better. But is the example of a country whose quantitative share of world trade in manufactures fell by nearly a quarter between 1931 and 1937 one to be followed in our present position?

The demand for our exports in the past, as we have seen, has been greatly influenced by the price at which they have been offered in the world market. There is no reason to doubt that this will continue to be so. Bilateral bargaining and other forms of pressure may be of temporary assistance, but in the long run they are much more likely to restrict our trade, especially when other countries follow suit.

The correct commercial policy for Britain is, of course, a matter of judgment. But if the analysis of this article is correct, it would be folly indeed to throw over the undoubted advantages offered by the current proposals for international agreements, just because we wished to reserve the right to use expedients which are more likely to be harmful than helpful.

This conclusion is not based on any theoretical arguments about the economic or political advantages of freer trade; it does not arise from any prejudice for international action for its own sake; nor have we even mentioned that this country is committed to a certain line of action by Article VII of the Mutual Aid Agreement and by the terms of the Financial Agreement with the United States. The sole criterion has been what is likely to be economically best for this country at the present juncture.

---

[80] See R. F. Harrod, *A Page of British Folly.* It may be that the detailed provisions of the scarce currency and related clauses require further examination, and perhaps amendment, but the principle is right.

6 Britain's foreign trade problem: a reply to Mr Balogh[1]

I have read Mr. Balogh's closely reasoned comments with much interest and respect. I should like to discuss every paragraph, but must confine my remarks to a few salient points.

First of all, what is Mr. Balogh attacking?

An eminent Oxonian was recently asked by a visitor from overseas about views on commercial policy in Britain. He replied that there were two schools of thought. One appeared to be the old-fashioned 'free trade' school. The other held that this was all 'my eye.'

Mr. Balogh seems to be under the same misapprehension. While there may well be views meriting the description 'my eye', I think supporters of I.T.O. and I.M.F. can hardly be called 'free traders.' Yet Mr. Balogh, who regards my article as a 'plea' for these agreements (although it was largely factual), claims that I want an 'unplanned world,' and talks of the *completely open* system prescribed by Bretton Woods and I.T.O.,' with *'uncontrolled* and non-discriminating multilateral trade in a monetary setting of *unconditional* convertibility of currencies.'[2] 'Surely,' he argues in effect, 'we tried all this between the wars – and you have only to look at Mr. MacDougall's statistics to see what a sorry failure it was.'

From one so versed in the subject, these are strange descriptions of agreements that permit discrimination for nearly a dozen reasons, and provide for high tariffs, quantitative restrictions, state trading, commodity agreements, suspension of convertibility and devaluation of currencies. Nor is it true that I want, or that a successful I.T.O. and I.M.F. would mean, an 'unplanned' world, or a world like that of the inter-war years. It is true I do not want a 'planned' world in

[1] *Economic Journal,* March 1948. Mr. (now Lord) Balogh's comments on Study No. 5 appeared in the same issue of the *Economic Journal.*
[2] Italics mine.

which the pricing system has been entirely superseded. But I do want international 'planning' (if this is a legitimate use of that much abused word) to ensure that foreign trade conforms to a sensible code of rules — a very different state of affairs from that of the inter-war years.

Then we had the worst of both worlds. On the one hand were unduly rigid beliefs in a gold standard and unconditional non-discrimination. On the other hand, when countries threw over these doctrines, there was nothing to restrain the reaction. There was unwarranted competitive depreciation, and discrimination restrictive of trade. But I.T.O. and I.M.F. neither insist on complete non-discrimination, nor allow full freedom to discriminate. They neither impose a rigid gold standard nor allow full freedom to devalue. They neither insist on free trade nor allow unlimited restriction. Had the conferences of recent years insisted on rigid doctrines little could have emerged but pious resolutions — the only outcome of most pre-war conferences. The new international bodies recognise that discrimination, restriction and devaluation may be desirable, or at least inevitable, in certain circumstances. But they try to prohibit them when unjustified and harmful.

II

Mr. Balogh professes belief in an international code. He takes me to task for implying the contrary. He would not 'refuse to consider the acceptance of any limitation on national sovereignty in commercial and monetary matters.' Splendid. But what kind of rules would he accept? Frankly I doubt whether any that were both acceptable to other countries and effective would be consistent with his policy for Britain.

If this were followed, we should have to be virtually free to do what we liked — to conclude reciprocal agreements with almost any country, to form a preferential U.K. bloc, to subsidise exports, and so on. But since Mr. Balogh rarely considers the consequences of similar action, by other countries, injurious to British interests, one is apt to conclude that he would expect this to be disallowed by the rules. He even suggests that other countries should, in effect, discriminate in our favour — that demand for investment goods should be diverted to 'mature deficit' countries[3] — even, apparently, if we are trying to live permanently beyond our means, or to maintain an artificially high value for the pound. Now I naturally favour a code that gives us special privileges while denying them to

[3] 'The Charter of International Trade,' *Oxford Institute of Statistics Bulletin,* Vol. 9, Nos. 3 and 4, and 'The Foreign Balance and Full Employment,' Vol. 5, Supplement.

others; and we stand to gain under I.T.O. and I.M.F. as a country in balance of payments difficulties and suffering from a world-wide disequilibrium. But there is a limit to this sort of thing. If the provisions of a code too obviously favour a few countries of one type — if they are clearly aimed at maintaining in Britain a substantially higher standard than we are entitled to — they will not be internationally accepted.

The only alternative type of code, if Mr. Balogh's policy for Britain is to be pursued, is one with so many escape clauses as to be completely ineffective. (The I.T.O. charter already runs this risk, unless carefully administered; more escape clauses might well prove fatal.) But if Mr. Balogh will accept only rules that would be unacceptable to other countries or ineffective, this really amounts to a refusal to accept any rules at all. It is not I who misrepresent his proposals by saying they would involve an international free-for-all. It is he who misrepresents my case, and prejudices a true understanding of the proposed international organisations, by saying that I want an 'unplanned' world like that of the 1920's and 1930's.

Mr. Balogh finds much that is distasteful in the new organisations. I agree that they are far from perfect. No individual and no nation can be wholly content with widely accepted agreements. But if we accept them, the rules can be improved and developed as time goes on. Mr. Balogh disputes this. 'No useful purpose,' he says, 'is served by general willingness to reconsider some of the schemes; we have passed that stage.' But has he not admitted that the London meeting of the Preparatory Committee was able to make 'remarkable progress'[4] in revising the draft I.T.O. charter? The latest version, too, gives the Organisation wide scope to allow all manner of practices, and much will depend on the interpretation of the clauses. The agreements may, of course, prove unworkable even if we accept them. But if we reject them, or do not try wholeheartedly to make them work, they will not even be given a chance — and it may be our last chance of widespread co-operation to regulate and expand world trade. We shall be inevitably doomed to a world in which every country is entirely at liberty to pursue its own policy; and with Britain following Mr. Balogh's policy the rest will not be slow to follow suit. Discrimination and restriction will be practised, not only when these are right and proper; they will run riot. Other countries will be completely free to raise barriers against our exports, to discriminate against us, to use their bargaining power to win our markets, to form regional blocs from which we shall be excluded, to

---

[4] 'The Charter of International Trade,' *op. cit.,* p. 121.

indulge in competitive depreciation. It is for Mr. Balogh to show that we shall do better in such a world than in one where British liberty of action, but also that of other countries, is limited by international agreement.

III

But Mr. Balogh minimises the indirect consequences of his proposals. Take as an example the effects of bilateral agreements on multilateral trade. One can of course conceive in theory of a network of such agreements which did not reduce multilateral trade below the level it would otherwise have reached. But does not experience suggest that in practice (unless the agreements are limited by an appropriate international code) multilateral trade will be severely restricted?[5] I think Mr. Balogh really agrees, for he is at pains to challenge the figures I gave to illustrate Britain's dependence on multilateral trade. Since these refer to 1930, he argues, they can have 'no relevance to our present problems.' But is he entitled to brush this evidence aside without producing any of his own? Perhaps he relies on an analysis he has published elsewhere,[6] but this does not convince me since it is based largely on visible trade. As the value of visible exports in 1937 (the year chosen) was little more than half that of visible imports, it is hardly surprising that he found the visible export surpluses to individual countries very few and far between. But is it fair to conclude, with but a cursory reference to the large invisible items, that multilateral trade is of little importance to Britain?

The *pattern* of our trade has naturally changed since 1930, but is there any reason to suppose that our general interest in multilateral trade has been greatly reduced? In 1947, taking visible trade alone, although we had a total deficit of nearly £600,000,000, we had export surpluses to well over half the countries of the world, amounting in all to some £300,000,000.[7] Mr. Balogh has in no way shaken my belief that profitable multilateral trade is a vital British interest.

---

[5] Some further considerations will be found in my 'Notes on Non-Discrimination,' *Oxford Institute of Statistics Bulletin*, Vol. 9, No. 11 (Study No. 7 below).
    Bilateral agreements will never, of course, lead to an exact balance between every pair of countries, nor did I intend to accuse anyone of working for such a state of affairs, as Mr. Balogh suggests. But the *tendency* of bilateral agreements is undoubtedly in this direction and it was surely legitimate to consider the extreme case as an indication of the maximum loss that might be involved.
[6] 'The Importance of Multilateral Trade for Britain,' *Oxford Institute of Statistics Bulletin*, Vol. 6, No. 11
[7] Estimate based on first eleven months of the year. There were deficits of roughly £250,000,000 with the U.S. and of £650,000,000 with various other countries.

IV

He maintains, however, that it could be largely preserved within the groups of his 'coherently planned regional system.' I propose to examine this 'regional system' in some detail. It is a central theme in Mr. Balogh's proposals, and the discussion will illustrate some of the difficulties I find in his paper.

It is attractive to think of a British 'region' in which we got larger and more stable markets. But I should have thought the first and most obvious fact about a regional system was that ours would not be the only region. Should not Br. Balogh consider the effects of other regional blocs being established?

In the first place, might there not be one or more 'regions' in Western Europe — Mr. Balogh mentions the possibility in several places. Now he must be aware of the serious obstacles to our joining such a group, especially Imperial Preference. Should he not then consider the consequences for our trade of European preferential arrangements that excluded Britain? These might, of course, enable the countries concerned to raise their scale of manufacture and so, through economies of mass production, to increase their prosperity. They might then import more from the outside world, and possibly more from Britain. But is it not equally likely in practice that they would buy less from the outside world? Even if they bought more, might we not find that, with a larger industrial production, they took fewer British manufactures, and more primary products from abroad in competition with us? Sir Hubert Henderson has expressed his belief that preferential arrangements in Europe might prove 'extremely dangerous to our interests.'[8]

In the second place, there would presumably be a region consisting of Russia and Eastern Europe.

In the third place, can Mr. Balogh be certain that there would never be an American 'region'? He may argue that we need not fear such retaliation, for so long as there is a dollar shortage, the rest of the world will in any case spend all the dollars they can get. But could we rely on the continuation of such enlightened altruism, remembering (1) that his regional system might well demolish I.T.O. and I.M.F., (2) that it would injure individual American exporters, and (3) that he justifies it more as a method of redressing international inequality than of dealing with the dollar shortage (see below)? The United States, confronted by regional blocs affecting half their trade, might well become interested in his 'planned exchange of manufactures against primary products.' Their region would probably, as I

---

[8] *The Times,* September 20, 1947.

have tried to show,[9] include most of the American continents and the Far East. It might also include European and other countries dependent on American finance. Mr. Balogh seems to imply that such a group would not greatly interfere with our trade because British and American imports are 'complementary rather than competitive.' Now it is true that we are the big buyers of meat, dairy produce, timber and tea, while they are the big buyers of such things as rubber, tin, coffee, cocoa and gold. But Mr. Balogh's analysis does not go quite deep enough. Although we are not large buyers of rubber, tin, coffee, cocoa and gold, we depend greatly on our export market in the countries that produce these things. Mr. Balogh in no way disproves my contention that up to one-third of our pre-war exports went to countries likely to be in any American 'region.'

If these are the sort of regions that would emerge in his system, we should be left with little more than the Empire for our region — an Empire perhaps shorn of Canada, and possibly South Africa, Malaya and other countries dependent on the American market. We might be left with countries with which we did perhaps 30 to 40% of our pre-war trade.[10] These are countries whose pre-war net exports of food could have met little more than one-third of our import needs. They were already taking a high proportion of their manufactures from Britain, so that the possibilities of diverting trade from our industrial competitors are limited; and since many of them are keen to develop their own industries the prospects of an increase in their total imports of manufactures are not very bright. Would it be safe to rely on a group of this kind and this size for the very large expansion of mutual trade necessary to make good the loss of trade with other groups? Mr. Balogh may assume away this loss in theory. Is he really prepared, as a matter of practical policy, to ignore its possibility?

V

What powerful arguments has he, then, in support of a 'regional' policy that would so seriously endanger our markets in a large part of the world?

(a) At times he appears to base his case on the existence of large-scale disequilibrium in the balance of payments between one part of the world and another. Now I entirely agree that, when such disequilibrium exists, countries suffering from it should be allowed

---

[9] *Economic Journal,* March 1946 and March 1947.

[10] The Colonial Empire proper, over whose economic policy we still have a measure of control, has hitherto accounted for only about 5–10% of our trade. However important we may regard colonial development, it clearly cannot make more than a minor contribution to a solution of our difficulties for many years to come.

to discriminate in each others' favour. I said this in my article, when
discussing the possibility of an American slump, and I have discussed
it more fully elsewhere.[11] The principle is recognised in the scarce
currency clause of I.M.F. (which, however, as I stated, requires
re-examination), and in the I.T.O. Charter (which also requires
revision). It is right that international bodies should permit discrimination in these circumstances while at the same time they prevent
less desirable forms,[12] and explore other methods of restoring a
balance.[13] But this is quite a different thing from a permanent
regional system. We have much to gain from an attempt, in the face
of world-wide disequilibrium, to preserve the unity of the world
market, while preventing an unnecessary fall in trade and a general
deterioration in standards of commercial policy. We have much to
lose from a regional system which would shut us off from a large part
of the world's markets. It will be hard enough to make both ends
meet with all the markets in the world at our disposal.

(*b*) I think, however, that Mr. Balogh advocates regional groups,
not so much to maintain trade in the face of balance of payments
disequilibrium, as to redress international inequality. He believes, it is
true, that inequality and disequilibrium will go together. But he does
not fully explain why a poor nation cannot compete with a richer
one. Japan was not particularly unsuccessful in her competition with
Britain before the war. Is there any compelling reason why
equilibrium should never be achieved between richer and poorer
countries, unless of course the latter attempt to maintain higher
standards than their productivity warrants, or artificially high rates
of exchange? Is there not something in the theory of *comparative*
costs, and do we not in practice find wide variations from industry to
industry in the degree of superiority of the more productive nations?
Mr. Rostas has shown, for example, that American output per head
varies from little more than the British in some industries to four or
five times the British in others.[14]

But let us take Mr. Balogh's very understandable plea for greater
equality on its own merits. 'It is the perpetuation of the present
inequality of opportunity,' he says, 'which is the most objectionable

---

[11] 'Notes on Non-Discrimination,' *op. cit.*
[12] For example, the need of countries suffering from the lack of balance to discriminate
against the 'scarce currency' countries (using the term loosely) must not be allowed as an
excuse for discrimination against each other. Nor must the 'scarce currency' countries be
allowed to form their own preferential arrangements in retaliation.
[13] Such as adjustments of exchange rates; appropriate policies of international lending, tariff
reduction and full employment in the 'scarce currency' countries; and 'disinflationary'
measures in others.
[14] *Economic Journal*, April 1943.

feature of the post-war international economic arrangements.' He fears that they will 'freeze an international division of labour unfavourable to the poorer and smaller countries.' 'Unless, therefore, smaller countries are permitted to combine in co-ordinated planning of their economic reconstruction, their inferiority will in all probability be perpetuated.'

Now which are these 'smaller' countries? Presumably countries much smaller than Britain, which is after all the oldest and still the third largest manufacturing nation, and even in population eighth largest in the world. If Mr. Balogh is thinking of such countries, I agree that their internal market may be too small to support certain mass production industries, even with 'infant industry' protection. Where this is so he would presumably advocate preferential arrangements between a number of countries to guarantee a large enough market. This may be sound in theory, but I am less certain how far it is necessary in practice; as Mr. Balogh admits, many small countries are in any case making rapid industrial progress. Nor will such arrangements always benefit the small countries; as Mr. Rothschild has shown,[15] their industrialisation and welfare may be prejudiced rather than aided by membership of a bloc containing stronger neighbours, quite apart from the reduction in trade that I believe would occur in a 'regional' world.

But whether the smaller countries would gain or lose is in any case irrelevant to our present discussion. We are concerned with *Britain's* foreign trade problem, and Mr. Balogh admits that the industrialisation of primary producing countries is likely to be to our disadvantage. We have seen, too, how a regional bloc formed to foster large-scale manufacture might well reduce the demand for our exports and the supply of our imports.

At times, however, Mr. Balogh appears to include in his 'small, poor countries,' not only those that spring to one's mind, but even the U.K.[16] Now I can think of only one country neither smaller (in population or industrial production) nor poorer (per head) than the U.K. That is the United States. I conclude that, in Mr. Balogh's opinion, all other countries[17] should be free to make preferential arrangements to assist their industrialisation. The splitting up of the world is to be even more widespread than we had feared. What, then, is to compensate us — indeed more than compensate us — for the loss

---

[15] *Ibid.*, 1944.
[16] See, for example, 'The Charter of International Trade,' *op. cit.,* p. 115.
[17] Mr. Balogh might exclude Russia which, although poorer than the U.K., has a larger population and industrial production. He might also exclude China, India, Japan and Germany because of their larger populations.

of markets in so many groups, each bent on its own industrialisation? It is, in Mr. Balogh's words, the ability to 'plan for the regional development of a wide enough area to secure the advantages of mass-production.' In other words, we are to get guaranteed markets in our 'region' which will make our total market for manufactures comparable in size to that of the United States. We can then enjoy the same economies of mass-production, and so compete on equal terms. Let us examine this proposition.

(i) In the first place, could we really hope for a market anything like as great as America's? According to Mr. Balogh,[18] her national income and manufacturing output are now about two-thirds of the world total, outside the U.S.S.R. and China. Even, then, if the whole world (outside the U.S., the U.S.S.R. and China) agreed to let Britain make all their manufactures, our market would be but one-half the American. The most spectacular recovery could hardly, even on these assumptions, give us a market as large as theirs for many years to come. But the assumptions are, of course, ridiculously favourable. Our group could include only a fraction of the world, and the member countries would naturally insist on making a large part of their own manufactures. Before the war we exported, say, one-fifth of our manufactures. Even a doubling of our exports would increase our total market by only one-fifth — not a great advance towards a market of the American size, perhaps five times our own. Even with a deliberately planned division of labour under which, say, Australia made one type of steel and we another (a type of planning whose practicability on a large scale has yet to be proved) it is hard to see how the combined market could be more than a fraction of the American for any appreciable number of products. In fact I think it much more likely that the British market would be reduced under a regional system, through our loss of markets elsewhere.

(ii) But even if we could greatly enlarge our market, how far would this increase our productivity? In most industries our market is already large enough for several *firms* of the optimum size; and our firms are often no smaller than the American. When this is not so, is it not often due more to lack of standardisation than to our smaller market? There may, of course, be *external* economies resulting from the larger size of American industries and of their whole economy. But before rushing to the conclusion that this explains our lower productivity, let us ponder on such facts as that industrial productivity in Canada, with a quarter of our population, is nearly as high as

[18] 'The U.S. in the World Economy,' *Oxford Institute of Statistics Bulletin*, Vol. 8, No. 10, p. 314.

the American, and that the latter greatly exceeded our own even in 1870, when their market was smaller than ours.[19] When we remember, too, the many other possible reasons for our lower productivity, would it be wise to rely on a larger market for a striking improvement?

It seems unlikely then that regional agreements would alter the order of magnitude of our market; and even if they did we could not rely on much increase in output per head. We must look elsewhere for ways of increasing our productivity — more standardisation, wider dissemination of technical knowledge, improved factory management, better methods of wage payment, more capital per head, perhaps even more scope for enterprise and competition, and all the other methods so widely canvassed. No doubt we should be told all this if we asked countries in our proposed 'region' to give us preference on 'infant industry' grounds. We already have substantial preferences, and a large share in the market for manufactures, in Empire countries which would form the bulk of any U.K. group. Are we to ask them to forgo cheaper American goods still more, to say nothing of their own industrialisation, in the name of increased productivity in Britain which can only be won by other means?

For all these reasons I am sceptical of the value to Britain of regional groups. But I am acutely conscious of the dangers. One possibility is that other substantial groups would be formed, with which our trade would fall. Even more likely, the whole scheme would prove impracticable. But by insisting on preferential arrangements to assist the 'economic development' of Britain, we should have driven a coach-and-four through all attempts to *limit* discrimination. Any international code which tried to distinguish good from bad discrimination would either break down or become ineffective; for virtually any pair of countries would have to be allowed to discriminate in each other's favour in the sacred name of economic development.

VI

Where would Britain be in this free-for-all, in a world atmosphere of *sauve-qui-peut*? We should of course have to use our bargaining power to the full, but would it get us very far? Mr. Balogh has hardly challenged my contention that it is much weaker than is commonly supposed. We may have a large market, but it is also a hungry one; and I have still to be convinced that beggars can be choosers. In the last resort, the bargaining power of an industrial nation like Britain,

[19] See Rothbarth, *Economic Journal,* September 1946.

with little land and virtually no other natural resources save coal and iron, is weaker than that of the primary producers, especially advanced countries like Australia, New Zealand, the Argentine, Canada or Denmark. The latter can, if necessary, expand their industrial production without much difficulty, and so dispense with our exports. We are far less able to increase our output of food and raw materials. To quote Mr. Balogh, 'Britain is more dependent on the import of primary products than other countries,' while 'Britain's exports consist of goods which can most easily be forgone.' Does this sound like a country that can pin great faith in its bargaining power?

VII

Before concluding, a few words on devaluation. I never argued, as Mr. Balogh claims, that this was a 'sovereign remedy' for international disequilibrium. I was at pains to show that it might do more harm than good, and would not, at the time of writing, solve Britain's problems. But I was equally insistent that an orderly revaluation of currencies might at times be an appropriate method of helping to restore equilibrium. If I understand Mr. Balogh correctly, he objects to devaluation for two reasons.

First, he argues, a more effective policy would be one of export subsidies and import restrictions.[20] Now it is well known that this can benefit a single country if there is no retaliation. But is it not also established that, if each country seeks its maximum advantage in this way, all are most likely to suffer? Surely, then, Mr. Balogh cannot wish this to become the general method of restoring equilibrium, even when revaluation can be effective without undue hardship.

In the second place, Mr. Balogh is (for once) afraid of counter-measures, or automatic deflationary reactions by other countries.[21] But the I.M.F., as I emphasised, is intended to prevent unwarranted competitive depreciation. As regards the deflationary effects on other countries, we must remember that any method of restoring equilibrium, when a country is importing more than it can afford, will reduce the favourable balance of the rest of the world. I agree that other methods may sometimes be more appropriate than devaluation, even if they involve discrimination,[22] but I can hardly accept the general tenor of Mr. Balogh's argument, that revaluation of currencies can be largely discounted as a method of restoring

---

[20] See, for example, 'The Foreign Balance and Full Employment,' *op. cit.*
[21] He claims that my figures veil these secondary effects because they show British exports of manufactures as a *percentage* of the world total. If I had taken *absolute* figures I could have shown a still greater rise in British exports from the depreciation in 1931 up to 1937; but this would have been an outrageous example of *post hoc ergo propter hoc.*
[22] See 'Notes on Non-Discrimination,' *op. cit.*

equilibrium. If exchange rates and relative prices throughout the world are to be taken as a datum, can we ever hope to reconstruct a balanced and expanding world trading system? The maze of discriminatory arrangements will grow more and more involved. The most far-seeing international bodies, supported by the most enlightened governments, could hardly solve the puzzle of maximising world trade in these circumstances. If this is what Mr. Balogh means by a 'planned' world, I am convinced it will end in economic anarchy.

VIII

Mr. Balogh is deeply concerned with our economic position, as we all are. He is looking for ways of improving our standard of living, and has a natural tendency to dismiss any policy that does not seem certain to do so. What I fear is that his alternative policies attempt the impossible, and that in seeking a higher standard than we *can* get we may get a lower standard than we *could*. 'The maintenance of the British standard of life,' he says 'will be very difficult, if at all possible,' unless we accept his proposals. But may it not be still more difficult if we do? 'We can, of course, compete by cutting real wages, but that cannot be the aim of the British policy.' Of course it is not the aim. But if we try, by bullying, by blocs, or by insisting on unacceptable rules, to maintain higher real wages than we are entitled to, if we try to sell our goods for more than they are worth on the world market, we shall not succeed for long. And in attempting to do so we shall make an effective international code impossible. We shall shatter the unity of the world market and help to start a free-for-all, the state of affairs we must avoid at all costs. It is tempting, when things look bad, to throw over the old beliefs lock, stock and barrel, to pursue a policy that shows immediate and visible benefits. But a market gained in, say, a bilateral agreement may often mean a couple of markets lost in countries indirectly affected. Let us hope that those who direct our policy weigh carefully these indirect consequences. Otherwise, our last state may be worse than the first.

7 Notes on non-discrimination[1]

In the *Bulletin* for August 1947, Sir Hubert Henderson expresses doubts 'whether plans based on *non-discrimination as the key principle* (italics mine) are likely, in the conditions left behind by a second major war, to secure a large volume of international trade.' He contends that 'with large scale disequilibria in the international balance of payments to be corrected, *insistence on non-discrimination* (italics mine) is likely to prove a contractionist influence of great potency'.

These statements offer an opportunity of reconciling what appear to be widely divergent views on the vexed question of non-discrimination.

Possible views on this matter may be divided into three categories:
(a) Insistence on non-discrimination in all circumstances;
(b) Insistence on complete freedom for countries to discriminate in any circumstances;
(c) The view that non-discrimination is desirable in some circumstances and discrimination in others.

Many — perhaps most — of those who think seriously about this subject hold views that would fall into the half-and-half category (c). But there is a tendency for those who emphasise the dangers of non-discrimination to be regarded as holders of the extreme view (b), that countries should be free to discriminate in all circumstances, while, conversely, we find Sir Hubert Henderson implying that those who believe in 'non-discrimination as the key principle' must hold the extreme view (a), 'insistence on non-discrimination' in all circumstances.

It is important that as much agreement as possible should be reached on this matter. The first step is to agree on the undesirability of insisting either on non-discrimination in all circumstances or on complete freedom to discriminate. The next step is to agree, in broad principle at least, on the circumstances in which non-discrimination is desirable, and on those in which it is desirable to permit discrimination. Agreement on these matters would be a great step

[1] *Bulletin of the Oxford University Institute of Statistics,* November 1947.

forward. There would still be room for differences of opinion on the commercial policy that should in fact be pursued, but these could fairly easily be attributed to differences of judgment as to the future course and pattern of world trade, the importance of multilateral commerce, the practicability of international agreements, and so on. It may, therefore, be useful to set out briefly some of the main arguments for and against non-discrimination. We shall not discuss questions of international justice or morality (will non-discrimination reduce international friction; is Imperial Preference any more discriminatory than free trade, behind a high tariff, between the 48 states of the U.S.A. or than a Customs Union between Belgium and Holland,[2] and so on). We shall concentrate here on the more 'economic' aspects, and in the main on the effects of discrimination and non-discrimination on the world total of international trade — the principal question raised by Sir Hubert Henderson. This does not, of course, imply that a greater world trade will necessarily mean greater welfare for the peoples of the world, or for particular nations; and something will be said in later Sections and in the Annex about the particular interest of Britain, the divergent interests of individual nations, the quality as opposed to the quantity of international trade, and the objective of stability.

II. THE CASE FOR NON-DISCRIMINATION

First, then, the arguments for non-discrimination. Non-discrimination can mean many different things, but in this context we shall take it to mean that countries in general buy their imports in the cheapest foreign market. This is a very broad definition, but there is no space to discuss here such questions as the allowance to be made for 'commercial' considerations other than the price (a provision of particular significance for long-term contracts), the discrimination between foreign countries that may be indirectly involved in import duties and restrictions of varying severity on particular products, the difficulty of defining non-discrimination when quantitative import restrictions are imposed, and so on.

The most general argument for non-discrimination as a means of maximising world trade follows, I suppose, directly from our definition. The more countries take advantage of the cheapest sources of supply, the greater will be international trade; and, conversely, to forgo such advantages means forgoing desirable consumption, the stimulation of less efficient domestic production,

---

[2] It is not suggested, of course, that the question of Customs Union versus Preference is wholly one of justice or morality. Whether, and in what circumstances, the former or the latter will be more conducive to a large world trade is an important 'economic' question, but there is no space for a discussion here.

and a limitation on the international division of labour. More particularly, a country will often use freedom to discriminate to buy more from countries which are disposed to buy from it and less from other countries; and more from countries with which it has a favourable balance, and less from countries with which its balance is unfavourable. This will reduce the possibilities of triangular, or multilateral trade, and so the total of world trade, for the same kind of reasons that barter between individuals will permit a much smaller volume of trade than the multilateral commerce that is a characteristic of all advanced communities. This argument for non-discrimination does not at all imply that those who stress its dangers desire, in Sir Hubert Henderson's words, 'to work for a state of things in which there would always be a precise equation between imports ˉand exports in the trade between each pair of countries'; clearly no sensible person would 'work for' such a state of affairs. But it is vital to remember that if nations are left completely free to discriminate in all circumstances, and for all purposes, on the ground that discrimination can in certain circumstances promote trade, and even do so without reducing the total of multilateral trade, then there will almost certainly in practice — or so experience suggests — be a severe limitation of multilateral trade; and a consideration of the extreme case of completely bilateral trade gives some measure of the maximum loss that might be involved.

Before the nineteen-thirties a large part of world trade was multilateral. While the payments and receipts of each country vis-à-vis the rest of the world were normally in balance, or nearly so, most nations had large favourable balances with some countries and unfavourable balances with others.

This is hardly surprising where countries specialised in one or two commodities. For example, some nine-tenths of New Zealand's exports consist of meat, diary products and wool. The United Kingdom is by far the largest market for these products; we took four-fifths of the world's exports of meat and butter before the War and nearly one-third of the world's exports of wool. It is therefore not surprising that the great bulk of New Zealand's exports came to this country. But it would have been surprising if New Zealand could have obtained from us all the goods she wished to import. We cannot possibly produce tropical products, and there are certain things that we are physically capable of producing, but which New Zealand prefers to buy from other manufacturing countries that can either sell them more cheaply or provide more suitable qualities. In fact New Zealand took only about half her imports from the United Kingdom and she therefore had a large export surplus to this country (this is true even after allowing for the interest payments due to this country). The currency she earned by her favourable balance with the United Kingdom, New Zealand spent on imports from other countries. If we had been reluctant to convert more than a small proportion of this currency, New Zealand would have been unable to obtain many of the products she needs.

Other countries that specialise on one or two products are usually in the same position as New Zealand. Coffee, for example, accounted for nine-tenths of El Salvador's total pre-war exports; two-thirds of Panama's exports were bananas; two-thirds of Cuba's exports were sugar; two-thirds of Bolivia's were tin; two-thirds of Ceylon's were tea. It would be surprising if the countries that required these products were also the countries that had the things required by El Salvador, Panama, and the rest, in exactly the same proportions. But so long as there is multilateral trading throughout the world, this does not matter. Nations can sell to countries that want their products and buy from countries that have the products they want.

The value of multilateral trade is equally great for countries that do not specialise so much, only it is not quite so obvious. A good description is contained in 'The Network of World Trade', from which the following illustration is largely taken. Table I shows the trade of the United States in 1928 with various parts of the world. It will be seen that the United States exported roughly twice as much to Europe and to the 'Regions of Recent Settlement' as she imported from them, while she imported twice as much from the tropical countries as she exported to them. (The last column of the table shows that this general pattern of United States trade was not affected by the inclusion of 'invisible' trade and new long-term loans.)

The large United States export surplus to Europe is explained by the availability in the United States of many commodities (such as tobacco, films, up-to-date machinery, etc.) which are required by the European countries, but which cannot be obtained in sufficient quantities or at competitive prices from countries other than the United States. Europe, on the other hand, has comparatively few products urgently required by the United States; there are few primary products of which she has an export surplus, and most European manufactures can be easily produced in the United States.[3]

[3] This does not, of course, imply that more European manufactures could not be sold in the U.S. if American tariffs were reduced. Recent comparative studies of industrial output per head in Britain and America show a wide variation from industry to industry in the degree of American superiority. (See, for example, Table V of Mr. Rostas' article in the *Economic Journal* for April, 1943, which shows American output per head varying from little more than the British in some industries to four or five times the British in others.) Although output per head is by no means the whole story, the figures suggest that a considerable increase in trade might be possible if tariffs were reduced.

TABLE I

United States Trade, 1928

$ millions

	Visible Imports*	Visible Exports*	Balance of Visible Trade	Total balance, allowing for invisible trade, interest, service of war debts, and new long-term loans
Europe	1130	2360	+1230	+340
'Regions of Recent Settlement'†	780	1380	+ 600	+370
Tropics	1820	870	− 950	−930
Rest of World	680	550	− 130	−280
Total	4410	5160	+ 750	−500‡

Source: Network of World Trade.
*Adjusted figures—'frontier values'.
†Broadly, Australia, New Zealand, S. Africa, Canada, Argentine.
‡Offset by reduction of gold reserves (290), and other capital items (210).

The 'Regions of Recent Settlement' (broadly the British Dominions and the Argentine) have a high standard of living and a scattered population and have, therefore, a large demand for such products as radios, refrigerators, motor vehicles and labour-saving devices, in the production of which the United States has an advantage over most of her manufacturing rivals. On the other hand these countries, like the United States, are situated mainly in the temperate zones, and have large amounts of agricultural land per head. Their main products, such as meat and wheat, are therefore easily produced in the United States, and their exports to that country are relatively small.

The tropical countries produce many things that cannot be produced, at least in sufficient quantities, in the United States, either because of the difference in climate or because of the absence in the United States of certain types of mineral deposits. These products include rubber, sugar, bananas, coffee, tea, cocoa, vegetable oils, jute, and various ores and metals such as tin. The tropical countries, on the other hand, mostly have a low standard of living and, therefore, a relatively low demand for high grade products in which the United States has an advantage; they have a large demand for lower quality consumer goods, many of which can be more easily obtained in the United Kingdom, Continental Europe and Japan; and we find in fact that the United Kingdom had a favourable balance with many of the tropical countries.[4]

An example of the working of the multilateral trading system in the nineteen-twenties is thus given by trade between the United States, the United Kingdom and the tropical countries. The United States had a large favourable balance with the United Kingdom; we had a favourable balance with the tropical countries such as Malaya; while the tropical countries had large favourable balances with the United States.

If multilateral trading had been restricted, many nations would have found it difficult to obtain a large number of products which they required from abroad. New Zealand and the United States would have found it difficult to obtain tropical products, while the tropical countries would have found it difficult to buy from the United Kingdom. Most countries would have had either to restrict their consumption of various products, or to produce more for themselves. The United States might have had to restrict her consumption of coffee and tea; the tropical countries would have been unable to buy such a large volume of textile goods because they would have had to buy the more expensive products of the United States rather than the cheaper products of Britain and Japan; the United States, finding it more difficult to pay for natural rubber from Malaya, might have been induced to make more synthetic rubber for herself. All this would have meant a reduction of international trade and less international division of labour. It would also have led to the widespread use of their bargaining power by large importers. For example, the United States might have tried to force the tropical countries to buy American goods rather than British.

In the 'twenties, something like one-quarter of all international trade was multilateral, which gives some idea of the magnitude of the loss that might be involved by discriminatory practices that reduced the possibilities of multilateral trade. It may be argued that a large part of this multilateral trade was accidental. For example, if a reduction in multilateral trade meant merely that we took more wheat from countries with which we had hitherto had a favourable balance and less from other countries, this would involve simply a re-channeling of trade at no great extra cost, so that the total of world trade would not be appreciably reduced. It seems likely, however, that the potentialities of such reciprocal trade had already

---

[4] It is true that some of the tropical countries with which the United States had close trading relations, especially those in Central America, took a much higher proportion of their imports from the United States than from the United Kingdom; but nevertheless they had an export surplus to the United States.

been fairly well exploited. This is suggested by the mere fact that ships or railway waggons taking goods from one country to another can offer low freight rates for return traffic; by the existence of Imperial Preference, preferential arrangements between the U.S., Cuba, and the Philippines, etc.; and by the commercial relations formed by trade in one direction which naturally encourage trade in the opposite direction. We also find, for example, that the tropical American Republics and the Philippines, which export largely to the U.S., took 46 per cent of their imports from the U.S. in 1938 and only 8 per cent from the U.K., although we have a comparative advantage in many of the goods demanded by such countries; while Australia, New Zealand and Eire, which export largely to the U.K., took 46 per cent of their imports from the U.K., and only 14 per cent from the U.S., although America has a comparative advantage in many 'high-income-goods'.

The main reason then why non-discrimination will tend to increase world trade is that it allows full scope for multilateral trade, while the main danger of unbridled discrimination is that it would severely limit such trade, which, as we have seen, is a most important and vital part of world trade.

III. THE CASE FOR DISCRIMINATION

But it is not always true that insistence on non-discrimination will maximise world trade; it may lead to higher trade barriers[5] and a lower world demand than would be possible if certain forms of discrimination were permitted, and the resultant losses may more than offset the advantages of buying in the cheapest market and of full multilateral trade. This may be illustrated by a few hypothetical examples.

(*a*) Let us suppose in the first instance that world employment, production and trade are running at high levels and that countries are in general not in balance of payments difficulties. Suppose now that a severe depression in, say, the United States reduced her imports by one-half while her exports were, for a time, maintained at the old level owing to the maintenance of full employment in the rest of the world. (United States exports might actually be stimulated by a relative fall in American prices.) This is the sort of situation that arose in 1938. American imports fell in volume between 1937 and 1938 by 28 per cent, while American exports were maintained.

Let us assume further that it is impossible or impracticable to restore equilibrium by changing the relative values of the dollar and

---

[5] Throughout this study, more and less restrictive state purchase of imports are comprised in the phrases higher and lower trade barriers.

of other currencies, by a reduction in American import barriers, or by an increase in American lending. Other countries, as their liquid reserves were reduced, would then have to cut down their imports.

If they cut down wholly on imports from the United States, full world equilibrium would at once be restored. The effect of the American slump on trade in the rest of the world would not in general be very serious. Let us suppose that countries had been sending, on the average, 10 per cent of their exports to the United States (this is not far from the pre-war proportion). A cut of one-half in United States imports would then reduce the exports of other countries by, on the average, 5 per cent. If they now cut their imports from the United States by on the average one-half, and made no cuts in imports from each other, world equilibrium would be restored with the total import and export trade of countries outside the United States reduced by only 5 per cent; while the trade of the United States would, of course, be reduced by 50 per cent. (It might even be possible to prevent the 5 per cent fall if countries outside the U.S. took more of each others' products.)

If, on the other hand, strict non-discriminatory principles were followed, countries other than the United States would cut down their imports in roughly equal proportions from the United States and from each other; an average cut of 5 per cent in their imports would then still leave them with a large overall adverse balance with the United States, and the United States with a large favourable balance. Further cuts would, therefore, have to be made until total imports from the United States were reduced to half of the original level; world trade would then once more be in equilibrium, but at only about one-half of the original level.

This is clearly a case where departure from the principle that each nation should buy in the cheapest market may lead to a larger total of world trade. It should be noted, however, that this simple example takes no account of the widely divergent position of individual countries. Some of the complications that arise are discussed in the annex, where it is shown that clashes of interest would arise; that discrimination in the circumstances described in this section (*a*) and in (*b*) below would not necessarily benefit every country; and that discrimination based on the suspension of the free convertibility of currencies into dollars would not necessarily give such a favourable result as that described in the previous paragraphs.

(*b*) Alternatively, let us suppose that foreign loans or gifts by the United States have been used to finance a large favourable balance on current account, and that these loans or gifts are now seriously reduced. Whether or not this reduced employment in the United

States, an analysis similar to that in (*a*) would again be appropriate, and a departure from the principle of non-discrimination justified.

There are, however, two important assumptions implicit in the analysis under (*a*) and (*b*), apart from the assumption that it is impossible or impracticable to restore equilibrium by an adjustment of exchange rates, by deflationary or 'disinflationary' measures in non-American countries that would not appreciably increase unemployment, by a lowering of American tariffs or by other methods not involving direct restriction of imports by non-American countries.

(*i*) It is assumed that discrimination against imports from America by the rest of the world would not induce Americans to curtail their imports still further, either in retaliation or for other reasons, or to form their own preferential arrangements with countries that agreed not to curtail imports from America but to cut imports from Britain and other countries instead. (This is a possible form of discrimination that should be borne in mind by those who emphasise the disadvantages of the principle of non-discrimination.) These are very important provisos. If the response of the United States to discrimination against her goods were to reduce her imports still further, or to form her own preferential arrangements, the trade of the countries unfavourably affected might be reduced by as much as if the principle of non-discrimination had been strictly adhered to from the beginning. From the United Kingdom point of view, an attempt to isolate ourselves and other countries from the effects of an American slump or a large reduction in American loans or gifts might, if America retaliated, also isolate us from a large part of the world's markets.[6]

It may be argued that there is no reason why the United States should retaliate in these circumstances, because discrimination against United States goods would not reduce the *total* demand for them below the level to which it would have fallen in a world of strict non-discrimination; the world as a whole, we might argue, will always contrive somehow to spend in America all the dollars that America makes available by importing, lending and gifts. But this argument would not necessarily convince individual American exporters whose interests were damaged; nor might it convince the general American public, or Congress. The danger of American retaliation would thus be a very real one, unless the U.S. had given a firm undertaking in advance, by accepting an appropriate code of international behaviour or otherwise, not to retaliate.

[6] More details are given in the *Economic Journal* for March 1946 and March 1947.

(*ii*) Another important assumption is that the discrimination is applied, in our examples, only against the United States. If the departure from the principle of non-discrimination, justified in the first place by the American favourable balance, led to the widespread adoption of discriminatory practices, world trade might fall by as much as, or more than, it would have fallen if non-discrimination had been rigidly adhered to. If countries other than the United States began to reduce their imports, not only from the United States but also from other countries that did not buy from them, the scope for multilateral trade would be greatly reduced and so the volume of world trade.

(*c*) A third case we may consider is that in which world trade has been restricted to a fraction of its previous or possible level, and an attempt is made to reduce world trade barriers all round in a non-discriminatory fashion. If now we assume that, say, United States imports do not increase much as a result of an increase in her exports (either because she will not reduce her tariffs, or because lower tariffs will have little effect in stimulating her imports, or because the extra income derived from higher exports does not result in a commensurate expenditure on imports), the process will soon come to a halt, because the exports of countries other than the U.S. will go up less than their imports. (This is largely the reverse of the analysis in (*a*) and (*b*).)

In these circumstances trade might be more easily increased if there were a lowering of obstacles to the mutual trade of countries other than the United States but not of barriers imposed against imports from the United States by the rest of the world. Again, however, we must enter the same provisos that the United States does not retaliate and that the departure from the principle of non-discrimination does not get out of hand.

(*d*) Quite apart from the existence of countries like the United States in our example (*c*), whose imports do not readily respond to an increase in their exports, world trade may sometimes be more easily revived from a low level resulting from all round restrictions through discriminatory agreements to lower trade barriers than by strict adherence to non-discrimination. The reason is that it is easier to reach agreement between a fairly small number of countries than it is to reach agreement between every country in the world.

The extreme case is an agreement between two countries, in which each agrees to increase its imports from the other by the same amount. In this case, apart from retaliation or other indirect consequences, each will have a guarantee that it will be able to finance the additional imports it agrees to take. Trade will thus be possible that would otherwise not have been possible, if we assume that no such satisfactory guarantee could, in practice, have been given as a result of a multilateral agreement, between a number of countries, to take more imports, or if trade barriers had had to be reduced in a non-discriminatory manner.

Here again, however, we must enter two provisos.

(*i*) It is true that a bilateral agreement of the type described, or a network of such agreements, may increase the total of trade above its *present* level without reducing the total of multilateral trade below its *present* level. But before giving our blessing to such agreements we must also be sure that they will lead to a greater total of beneficial trade in the *future* than would have been possible in the *future* if trade barriers had been reduced in a less discriminatory fashion. For if, on grounds of practicability, we attempt to increase trade by such bilateral agreements, we reduce the potential scope for expansion[7] and force the additional trade into bilateral channels, some of the disadvantages of which have already been described; once these channels have been formed it will, moreover, be difficult to alter their course.

(*ii*) The second proviso is that the bilateral agreements do not unduly affect the trade of third countries, which they may well do in practice if unconditionally permitted. An agreement between two countries, under which each merely took more of the other's products at the expense of imports from third countries, might well reduce rather than increase the total of world trade.[8] Even if the two

---

[7] If, for example, we wished to expand our trade with Palestine, but could offer her, in return for an increase in her exports to us, only an equivalent amount of British goods, the possibilities of expanding our mutual trade would be limited because Palestine needs things other than British manufactures. The sources of Palestine's imports are extremely varied. In 1937, for example, her largest supplier (Germany) supplied only 17 per cent of her total imports. She took, in addition, 16 per cent from the U.K.; 9 per cent each from Syria and Romania; 7 per cent from the U.S.A.; 4 per cent from Egypt; 3 per cent each from Belgium, Japan, Czechoslovakia and Poland; 2 per cent each from Iraq, India, France, Italy, Turkey; and 16 per cent from other countries. It is likely that, if she were free to do so, Palestine would use the proceeds of an increase in exports to Britain in purchases from a wide range of countries. If she were permitted to spend the proceeds only on British goods, the practicability of negotiating an agreement might be greater, but the scope for an expansion of trade would be smaller. (The scope for bilateral expansion of trade between two countries, neither of which has such a wide range of goods to offer as the U.K., would be still more limited.) The importance of the limitation mentioned will, of course, vary with the type of world we are considering. A greater bilateral expansion of trade will be possible with a Palestine with a large surplus of oranges and desperately short of manufactured imports than with a Palestine, without such a surplus of oranges or shortage of imports, that is anxious to develop her own industries.

[8] To take a highly simplified example, suppose each of two countries A and B increases its imports from the other by *x*, and reduces its imports from a third country C by *x*. The balance of trade of both A and B will be improved by *x*, and that of C worsened by 2 *x*. If there are no secondary consequences, each country being satisfied with its new balance of

countries made some compensatory increase in their imports of other articles from the outside world, many individual third countries would be adversely affected by the diversion and would be forced, through loss of importing power, to reduce their imports and possibly to form their own preferential arrangements; while others, with a margin in hand, might be provoked to retaliatory action of a similar nature. It is clear, without further elaboration, that the indirect consequences of a discriminatory agreement, between two or a small number of countries, that involved a measure of diversion of trade from the rest of the world, would have to be carefully assessed before we could be certain that it would promote the trade of the world as a whole.

IV. STRIKING A BALANCE

We outlined in Section II the case for non-discrimination, and in Section III some of the circumstances in which a departure from non-discrimination may lead to a greater world trade. Our first three examples in Section III related to circumstances in which there is a large-scale disequilibrium in the balance of payments between one part of the world and another which cannot be corrected on a non-discriminatory basis without restricting world trade to an unnecessarily low level; the fourth was an argument for discrimination on grounds of convenience of negotiation when an attempt is being made to increase international trade. These four examples are not intended to be exhaustive. We have not dealt, for example, with the case for discrimination in order to form a 'full employment club' of nations—this must be distinguished from the case discussed in example (*a*) of Section III; a primary object of the club would be to isolate its members in advance, and permanently, from the economic instability of, say, the U.S., and this would be more likely to provoke retaliation. Nor have we dealt with the case for discrimination to encourage the development of production by long-term contracts above the world price, a case to which many of the 'infant industry' tariff arguments apply. We have not dealt either with discrimination to soften the effects of rapidly changing conditions of world supply and demand, or with many other proposals that have been made.

But the fact that discrimination may in certain circumstances

---

trade, the total of trade will be unaltered. If C reacts by reducing her imports from both A and B by *x*, the balance of trade of each country will be restored to the original level, and total trade reduced by 2 *x*. If, however, before the reaction of C, A and B are induced by their improved balance to increase their imports, the fall in total trade may be lessened, avoided, or even, if the reaction of A and B is sufficiently strong, reversed. (There is no space for further elaboration.)

permit a greater, or more stable, world trade than strict adherence to the principle of non-discrimination does not mean that we should abandon the latter principle and permit discrimination in all circumstances. This might lead to a smaller world trade than uncompromising adherence .to non-discrimination; it would certainly lead to a smaller trade than would result from adherence to a code of international behaviour under which discrimination was allowed only in certain carefully defined circumstances, and within carefully prescribed limits. For example, discrimination may be justified on grounds of convenience in negotiating an increase in trade; but we must ensure that it is in fact being used solely for this purpose, that the trade of countries other than those negotiating is not unduly affected, and that a greater or more beneficial increase in trade might not have been obtained by non-discriminatory reductions in trade barriers. Or again, discrimination may be justifiable, when there is large scale disequilibrium in the international balance of payments, against what may be loosely called 'scarce currency' countries (the term is not used in the Bretton Woods sense); but to ensure that such discrimination makes possible a greater world trade we must make sure that it is exercised only against the 'scarce currency' countries and not against other countries, and that the 'scarce currency' countries do not retaliate. It is also important that everything possible should be done to remove or to minimise the disequilibrium by adjustments of exchange rates, by appropriate policies of international lending, tariff reduction and full employment in the 'scarce currency' countries, by 'disinflationary' measures in other countries, and by other such means.

It may, of course, be impossible to devise a workable international code of the type described, because of the difficulty of defining clearly all the circumstances in which discrimination should be permitted, or deciding in particular cases whether the necessary conditions are fulfilled, and of deciding also whether discrimination, once permitted, is being carried beyond the proper limits. It may be impossible to reach agreement on a code that does not contain so many escape clauses as to be worthless. The practicable alternatives might then be (*a*) to attempt to secure widespread adherence to the principle of non-discrimination with the minimum number of exceptions, or perhaps even with no exceptions at all, (*b*) to abandon the principle entirely and to give full rein to discriminatory practices. The choice between these two alternatives would be influenced by such considerations as the likely degree of chronic disequilibrium in the future international balance of payments, the quantitative importance of multilateral trade and the extent to which nations would be likely to abuse a freedom to adopt discriminatory practices.

Sir Hubert Henderson adduces historical evidence, and claims that the non-discriminatory system built up in the 1920's 'led to the disasters of 1930-32'. It is true that the volume of world trade fell by a quarter between 1929 and 1932, but can this fall be wholly attributed to non-discrimination? Would there not have been a serious fall in any case, discrimination or no discrimination? The fall in trade between 1929 and 1932 does not in itself prove that it would have been better never to have attempted to rebuild a non-discriminatory system in the 1920's. To prove this it would be necessary to show that trade would have fallen by less if the world had been free of any doctrine of non-discrimination; but this is by no means obvious, because, as we have seen, freedom to discriminate will lead to discrimination not only where this is right and proper, but also for purposes that are destructive of trade. It would also be necessary to prove, not only that the fall in trade between 1929 and 1932 would have been smaller had there been complete freedom to discriminate, but also that the absolute level of trade in 1932 would have been higher. This again is by no means obvious. The volume of world trade rose between 1924 and 1929, a period when non-discrimination was the general rule, in the ratio 75:100, and fell again between 1929 and 1932 in the ratio 100:75. Even if complete freedom to discriminate had, on balance, reduced the fall during the latter period (which is uncertain), would it have allowed the large rise that took place between 1924 and 1929, a period when large-scale disequilibria in balances of payment were at least masked by large scale lending? (This, of course, raises the further question of the unsettling influence of large uncontrolled international lending.)[9]

It is sometimes argued further that the recovery in trade between 1932 and 1937 demonstrates the value of abandoning the principle of non-discrimination. But would there not have been a recovery in any case? The question is whether the radical departure from non-discrimination in the 1930's made possible a larger recovery than would otherwise have taken place. It is impossible to give a definite answer, but it is worth recording (*a*) that the volume of world trade failed to recover by 1937 to the 1929 pre-depression level, although world production rose well above that level, (*b*) that during the years 1932-37 the recovery in international trade lagged behind that in

[9] See *Economic Journal*, March 1947, p. 98.

production, whereas during the 'non-discrimination' years 1925-29 trade seems to have increased more rapidly than production.[10]

It is not claimed that these statistics of the inter-war years prove the case for non-discrimination, but simply that they cannot prove the case against it. Even, however, if it could be shown that complete freedom to discriminate throughout the inter-war years would have been preferable to the fairly strict doctrine of non-discrimination which characterised at least part of the world for at least part of the period, it remains true that an international code, working properly, which allowed discrimination in certain circumstances but not in others, would have been better still.

The history of the inter-war years provides a good illustration of the need for such an international code. The fact that it would have been particularly valuable in the critical periods of the 30's reminds us that what we want is not just a 'fair weather' code, to be introduced when 'normal' conditions return. It may be hard to secure acceptance of a code during a difficult period such as the present. But it is precisely during periods of crisis that a workable code is most needed to prevent discriminatory practices getting out of hand.

In discussing the merits of discrimination and of non-discrimination our main criterion so far has been the total of world trade—the criterion used by Professor Henderson. But even if it could be shown that freedom to discriminate would not lead to a greater world trade, it might still be argued that British trade could be increased, at the expense of other countries, by a departure from non-discrimination.

This would enable us, for example, to use our bargaining power in an attempt to force other countries to buy more from us, often at the expense of our industrial rivals. The question is not whether we should depart from the principle of non-discrimination if most other

---

[10] The following figures, which are derived from League of Nations publications, are not all strictly comparable, but seem to bear out these general conclusions:

		Percentage change in Volume of World	
		Production	Trade.
1925–29	Primary Products	+11	+15
	Manufactures	+27	+32
1932–37	Food and Fodder	+ 6	+ 5
	Raw Materials	+57	+33
	Manufactures	+73	+46
1929–37	Food and Fodder	+ 6	− 6½
	Raw Materials	+16	+ 8
	Manufactures	+20	−13
	Total	..	− 3½

countries had already done so, but rather whether, if there were in operation, or in prospect, an international code of the type described, it would pay us to denounce it (which would almost certainly lead to its universal abandonment), so as to be free to exercise our bargaining power. Nations would then be free to discriminate in all circumstances, so that world trade would be smaller than under a properly working international code; could we hope to gain on balance by securing an increased share of a smaller total of trade? The answer will depend on the extent of our bargaining power (which, it has been argued elsewhere,[11] is not so great as is sometimes supposed), in comparison with the unfavourable consequences that would result. These include the loss of importing power by countries adversely affected, which would react, directly and indirectly, on British trade; the danger, which is a serious one, of retaliation, especially by the United States, and a general deterioration in standards of commercial conduct throughout the world, which would, *inter alia*, reduce the possibilities of multilateral trade — a serious consideration for a country, like the U.K., which depends greatly on such trade.

Quite apart from the exercise of bargaining power, we might, for example, use freedom to discriminate to switch our imports from one country to another in the hope that we should thereby increase our exports without obtaining concessions from other countries in the way of reduced barriers against our goods. This could be done by taking imports from countries with a high propensity to import from the U.K. instead of from countries with a low propensity. For example, we might buy more South African oranges and fewer Brazilian oranges. Since Brazil took only 10 per cent of her imports from the U.K. in 1938, while South Africa took 43 per cent of hers, it might be assumed that the gain of importing power in South Africa would increase the demand for U.K. exports more than it would be reduced by the loss of importing power in Brazil. It must, however, be remembered:

(i) that our oranges would almost certainly cost more than before;
(ii) that Brazil might in turn discriminate against the U.K., and cut down her imports mainly from this country;
(iii) that even if she did not do this, the loss of importing power in Brazil might affect British exports indirectly through the loss of importing power of countries that export to Brazil;
(iv) that other countries might play the same game; for example, Brazil drew 25 per cent of her imports from Germany, South

[11] See *Economic Journal*, March 1946, and March 1947.

Africa only 8 per cent of hers; so that Germany, who would be affected by Brazil's loss of importing power, might in pre-war conditions have decided to buy more Brazilian oranges and fewer South African.

The final result of our discrimination in favour of South Africa might thus not be very favourable, and it might be unfavourable.

A few very general remarks may finally be made about Britain's interest in discriminatory arrangements justified on the ground that they increase stability. If the stability helps to increase trade, well and good; long-term contracts may serve this end, but these need not necessarily, in my opinion, be considered discriminatory. Stability may sometimes, however, be bought at the expense of trade—a 'full employment club' of nations, for example, might well have this result, the limitation of the area of trade more than offsetting the gain of confidence. Such an exchange of trade for stability we could hardly afford. The acquisition of our necessary food and raw materials is our most difficult problem, and must surely be our primary objective even if it involves some internal instability; this we can somehow deal with by domestic measures, and if the two aims of 'maximum imports' and 'full employment' are in conflict, the latter must, up to a point at least, give way. Stability may, in the third place, mean the preservation of existing channels of trade, the slowing down of economic change. But for a nation that must welcome any new and cheaper source of primary production and greatly increase its own share of world exports of manufactures, to accept general discriminatory arrangements aimed at the preservation of the *status quo* would surely be a counsel of despair.

No attempt has been made in these notes to give an exhaustive analysis of the case for and against non-discrimination either from the British or from the world point of view; nor have we discussed any of the details of plans for international co-operation such as Bretton Woods and I.T.O. The discussion has been largely theoretical and hypothetical. But when views on commercial policy vary so widely as they have recently done, it seems desirable to seek agreement, at least on general principles, where agreement is possible, and so to isolate the reasons for disagreement. It is desirable at least to reach agreement that there is a case for as well as against non-discrimination. It is particularly important at present that, in applying discriminatory principles for good reasons, the world should not allow discrimination to get out of hand. It is vital not to lose sight of the fundamental case for non-discrimination, and those who emphasise the arguments in its favour (which tend to be forgotten) may perhaps be performing as useful a function as those who concentrate on its shortcomings. It is equally important to recognise that, when there is a large scale lack of balance in international transactions, universal non-discrimination cannot be justified or maintained; hence the need, not only for an international code to prevent the complete abandonment of the principle, but also for the fullest possible exploration of policies to minimise the disequilibrium, and so to restore conditions in which a large measure of non-discrimination may be possible.

ANNEX

The simple examples (*a*) and (*b*) in Section III above, of how discrimination against the United States may help to maintain world trade in the face of an American slump or of a reduction in American lending, took no account of the widely divergent effects on individual countries.

We assumed that, on the average, countries had been earning 10 per cent of their foreign purchasing power by exporting to (or borrowing from) the U.S., so that a fall of one-half in U.S. imports and loans would necessitate an average cut of 5 per cent in the imports of other countries.

But countries like those of Central America, many of which send over half their exports to the U.S., would have to cut their total imports by much more than 5 per cent; while the total imports of countries like Eire, Denmark and Romania, which sent only one or two per cent of their exports to the U.S. before the war, would hardly be effected although the proportionate fall in their imports from the U.S. might be large. Countries of the first type would not have a great deal to gain by agreeing, with other countries outside the U.S., to discriminate against U.S. goods, and to cut down their imports wholly from the U.S. Honduras, for example, which before the war sent nearly nine-tenths of her exports to the U.S., would, even if she discriminated against the United States, have to cut her total imports by approximately 45 per cent to meet a fall of one-half in her exports to the United States; this is little better than the fall of 50 per cent in her imports that might theoretically be necessary if the world adhered strictly to the principles of non-discrimination.[12] Honduras might well prefer not to discriminate against the United States, in the hope that she might thereby obtain concessions from that country.

Then again countries like Malaya, with a large export surplus to

---

[12] For the sake of simplicity, the rather unrealistic assumption is made throughout that non-discriminatory cuts in imports will mean equi-proportional cuts in imports from every country.

the U.S. (in 1938 Malayan exports to the U.S. were 98 million dollars, her imports only 10 million), might find it arithmetically impossible to balance their accounts wholly by cutting imports from the U.S.

Even where this was arithmetically possible it would involve cutting their imports from the U.S. much more than in proportion to the fall in their exports to the U.S., *i.e.* by much more than one-half in our example. It is true that adherence to a general agreement to discriminate against the U.S. would maintain their *total* trade at more than one-half the original level (to which it would fall under universal non-discrimination); but this trade would be very unbalanced, with imports from the United States cut to less than half the original level. It is not impossible, if the goods previously imported from the U.S. could not easily be obtained from other countries, that such an unbalanced total of imports would contribute less to the welfare of countries like Malaya than the lower, but balanced, imports that would result from universal non-discrimination.

In this case 'Malaya' (using the term to denote countries which initially have a favourable balance with the U.S.) might be reluctant to discriminate against United States goods; and even if co-operation with other countries in such discrimination were ultimately to her interest, it would be politically difficult for a country which is a large dollar earner to cut down unduly on United States goods desired by her citizens.

'Malaya' might well prefer to cut down her imports, so far as possible, in a non-discriminatory manner, but to suspend the free convertibility of her currency into dollars (either to forestall the reduction of imports from Malaya by other countries acting in a like manner, or to safeguard her reserves in the face of such reductions.)[13] This would lead to a widespread discrimination against United States goods according to quite different principles from those hitherto discussed. Currencies would no longer be freely convertible into dollars, and many countries' purchases in the U.S. would be limited, not by any international agreement, nor by their total earnings of foreign exchange, but by the amount of dollars

[13] In a sense, Britain was perhaps a 'Malaya' during, for example, at least part of 1947, if, as in case III(b) above, we include borrowing from the U.S. in a country's dollar receipts. Our sales to, and loans from, the U.S. exceeded our purchases from her, and we used part of the difference to finance deficits with other countries. When borrowing ceased, we suspended the convertibility of sterling into dollars, and we did not cut our flow of imports from the U.S. by as much as our borrowing had been reduced; apart from drafts on our reserves, we also cut our imports from countries other than the U.S.
(There is no space to pursue the analogy further.)

earned directly by exporting to the U.S. together with any dollars they could procure by exports to other countries that were prepared to pay, in part at least, in dollars. Discrimination of this type would not necessarily lead to the same results as discrimination under which each country cut its imports from the U.S. by the whole amount of the fall in its exports to the U.S.; it might well lead to a greater contraction of world trade (although it would not necessarily do so).

The reason is that countries of the 'Malaya' type, even after the fall in their exports to the U.S., may as we have seen still have large dollar earnings; if they are then free to cut their imports in the least inconvenient manner to themselves, the only limit to purchases from the U.S. being the amount of their dollar earnings, they are likely to cut imports not only from the United States but also from other countries. This will tend to initiate a contraction in trade between countries other than the United States. Countries of the 'Canada' type in particular, which have large deficits with the United States, will be adversely affected. Not only will they suffer a reduction in their exports to the 'Malaya' countries, as well as in their exports to the U.S., but the inconvenience of discriminating to the necessary extent against United States goods will be extreme. 'Canada' (using this term to stand for countries of the type described) will have to cut her imports from the United States, not only by an amount equal to the fall in her exports to the United States, but in addition by an amount equal to her original deficit with the United States (less any dollars which 'Malaya' may be willing to pay for 'Canadian' exports).

These points are illustrated by the hypothetical example in the accompanying table, which also shows that, under certain different assumptions, the results may not be so unfavourable.

Column (1) shows the original equilibrium position. 'Malaya' has an export surplus of 20 to the 'U.S.', the 'U.S.' an export surplus of 20 to 'Canada', and 'Canada' an export surplus of 20 to 'Malaya'.

Column (2) shows the position after a slump in the U.S. has reduced her imports from both Canada and Malaya by one-half (the example can be readily adjusted to cover the case of a reduction in American lending).

Column (3) shows what happens if Canada and Malaya both cut their imports from the U.S. (presumably by agreement) by an amount equal to the fall in their exports to the U.S. (Case I). Equilibrium is regained with U.S. trade at 50 per cent of the old level, Canadian trade at 73 per cent and Malayan trade at 75 per cent. Malayan imports, which now stand at 75 compared with the original level of 100, are bigger in total than they would have been if non-discrimination had been adhered to from the beginning; in that

Possible Readjustments by Malaya and Canada

Currencies no longer freely convertible into dollars; countries discriminate against
U.S. only to extent required by shortage of dollars

	Original Position	After U.S. slump which reduces U.S. imports from both Canada and Malaya by one-half, but before readjustment of imports by Malaya and Canada	Case I — Both Canada and Malaya cut imports from U.S. by full amount of fall in their exports to U.S.	Case II — Malaya cuts imports first		Case III — Canada cuts imports first but does not increase imports from Malaya			Case IV — Canada cuts imports first and increases imports from Malaya
				Position (i) After Malaya has cut imports	Position (ii) After Canada has cut imports	Position (i) After Canada has cut imports	Position (ii) After Malaya has cut imports	Position (iii) After further readjustment by Canada	
	(1)	(2)	(3)	(4)	(5)	(6)	(7)	(8)	(9)
MALAYA *Exports*									
To U.S.	50	25	25	25	25	25	25	25	25
To Canada	50	50	50	50	50	50	50	50	70
	100	75	75	75	75	75	75	75	95
Imports									
From U.S.	30	30	5	22½	22½	30	22½	22½	25
From Canada	70	70	70	52½*	52½*	70	52½*	52½*	70
	100	100	75	75	75	100	75	75	95

CANADA *Exports*									
To U.S.	80	40	40	40	40	40	40	40	40
To Malaya	70	70	70	52½*	52½*	70	52½*	52½*	70
	150	110	110	92½	92½	110	92½	92½	110
Imports									
From U.S.	100	100	60	100	42½	40	40	42½	40
From Malaya	50	50	50	50	50	50	50	50	70
	150	150	110	150	92½	90	90	92½	110
U.S.A. *Exports*									
To Canada	100	100	60	100	42½	40	40	42½	40
To Malaya	30	30	5	22½	22½	30	22½	22½	25
	130	130	65	122½	65	70	62½	65	65
Imports									
From Canada	80	40	40	40	40	40	40	40	40
From Malaya	50	25	25	25	25	25	25	25	25
	130	65	65	65	65	65	65	65	65

* of which 2½ paid for in dollars.

case the halving of U.S. imports would eventually have reduced Malayan imports to 50. But this smaller total would at least have been better balanced. Malayan imports from both the U.S. and Canada would, we may assume, have been cut by one-half; imports from the U.S. to 15, imports from Canada to 35. Instead of this, Malaya now has imports of only 5 from the U.S. and of 70 from Canada; and this does not necessarily contribute so much to Malayan welfare as the smaller, but better balanced total of 50. It is not impossible, therefore, that Malaya may be even worse off under the agreement to discriminate against the U.S. in the manner described than she would have been if the world had adhered strictly to non-discrimination throughout.

The remaining columns of the table show what may happen if free convertibility into dollars is suspended, and discrimination against U.S. goods is carried only to the point required by each country's supply of dollars.

Case II (columns (4) and (5)) is where Malaya cuts her imports first (Canada meanwhile drawing on her liquid reserves to maintain her old imports in the face of a fall in American demand). Column (4) shows the first stage. Malaya's total earnings have been reduced from 100 to 75 and she must therefore cut her imports from 100 to 75. The most convenient way for her will, we assume, be to cut imports from both Canada and the U.S. by one-quarter, from 30 and 70 to 22½ and 52½ respectively. As her dollar earnings are still 25, she can do this, and still have 2½ in dollars to pay for her import surplus from Canada. Column (5) shows Canada's reactions. She now has to cut her imports from 150 to 92½, but she cannot cut imports from Malaya and the U.S. in the same proportion, because of her shortage of dollars. Her imports from the U.S. have to be limited to 42½ (40 earned by exports to the U.S., 2½ by exports to Malaya). The final position (Column 5) is, then, that U.S. trade is down to one-half, as before; Malayan trade is down to three-quarters, as before (but the reduction has involved much less hardship since no violent cut has been made in imports from the United States—Malaya was right not to co-operate in the alternative plan of discrimination); Canadian trade is down to 62 per cent compared with 73 per cent and the whole of the extra cut has had to be made in her imports from the U.S.

Canada is obviously worse off in Case II than in Case I, and she may even be worse off than she would have been under universal non-discrimination; for although this would have meant a still greater fall in her total trade, to 50 per cent, the smaller imports would at least have been better balanced.

Columns 6–9 show what happens if Canada makes the first cut, Malaya meanwhile drawing on her liquid reserves. On the assumption (Case III) that Canada does not attempt to make good the cut in imports from the U.S. by extra imports from Malaya, we reach exactly the same result as before (Column 8 being identical with Column 5). On the alternative assumption (Case IV) that Canada, after cutting her imports from the U.S. to an amount equal to her earnings in the U.S., increases her imports from Malaya until they equal her exports to Malaya, we get a greater total of trade, but Canada's imports are even more unbalanced than before.

The discussion in this annex has shown that discrimination against, say, the United States, in the event of an American slump or a reduction in American lending, may take several forms, and lead to various results according to the assumptions made (no attempt has been made to cover all the possibilities). It has also brought to light the divergent interests of countries of various types.

Countries of the 'Honduras' type, whose exports are sold mainly to the U.S., may have little or nothing to gain from discrimination.

Countries of the 'Malaya' type, with export surpluses to the U.S., may have more to lose by agreeing to cut imports only from the U.S. and to maintain trade with other countries, than they would lose in a world that adhered strictly to non-discrimination; and their best course, in our example, would be to avoid discrimination so far as possible, but to suspend the free convertibility of their currencies into dollars.

This reaction to an American slump would be disadvantageous to countries of the 'Canada' type, with import surpluses from the U.S.; they may even have more to lose from such a development than from universal adherence to non-discrimination.

It may be that countries outside the U.S. as a whole can benefit from discrimination which helps them to concentrate their limited power to import from the U.S. on essential products not easily obtainable elsewhere, and to maintain their mutual trade; but individual countries may suffer, because of the redistribution of dollar purchasing power involved.

All this tends to weaken the case for discrimination made on pages 202–4 of the text, which took no account of the unequal effects on individual countries, of the possibility that some countries would refuse to co-operate, or of the less favourable results that might ensue if discrimination took a form different from that assumed. It also reinforces the case for a carefully worked out international code, if the whole scheme is not to break down through the clash of interests that has been revealed. Finally, it reminds us that the quality, or composition, of international trade is important, and that the quantity alone does not tell the whole story.

8 Notes on Britain's bargaining power[1]

1. INTRODUCTION

Britain has hitherto been the largest importer in the world. Table I shows that, in 1937, her imports were 17 per cent of the world total, and that she took no less than 30 per cent of the world's imports of

TABLE I

United Kingdom and World Imports 1937

	U.K. imports (Billion dollars)	World imports (Billion dollars)	U.K. as per cent. of world imports
Food	1.9	6.4	30
Raw materials	2.0	11.6	17
Manufactures	0.8	10.2	8
	4.7	28.2	17

food. Her share in world imports of certain commodities was even larger — four-fifths of the world's imports of meat and butter and half the world's imports of eggs, cheese, and tea. Certain countries, too, depended greatly on the United Kingdom market. More than half of Denmark's exports came to this country, over four-fifths of New Zealand's, and over nine-tenths of the exports of Eire.

The British market is thus of vital importance to many primary producers throughout the world; and it is often argued that, by threatening to reduce, to eliminate, or not to increase our imports from particular countries we might induce them to help us pay for our essential imports. We might, for example, induce them to charge us a lower price for their produce or to pay a higher price for our exports; to take more of our exports, either in addition to those they were already taking from other countries or in their place; to reduce their import barriers against manufactures from all countries; or to assist us in other ways.

[1] *Oxford Economic Papers*, January 1949.

It is clearly of some importance to evaluate, in more detail, our bargaining power as a large importer, and to consider the possible repercussions of the use of this power as part of our commercial policy.

In the *Economic Journal* for March 1946 I published a brief analysis.[2] This seemed to show that many countries were less dependent on the British market than was commonly supposed, and that many were even more dependent on the market of the United States. The measure I then used of a country's dependence on our market was the proportion of its total exports sent to the United Kingdom. But, as I explained, this is by no means the only measure. The main object of these further notes is to consider certain others. Thus, for example, a more useful measure may sometimes be the proportion, not of a country's exports, but of its total output, sent to the United Kingdom. We shall also make an analysis commodity by commodity; for it has been argued that my analysis by countries understates the bargaining power of Britain.

This article is by no means exhaustive. Many other considerations, which are not treated here, are highly relevant. We shall have nothing to say, for example, on the stability of our market as compared with that of other countries, or on the relative ability of this and other countries to offer loans and gifts, or to offer scarce commodities – a bargaining weapon of much potency in recent years. Nor shall we discuss the lessons to be learned from recent exercise of our bargaining power.

The figures relate to pre-war years throughout and are thus some 10 years out of date. This clearly needs some explanation. One reason is, of course, that many of the statistics required are not readily available for 1946 and 1947. But even if they were I should be reluctant to use them. It is doubtful whether the pattern of world trade in 1946–7 was any nearer a post-war norm than the pattern existing in 1937–8. Even more important, I believe that figures for 1946–7 would show Britain's bargaining power, according to the measures I have chosen, to be less than it was in 1938. British imports were only 13 per cent of world imports in the later years compared with 18 per cent in 1938 (while United States' imports rose from 9 per cent of the world total in 1938 to 13 per cent in 1946–7).[3] The exports of many countries have, moreover, recovered less quickly than their production, and have been a smaller

---

[2] 'Britain's Bargaining Power.' A later article (*Economic Journal*, March 1947) included a further analysis of the bargaining power of the United States.

[3] Calculated from the International Monetary Fund's *International Financial Statistics* for July 1948. The figures for the United States and for the United Kingdom refer to general trade. Elsewhere I have used figures for special trade.

proportion of their output than before the war. The proportion taken by the United Kingdom of the exports, and of the output, of many countries and commodities must thus have been lower in 1946–7 than before the war. But, as 1946 and 1947 were years of transition, it might be thought that figures relating to them would underestimate Britain's bargaining power in the future, and so unduly strengthen the general tenor of my argument. I therefore prefer to use pre-war figures for fear of giving a false general impression, although the details might be very different had more recent figures been used. I shall return in section 7 to the comparison of our pre-war and post-war bargaining power.

One final introductory remark. This paper is intended to give a general impression. The method is to present tables covering a fair number of countries and commodities but to avoid excessive detail and refinement. This means that some of the figures may be misleading if taken in isolation. It may be misleading, for many purposes, to combine the figures for mechanical and chemical wood-pulp, or for all types of cotton, in Table VI. Some of the national income figures on which Table V is based may be too high, others too low. When a table refers to a single year, some individual figures may be freaks. Those with expert knowledge of particular countries and commodities will find some of my figures hard to swallow. I freely admit in advance to any technical howlers they may discover. But I have a faith in the 'law of compensating errors', and I do not think the general picture will be affected. Clearly, however, no significance should be attached to the precise figures given. These depend on the choice of years and the method of calculation. I have given the sources from which the figures have been derived, and the reader may refer to these for definitions and qualifications. To mention them all would double the length of this paper.

2. INDIVIDUAL COUNTRIES' EXPORTS TO THE UNITED KINGDOM AS A PROPORTION OF THEIR TOTAL EXPORTS

Before considering other measures of our bargaining power it will be convenient to recapitulate the results of my earlier analysis and to suggest some morals that can be drawn from them.

Table II shows the proportion of their total exports sent to the United Kingdom in 1938 by the various countries of the world. (The gold exports of the gold-producing countries — or their output if lower — have been included in their total exports but not in their exports to the United Kingdom since, even when their gold was in fact shipped to this country, it is clear that they did not depend on us for its sale.)

Ninety-eight countries are distinguished in Table II (including a

TABLE II*

Percentage of over-seas country's ex-ports† sent to U.K. in 1938	No. of countries	Percentage of all U.K. exports in 1938 sent to each category of country	Main countries included. (Figures show percentage of all U.K. exports sent to each country in 1938)
91—100	1	4.4	Eire 4.4
81—90	1	4.1	New Zealand 4.1
71—80	1	0.2	—
61—70	1	—	—
51—60	6	5.1	Denmark 3.4
41—50	6	11.4	Australia 8.2
			Finland 1.2
31—40	11	20.6	India and Burma 7.9
			Canada 4.9
			Argentina 4.2
			Egypt 1.9
21—30	10	11.0	Netherlands 2.8
			Sweden 2.5
			Norway 1.7
			Iran 1.2
			'Other British West Africa' 1.1
11—20	24	28.5	South Africa 8.5
			U.S.A. 4.4
			France 3.3
			British Malaya 2.4
			Belgium 1.8
			U.S.S.R. 1.4
			Poland 1.1
			Misc. European countries 2.3
0—10	37	14.7	Germany 4.4
			Italy 1.2
			Brazil 1.1
			Misc. Far Eastern countries 3.6
			Misc. European countries 2.5
			French, Portuguese, and Belgian Africa 1.0
	98	100.0	

*Taken from *Economic Journal*, March 1946, with slight revisions.
†Gold exports (or gold output if lower) are included in the exports of gold-producing countries, but not in their exports to the United Kingdom, since the sale of the gold did not depend on our market.

number of 'composite countries'). Of these, two countries (Eire and New Zealand) were almost wholly dependent on our market; both sent over 80 per cent of their exports to us. Eight others depended on us for more than half their exports, but of these the only important trading country was Denmark, which sent 56 per cent of its exports to the United Kingdom.

Next we find twenty-seven countries that sent between one-fifth and one-half of their exports to this country, the most important being India, Canada, and Australia; the Argentine; Norway, Sweden, and the Baltic States.

Finally, we find sixty-one countries (three-fifths of the total) dependent on us for one-fifth or less of their exports. These include most European countries south of the Baltic; the United States; most of tropical America; most of the Far East; and South Africa. The sixty-one include, it is true, a fair number of unimportant trading nations, but they nevertheless took between them 43 per cent of our pre-war exports. There were also four countries that, while depending on the United Kingdom market for more than one-fifth of their exports, depended even more on the market of the United States, and might be unwilling to yield to pressure by us for fear of offending that country. If these four (of which Canada is the most important) are added to our list of sixty-one, we get a group of sixty-five 'unexploitable' countries which took roughly one-half of our exports before the war and supplied nearly one-half of our imports.

The conclusions so far seem to be (1) that while the number of countries to whom our market is of overwhelming importance is very small indeed, there is a fair number of important trading countries to whom our market is of very considerable importance; and (2) that the majority of the countries of the world, countries with which we did about half our trade before the war, would not be greatly susceptible to the use of our bargaining power as a large importer.

If, following my earlier nomenclature, we call this latter group of countries 'unexploitable' and the rest 'exploitable', we may draw up Table III, showing the geographical distribution of the two types of country.

Any attempt to force our exports by the use of our bargaining power as a large importer would be largely confined to the 'exploitable' countries. It may be that we should add one or two parts of the Colonial Empire, such as Malaya, which, although not greatly dependent on the United Kingdom market, might be controlled by us. But it is also true that the countries labelled 'exploitable' include the pre-war Baltic States, now part of Russia; other countries where our political power is uncertain; and Holland, which is forming a Customs Union with one of our industrial rivals. On balance, it is unlikely that the truly 'exploitable' countries took more than half our exports before the war.

To secure the necessary increase in our total exports by the use of our bargaining power would thus require a very large increase in

TABLE III*

'Exploitable' countries	Percentage of all U.K. exports in 1938 sent to 'exploitable' countries	'Unexploitable' countries	Percentage of all U.K. exports in 1938 sent to 'unexploitable' countries
Scandinavia, Baltic States, and Holland	12½	Russia, and most European countries south of Baltic	18
Australia and New Zealand	12	Most of North and South America	12
India, Burma, and Ceylon	9	Union of South Africa	8½
Argentina and Uruguay	5	Most Far Eastern countries	6
Eire	4	Miscellaneous, mainly African countries	5
Miscellaneous	8		
	50½		49½

Notes:

(1) 'Unexploitable' countries are those sending one-fifth or less of their exports to the United Kingdom in 1938, and other countries for which the United States was a larger market. 'Expoitable' countries include all others.

(2) Gold exports (or gold output if lower) are deemed to go to the United States.

*Taken from *Economic Journal*, March 1946.

exports to the 'exploitable' countries. This might, in principle, be achieved by an increase in their total imports of manufactures. But the exercise of our bargaining power would be likely to aim also at an increase in their imports of British manufactures at the expense of the manufactures of our rivals (*a*) in the United States, (*b*) in Europe.

(*a*) The United States did not, before the war, export very much to the 'exploitable' countries (some relevant figures will be found in Table IV), so that only a drastic discrimination by those countries against United States' goods and in favour of ours would be of appreciable benefit to our exports. This would raise the danger, at least in the long run, of retaliation by the United States which would endanger a large part of our markets in North and South America, the Far East, possibly South Africa, and perhaps other countries dependent on financial assistance from the United States. These markets (as can be seen from Table III) took a good quarter of our exports.

(*b*) We might in addition (or as an alternative) ask the 'exploitable' countries to buy from us rather than from our rivals in Europe. We might gain some of the pre-war German markets without provoking retaliation, but if we attempted to secure the pre-war export markets of the other European industrial countries (France, Belgium,

TABLE IV*

Imports (millions of dollars) in 1938 from

	U.K.	U.S.	Japan	Germany	Other industrial Europe	All main industrial countries
Australia	224	82	23	21	32	382
New Zealand	106	26	5	4	9	150
Eire	102	23	2	7	16	150
India, Burma, Ceylon	225	47	69	52	59	452
British Malaya†	59	10	7	6	13	95
African Colonies	86	17	9	11	18	141
Denmark	123	29	–	87	59	298
Norway	68	32	2	50	83	235
Portugal	17	12	1	17	24	71
Argentina	89	77	17	45	106	334
Total of above	1,099	355	135	300	419	2,308

*Source: *Network of World Trade.*
†British Malaya is included with other 'exploitable' countries because she is part of the Colonial Empire.

Switzerland, Sweden, &c.) which in the aggregate were even more important than the German, we should seriously reduce their importing power. This might well impel them not only to reduce their purchases from the United Kingdom but also, perhaps, to enter into preferential arrangements with the other countries of Europe (including possibly some of the countries labelled 'exploitable'). We should then find our exports restricted, not only in eastern Europe. but also in central and western Europe.

If we used our bargaining power to gain exports in the 'exploitable' countries by forcing them to discriminate against the goods of our rivals, in both Europe and the United States, we should thus risk the loss of markets throughout the 'unexploitable' world, as shown on the right-hand side of Table III. Since many of the 'exploitable' countries were already taking a high proportion of their manufactures from the United Kingdom before the war (the 'exploitable' countries in the Empire took about one-half) the gains to be made are limited, while the possible indirect losses are large.

It would be very difficult to sell the exports necessary to pay for our essential imports if our trade were largely concentrated on a group of countries roughly corresponding to those labelled 'exploitable'. Even if we could sell the volume of exports that would, in a world undivided into economic groups or spheres of influence, pay for our essential imports, it is doubtful whether this would suffice if we relied heavily on our trade with the 'exploitable' countries. This group of countries supplied, it is true, over 80 per cent of our meat, dairy produce, wool, tea, jute, and wood-pulp. This suggests, at first sight, that we could secure a large part of our essential imports by using our bargaining power with them. But they supplied only about one-third of all our other imports, and a very much smaller proportion of certain important commodities. A concentration of our trade on the countries with whom our bargaining power is greatest would, therefore, leave us deficient in many vital imported supplies, if our trade with the rest of the world was, as a result, greatly reduced.

This danger, which does not depend on the assumption of inconvertible currencies, may be illustrated by the following example (in which the figures are purely illustrative). The 'exploitable' countries took about half our exports before the war. If, by the use of our bargaining power, we induced them to take twice as great a volume as before, while, as a result of retaliation and other indirect consequences, our exports to the 'unexploitable' countries fell by one-half, our total exports would be 125 per cent of the pre-war volume. Let us now suppose that this would enable us to buy 75 per cent of the pre-war volume of imports, and that such a volume would just suffice to maintain a tolerable standard of living, *if we were free to buy throughout the world, and to apportion our import programme without regard to commercial agreements with particular countries.* But if we were not so free because, in order to push our exports in the 'exploitable' countries, we had agreed to take more from them than we should otherwise have done with a total import volume 75 per cent of pre-war, then our imports would *not* suffice to maintain a tolerable standard of living. We might have relatively plentiful supplies of meat, dairy produce, wool, &c., but this would mean that we had not sufficient foreign exchange left over to buy even the minimum necessary supplies of many other commodities. This would be especially true if we had diverted our demand for these other commodities from the 'unexploitable' to the 'exploitable' countries, and if the latter could supply the diverted quantities only at a higher price.

3. INDIVIDUAL COUNTRIES' EXPORTS TO THE UNITED KINGDOM AS A PROPORTION OF THEIR NATIONAL INCOME

The main criterion of our bargaining power used in section 2 was the proportion of a country's exports sent to the United Kingdom. This gives some indication of its dependence on our market for the balancing of its international accounts and for its power to buy imports. But it will usually give an exaggerated idea of how far its standard of living and level of employment depend on exports to the United Kingdom. If a country that sent 10 per cent of its exports to us lost the whole of our market, then, even if it gained no compensating markets elsewhere, it is unlikely that its level of employment or standard of living would fall by as much as 10 per cent, because only a fraction of its resources are employed in production for export. Suppose this fraction were one-fifth. The fall in employment or living standards would then be likely to be nearer 2 than 10 per cent.

The fall in employment might, it is true, exceed 2 per cent if the cumulative effect of a fall in export employment on employment in other industries were not offset. And, even if the displaced export workers were re-employed in production for the home market (and the old level of total employment maintained), the standard of living, in so far as it can be measured, might fall by more than 2 per cent. For the import economies that would be necessary might involve key raw materials or highly prized finished goods that could not be easily replaced by home production. In less unfavourable circumstances, however, if imports could be easily replaced by home production, the standard of living might equally well fall by less than 2 per cent. In general, the proportion of a country's *exports* sent to the United Kingdom is likely to exaggerate the dependence of its employment and standard of living on our market. The proportion of its total national *output* exported to the United Kingdom will, in some ways, give a truer picture.

Table V shows, in column 1, the exports of a number of countries in 1938 as an approximate percentage of their national incomes. This will overstate the percentage of the national effort going to export in so far as imports of raw materials and semi-processed goods are used in the production of exports; but it will understate the country's dependence on receipts from abroad by the amount of invisible exports. Many of the figures are not comparable with each other and some are subject to a wide margin of error, but the table probably gives a correct general impression of the relative importance of exports in the various countries' national outputs. The proportions shown in column 1 vary from 5 per cent or less for the U.S.A., China, and almost certainly Russia, to one-third in New Zealand and Belgium and nearly one-half in Ceylon. Column 3 shows each country's exports to the United Kingdom as an approximate percentage of its national income. This proportion varies from 1 per cent or less in a large number of countries to one-quarter in Ceylon and New Zealand. In the majority of countries it is 5 per cent or less. The table includes countries with which we did about 70 per cent of

TABLE V

	Total exports as approx. percentage of National Income, 1938 (c) (1)	Exports to U.K. as approx. percentage of:	
		Total exports, 1938 (2)	National Income, 1938 (3)
Ceylon	48	54	26
New Zealand	31	83	26
Bolivia (a)	27	63	17
Denmark	26	56	15
Ireland	16	93	15
Finland	29	45	13
Canada	23	37	9
Australia	18	49	9
Dominican Republic (a)	16	40	7
Chile (a)	24	23	6
Norway	21	28	6
Netherlands	21	23	5
Argentina	16	33	5
Belgium	33	14	4
Sweden	16	24	4
South Africa	23	13	3
Brazil (a)	23	9	2
Czechoslovakia	18	9	2
Switzerland	16	11	2
Philippines	29	3	1
Netherlands East Indies	24	5	1
Greece	17	9	1
Japan (b)	16	5	1
Mexico	12	12	1
Hungary	10	7	1
France	9	12	1
Italy (a)	9	6	1
Poland (a)	7	19	1
U.S.A.	5	17	1
Bulgaria (a)	10	4	—
Germany (b)	7	6	—
China (a)	2	8	—
U.S.S.R.	..	20	(Under 1)

Notes: Gold exports (or output if lower) are included in the exports of gold-producing countries, but not in their exports to the United Kingdom.

Sources: Except where otherwise noted the national income figures are from the United Nations' *Monthly Bulletin of Statistics,* q.v. for definitions. The export figures are from *The Network of World Trade,* and the gold statistics from the sources stated in *Economic Journal,* March 1946, p. 36.

(a) National income figures derived from p. 243 of United Nations' *Economic Report,* 1945–7.

(b) National income figures from League of Nations' *World Economic Survey,* 1938/9, p. 84.

(c) The corresponding figure for the United Kingdom is 10 per cent.

our trade in 1938. Making allowance for other countries it seems that about 60 per cent of our exports before the war went to countries whose exports to us were 5 per cent or less of their national incomes. This reminds us again of the limited nature of our bargaining power with many important countries. It also suggests that, in exercising what power we have, we should often have to rely more on the importance of our market to a small section of producers than on its importance to a country as a whole.

Table V also shows that the proportion of their total exports sent to the United Kingdom by the various countries (column 2) usually indicates the relative dependence of their economies on the United Kingdom market, as shown by column 3. There are, however, important exceptions. Belgium and South Africa, for example, depended more on our market than did the United States, Poland, or Russia, although the last three countries sent a higher proportion of their exports to us.

4. THE PROPORTION OF WORLD EXPORTS OF INDIVIDUAL COMMODITIES TAKEN BY THE UNITED KINGDOM

In some ways the proportion of world exports of particular commodities taken by the United Kingdom is a better indication of our bargaining power than the proportion we take of each country's total exports. This will be the case:

(a) *When the proportion of a country's produce sent to the United Kingdom could very easily be modified.* Thus we may take a large proportion of the world's exports of a commodity, but a small proportion of a particular country's exports because it is slightly more convenient for the country to send its produce elsewhere. For example, we took one-third of the world's exports of wheat and wheat-flour before the war, but only about one-sixth of the Argentine's wheat and flour exports. But the Argentine was greatly dependent on British purchases of wheat since these had a major influence on the world price. The proportion of its total exports sent to the United Kingdom by the Argentine tended, for this reason, to understate its dependence on the United Kingdom market; although there may, of course, have been offsetting tendencies.

On the other hand, the high proportion of Bolivia's total exports sent to the United Kingdom (over three-fifths in 1938) may have exaggerated her dependence on this country. Bolivia sent three-quarters of her tin ore (accounting for 70 per cent of her total exports) to the United Kingdom for smelting. But the U.S.A. was a far larger consumer of tin than the United Kingdom and, although she did no smelting, her consumption had a great effect on the demand for, and price of, tin and so of tin ore.

TABLE VI

	Pre-war share in world imports		U.K. retained imports, 1938 (£ millions) (3)	S = U.K. imports less than 20% of world total. U = U.K. imports less than U.S. imports (4)	
	U.K. % (1)	U.S. % (2)			
FOOD:					
Meat (a)	80	3	90	..	..
Butter	78	1	50	..	..
Eggs	52	—	15	..	..
Cheese	52	10	10	..	..
Wheat (incl. flour)	32	3	43	..	..
Rice	1	1	1	S	..
Maize	27	16(b)	18	..	..
Barley	34	8	7	..	..
Oats	8	—	1	S	..
Potatoes	16	2	2	S	..
Sugar	20	42(c)	19	..	U
Wine	5	1	5	S	..
Coffee	1	47	1	S	U
Tea	51	10	26	..	..
Cocoa beans	14	41	4	S	U
Citrus fruit	39	1	10	..	..
Bananas	12	55	5	S	U
Apples	45	—	6	..	..
Dates	9	11	—	S	U
Raisins	44	1	3	..	..
Grapes	21	2	2	..	..
Onions	47	—	2	..	..
6 Oilseeds (fat content) (a)	16	10	14	S	..
8 Vegetable oils (a)	14	25	4	S	U
Pepper	7	29	—	S	U
Hops	11	20	—	S	U
Dried kidney beans	7	5	—	S	..
MATERIALS:					
Timber	34	6	43	..	..
Wood-pulp	28	34	14	..	U
Rubber	10	43	9	S	U
Wool	30	13	28	..	..
Cotton	22	2	28	..	..
Silk	5	64	2	S	U
Jute	21	13	3	..	..
Hemp	28	12	2	..	..
Flax	16	2	4	S	..
Tobacco	22	6	22	..	..
Copper (unworked) (a)	18	11	11	S	..
Lead (unworked) (a)	47	1	6	..	..
Tin (unworked) (a)	6	40	1	S	U
Tin ore (a)	40	—	6	..	..

TABLE VI   *continued*

	Pre-war share in world imports		U.K. retained imports, 1938 (£ millions) (3)	S = U.K. imports less than 20% of world total. U = U.K. imports less than U.S. imports (4)
	U.K. % (1)	U.S. % (2)		
MATERIALS (*continued*)				
Zinc (unworked) (*a*)	36	1	2	.. ..
Bauxite (*a*)	11	20	–	S U
Iron ore (*a*)	11	5	7	S ..
Manganese ore (*a*)	9	23	1	S U
Crude petroleum (*a*)	4	7	5	S U
Petrol (*a*)	31	–	25	.. ..
Gas and fuel oil (*a*)	18	15	9	S ..
Cattle hides	14	10	4	S ..
Nitrates	2	30	–	S U
Potash fertilizers (*a*)	9	14	1	S U
Total of above	..	..	571	
Other Commodities	..	..	287	
ALL COMMODITIES	17	12	858	

Sources: *International Yearbook of Agricultural Statistics* (International Institute of Agriculture); *International Trade in Certain Raw Materials and Foodstuffs* and *Network of World Trade* (League of Nations); *Annual Statement of the Trade of the U.K.*

Note: The figures in columns 1 and 2 refer to 1937, except those for commodities marked (*a*) which refer to 1938. For commodities marked (*a*) the figures in column 1 include imports into Eire, Iceland, the Faroe Islands, and Spitzbergen.
(*b*) The large import of maize into the U.S. in 1937 was abnormal.
(*c*) Including imports from Puerto Rico, Hawaii, and U.S. Virgin Islands.

(*b*) *When there are influential 'lobbies' of producers of particular products in overseas countries.* Although a country sends a small proportion of her total exports to the United Kingdom, she may send us a high proportion of her exports of a particular product, the producers of which may be able to influence the commercial policy of their government.

In other ways the proportion of each country's total exports sent to the United Kingdom may often be the better measure of its dependence on our market.

(*a*) *When the world market for a product is imperfect, because of high transport costs, differences in quality, or for other reasons,* the proportion of a country's exports sent to the United Kingdom may be a better measure of its dependence on us than the proportion we take of world exports of the commodity. Suppose Denmark exported nothing but eggs. Then the fact that she sent nearly three-quarters of her pre-war exports of eggs to the United Kingdom would be a more accurate measure of her dependence on our market than the fact that we took only half the world's egg exports, if it were established that other markets for eggs were not so easily accessible to Danish exporters.

(b) *Even when a country sends a high proportion of its exports of certain commodities to the United Kingdom, it may send us a low proportion of its exports of many other things.* In this case the proportion of its total exports sent to the United Kingdom will be a better guide to its reliance on the United Kingdom market at least for the balancing of its international accounts and for its power to import. Provided there are no powerful 'lobbies', this proportion will also be a better indication of our bargaining power with the country.

With these considerations in mind, we may examine the proportion of world exports of particular commodities taken by the United Kingdom before the war. This is shown in Table VI for fifty-one commodities. These accounted for two-thirds, by value, of Britain's imports before the war, but will probably account for a higher proportion in the future since it is likely that our imports of manufactures will be severely restricted.

It will be seen that the United Kingdom took a very high proportion of world exports of a number of important commodities, especially animal products and tea; and, as we saw in section 2, we took a high proportion of the total exports of countries that specialized in these commodities, notably Australia, New Zealand, Argentina, Eire, Denmark, India, and Ceylon.

But there were also many commodities of which the United Kingdom took only a small proportion of world exports. She took less than a fifth of world exports of rice, oats, potatoes, wine, coffee, cocoa beans, bananas, dates, oilseeds, vegetable oils, pepper, hops, kidney beans, rubber, silk, flax, copper, tin, bauxite, iron ore, manganese ore, crude petroleum, gas and fuel oil, cattle hides, nitrates, and potash fertilizers. For the majority of these commodities the United States was a bigger market. If we add to the list sugar and wood-pulp, for which although the United Kingdom share was one-fifth or more, the United States was a still larger market, we get 28 commodities out of 51 for which the pull of the United Kingdom market cannot be regarded as the predominant factor.

By analogy with section 2 we might perhaps say that the producers of over half the commodities on our import list are 'unexploitable'. This would, of course, be misleading in so far as the twenty-eight items cost us only £124 million out of a total import bill of £571 million for the full list of fifty-one items. Over three-quarters, by value, of the imports in Table VI were thus of commodities for which the United Kingdom market was of great importance. Our bargaining power appears, at first sight, to be much greater when we take each commodity separately than it was when we made the analysis by countries. If we were to use our bargaining power with the producers of the 'exploitable' commodities to make them take payment for our purchases in British goods, could we not secure the great bulk of our essential imports?

But although the twenty-eight items were less than one-quarter, by value, of *Britain's* imports, they formed a much larger proportion — roughly one-half — of *world* trade in the fifty-one commodities. The producers of the twenty-eight commodities were therefore important *purchasers* of manufactured goods in the world market. If we add the exporters of coal (of which we imported none) and of manufactures (of which we imported only 8 per cent of the world total) it will be seen that a large part of the world's producers (and so a large part of the world's purchasers) were not greatly dependent on the United Kingdom market. But we depend greatly on their purchases of our manufactured goods. And since countries in which these producers are the most influential would not be very susceptible to pressure by us, the commodity analysis is quite consistent with the country analysis, which showed only one-half of our exports going to countries likely to be 'exploitable'.

5. THE SMALL NUMBER OF SUPPLIERS OF INDIVIDUAL COMMODITIES IMPORTED BY THE UNITED KINGDOM

Even where we take a substantial proportion of world exports of a particular commodity our bargaining power may not be very great if the number of suppliers is small. This is in large measure the case. Table VII shows the percentage of United Kingdom imports of various commodities drawn from our main suppliers, defined as those countries that, between them, sent us 75 per cent or more of our imports of each commodity. The table includes most of the commodities in Table VI of which we took more than one-fifth of world exports, and a number of others as well. It shows that at least three-quarters of our supplies of nearly every commodity came from a very small number of countries. Our most important single supplier usually sent a very high proportion of our total imports; always more than one-quarter and very often more than one-half.

This means, it is true, that only a small number of negotiations would be needed to cover the greater part of our requirements of each commodity. But it also means, first, that it would be easy for the main suppliers to co-operate in order to resist our demands;

TABLE VII

Proportion of United Kingdom Imports Obtained from Main Suppliers in 1938

Commodities of which ONE country supplied 75 per cent. or more of U.K. imports

		Per cent.
Nickel ore	Canada	100
Nickel (unwrought)	Canada	90
Jute	India	100
Molybdenum ore	U.S.A.	97
Tobacco	U.S.A.	76

Commodities of which TWO countries supplied 75 per cent. or more of U.K. imports

		Per cent.		Per cent.
Flax	Belgium	48	U.S.S.R.*	42
Tea	India	55	Ceylon	32
Rubber	Malaya	68	Dutch E. Indies	14
Mutton and lamb	N. Zealand	52	Australia	27
Beef and veal	Argentina	60	Australia	18
Cheese	N. Zealand	56	Canada	23
Tin ore	Bolivia	55	Nigeria	20
Wood-pulp	Finland	40	Sweden	35
Hemp	Philippines	46	Brit. E. Africa	32
Zinc (unworked)	Canada	54	Belgium	22

Commodities of which THREE countries supplied 75 per cent. or more of U.K. imports

		Per cent.		Per cent.		
Bacon	Denmark	49	Canada	19	Holland	7
Wheat	Australia	31	Canada	28	U.S.A.	16
Wool	Australia	41	N. Zealand	23	S. Africa	12
Lead	Australia	46	Canada	26	Burma	15
Maize	U.S.A.	40	Argentina	31	Canada	6
Cotton	U.S.A.	34	Egypt†	34	India	12
Motor spirit	Dutch W. Ind.	41	U.S.A.	22	Iran	22

Commodities of which FOUR or MORE countries supplied 75 per cent. or more of U.K. imports

		Per cent.		Per cent.		Per cent.		Per cent.
Butter	N. Zealand	27	Denmark	25	Australia	19	Holland	7
Barley	Canada	27	U.S.S.R.	19	Iraq	16	U.S.A.	14
Timber	U.S.S.R.*	37	Canada	17	Sweden	14	U.S.A.	9
Oranges	Palestine	37	S. Africa	15	Brazil	15	U.S.A.	14
Eggs	Denmark	34	Holland	21	Poland	9	Eire	8
							Romania	5

*Including pre-war Baltic States.
†Including Sudan.
Source: *Annual Statement of the Trade of the U.K.*

indeed, any serious attempt to use our bargaining power might lead to agreements that would not otherwise have been made, and to a higher price than would have had to be paid if we had refrained from such tactics. The small number of suppliers means, in the second place, that our bargaining power, with the more important at least, will be smaller than is suggested by the proportion of their exports sent to this country. It is most unlikely, for example, that we could dispense with the whole of our tea imports from India, the whole of our beef imports from the Argentine, or the whole of our tobacco imports from the United States. Our bargaining power with a country, or with a section of producers, is determined not so much by the proportion of their exports they have hitherto sent us, but by the proportion we might dispense with.

Even when we could dispense with the bulk of our imports from country A, by taking them from country B instead, this would be little hardship to country A if country B's exports could not be greatly expanded; A would merely divert her exports to the markets now vacated by B. The loss of exports with which we could threaten A would then be limited roughly to the possible increase in B's exports. But if A's exports form a large proportion of the world total this possible loss will not normally be of great importance to her, since it is usually difficult to make a rapid expansion in primary production.

Even, then, when we take a high proportion of the world's exports of a commodity, our bargaining power will be circumscribed if the available export surpluses are in the hands of a small number of countries; for this will reduce our power to play off one primary producer against another. In the limiting cases of, say, jute or Manila hemp, of which India and the Philippines, respectively, have virtual world monopolies, we can reduce our purchases only by reducing total consumption. There is no alternative source of supply unless other countries begin to produce.

We can, of course, substitute, up to a point, one commodity for another — other textiles for jute and Manila hemp; beef for mutton; even wheat and maize for bacon and eggs. But when we analyse our imports in broad groups, we still find a marked concentration of supplies in the hands of a small number of countries. Thus, for example, six countries (Australia, New Zealand, Denmark, Argentina, Canada, and the U.S.A.) supplied between them three-quarters of our imports of cereals, meat, and dairy produce of all kinds.

It might be argued that the high proportion of *United Kingdom imports* of particular commodities obtained from a small number of countries exaggerates the concentration of *world exports*, since we

TABLE VIII

	Percentage of 1937 World Exports supplied by four main exporters of each commodity								Total of four countries
Jute	97	India	1	Nepal	1	Belgium	1	China	100
Raw silk	83	Japan	11	China†	5½	Italy	½	France	100
Mutton	52	New Zealand	27	Australia	15	Argentina	2	Uruguay	96
Rubber	40*	Malaya	40	Netherlands E. Ind.	6	Ceylon	4	Indo-China	90
Hemp	49	Philippines	15	Italy	14	India	11	Yugoslavia	89
Cotton	45	U.S.A.	21	India	15	Egypt§	7	Brazil	88
Flax	39	France	19	U.S.S.R.‡	17	Netherlands	12	Belgium	87
Maize	70	Argentina	6	S. Africa	6	Yugoslavia	4	Indo-China	86
Wood-pulp	40	Sweden	23	Finland	12	Canada	10	Norway	85
Rice	33	Burma	23	Indo-China	16	Thailand	11	India	83
Tea	36	India	16	Ceylon	16	Netherlands E. Ind.	14	Brazil	82
Beef	50	Argentina	13	Australia	10	Uruguay	6	Brazil	79
Cocoa beans	41	Gold Coast	16	Brazil	14	Nigeria	8	French West Africa	79
Coffee	49	Brazil	17	Colombia	7	El Salvador	5	El Salvador	78
Motor spirit	33	U.S.A.	18	Curaçao	13	Iran	12	Iran	76
Butter	26	Denmark	25	New Zealand	14	Australia	9	Netherlands	74
Cheese	29	New Zealand	22	Netherlands	14	Canada	8	Italy	73
Wool	36	Australia	12	Argentina	11	S. Africa	11	S. Africa	70
Wheat	28	Argentina	19	Canada	15	Australia	7	Romania	69
Pig meat	34	Denmark	19	Canada	7	U.S.A.	7	Poland	66
Tobacco	38	U.S.A.	10	Netherlands E. Ind.	8	Greece	8	Turkey	64
Eggs	26	Denmark	19	Netherlands	7	Poland	6	China	58
Sugar	29	Cuba	13	Netherlands E. Ind.	10	Australia	5	Australia	57

*Exports of home-produced rubber only. †Including Manchuria. ‡Including pre-war Baltic States. §Including Sudan.
Sources: *International Trade in Certain Raw Materials and Foodstuffs* and *International Year Book of Agricultural Statistics.*

may take our imports largely from countries with which we have close trading relations. But this is unlikely to be an important source of error where we take a high proportion of world imports; and in fact world exports of most primary commodities are highly concentrated. This is illustrated in Table VIII. The last column of figures shows that, nearly as often as not, the four main exporters supply four-fifths or more of the world total. The first column shows that the largest single exporter always supplies one-quarter of the total and often two-fifths or more. This is true even though some of the categories are wide. The commodities included under cotton, wood-pulp, wool, tobacco, and hemp, for example, are by no means perfect substitutes. Had a finer classification been used the concentration would have been even greater.

It may be argued that, even where there is a small number of actual exporters of a commodity, there may also be potential exporters, and that this would increase our bargaining power with the actual exporters. But if the switching of our purchases to countries not yet producing, or not yet exporting, involved a large increase in the price of our imports, our bargaining power would not in fact be so great. If, on the other hand, it is held to be easy for primary producers to expand production at a cost not much greater than the old world price, then it will in general be easy for existing producers of one commodity to switch to the production of another. This would also limit the effectiveness of a threat by us to reduce our purchases.

6. PROPORTION OF THE WORLD'S, AND OF SINGLE COUNTRIES', PRODUCTION OF INDIVIDUAL COMMODITIES EXPORTED TO THE UNITED KINGDOM

When we take a high proportion of world *exports* of a commodity, it is salutary to remember the much smaller proportion of world *production* dependent on our market. This is illustrated in Table IX.

For the major exporting countries, it is true, the proportion of output exported to the United Kingdom is often much larger than the world proportion shown in Table IX. This is illustrated in column 1 of Table X. But column 3 of the same table reminds us that even the major exporting countries, the only ones shown, often consume a high proportion of their output themselves. Thus the United States consumed two-thirds of her tobacco production. Even Australia and the Argentine, two of our major suppliers of meat, seem to have consumed about three-quarters of their own output, although the figures may exaggerate the true proportion.[4]

---

[4] See note 3 to Table X.

TABLE IX

	United Kingdom imports in 1937 as percentage of	
	World exports (1)	World production (2)
Butter	78	11
Beef and veal	61	4
Cheese	52	7
Barley	34	2
Wheat	32	4
Maize	27	3
Tobacco	22	4
Cotton	22	9
Sugar	20	8

Sources: *International Year Book of Agricultural Statistics*; League of Nations' *Statistical Year Book* and *International Trade in Certain Raw Materials and Foodstuffs; Commodity Year Book*.

Note: Some of the figures in column 2 may be too high because of the incompleteness of world production figures.

This reminds us of the limitation of our bargaining power when aimed at producing interests in overseas countries. Even a cut of, say, one-third in our imports of meat from Australia or the Argentine would affect the total meat production in these countries by only about one-tenth. This could be fairly rapidly offset by increased domestic consumption, by the development of other branches of agriculture, or by more rapid industrialization.

7. SPECIAL CHARACTERISTICS OF THE POST-WAR POSITION

Unless there is a large expansion in world trade, British imports, especially of foodstuffs, are likely to remain well below the pre-war level, and well below the level we should like to take if our importing power were greater.

In some ways this may increase our bargaining strength. In the first place we shall be more willing to substitute one commodity for another. Secondly, we shall be more ready to offer to increase our imports of food from a country that gives us adequate concessions, since this will be less likely to harm the interests of British farmers. Thirdly, the low exports of our suppliers, resulting from our reduced importing power, may make them more anxious for a large share in the British market, and so more willing to give favourable treatment to our exports.

But in other ways our bargaining power may be reduced. In the first place, the more our main suppliers are depressed, the more likely they are to make agreements with each other, and this would reduce our bargaining power.

Secondly, it is by no means certain that, even if our imports are greatly curtailed, the primary producers will be in desperate straits. We must remember that our loss, through reductions in net invisible income and possibly through adverse terms of trade, will be their gain. Even, then, if we are importing from them a considerably lower

TABLE X

		Exported to U.K. (1)	Exported to other countries (2)	Used at home* (3)	Total (4)
Beef and veal	Argentina	20	5	75	100
	Australia	20	2	78	100
Mutton and lamb	New Zealand	73	—	27	100
	Australia	27	1	72	100
	Argentina	28	1	71	100
Pig meat	Denmark	58	4	38	100
	Canada	29	3	68	100
Butter	Denmark	62	21	17	100
	New Zealand	82	2	16	100
	Australia	42	4	54	100
Cheese	New Zealand	90	—	10	100
	Netherlands	9	41	50	100
	Canada	61	6	33	100
Wheat†	Argentina	5	29	66	100
	Canada	44	23	33	100
	Australia	36	30	34	100
Tobacco	U.S.A.	17	16	67	100
Jute	India	12	38	50	100
Cotton	U.S.A.	8	31	61	100
	India and Burma	9	50	41	100
	Egypt	30	57	13	100

*Including changes in stocks, quantities used for seed, etc.
†Exports include wheat equivalent of flour exports.
Notes: (1) The figures refer either to a single recent pre-war year, or, where it appears that this would be misleading, to an average of such years.
  (2) The countries shown are those that supplied more than 10 per cent. of world exports of each commodity in 1937, as shown in Table VIII.
  (3) The figures for meat may exaggerate the proportion of output used at home in so far as a higher proportion of the tonnage exported than of the tonnage produced consists of edible meat. The production figures used refer to dressed carcases, i.e. excluding head, extremities, and offal.
Sources: As for Table IX, together with certain national statistical sources.

volume of goods than before the war, they may be importing just as great, or possibly a greater volume from us.

Thirdly, our main suppliers have continued to industrialize during the war. This will make them less dependent on imported manufactures, and also help to provide employment for those displaced from primary production as a result of a fall in exports to Britain.

Finally, any fall in exports to Britain may well be offset by additional sales elsewhere. In the early post-war years, at least, there has been no surplus food in the world. The main reason has been the fall in production which it is hoped will be temporary. But the growth of population, together with full employment policies, are likely to keep the demand for primary products at a higher level than before the war, both within the countries exporting these products and in other countries. In particular, the level of industrial production in the United States is almost certain to be much higher than before the war, and this will greatly affect the world demand for primary products.

For all these reasons, our suppliers may not all be so desperately anxious to sell additional exports, or to get a better price, that they are willing to give very favourable terms to our exports.

We, on the other hand, shall be extremely anxious about our balance of payments. In bargaining with, say, the Argentine, we should be susceptible to a threat by them to buy more from the United States and less from us, even if this would mean quite a small fall in our exports, and so in our imports. A given proportionate fall in our imports will be a much more serious matter when they have already been cut to the bone than it would have been before the war. Our suppliers, on the other hand, may be more easily able to accept a cut in their exports.

We should never forget that, in the last resort, the bargaining power of a manufacturing nation like Britain, with very little agricultural land per head of the population, and with virtually no other natural resources save coal and iron, may well be weaker than that of primary producing nations, especially advanced countries like Australia, New Zealand, the Argentine, Canada, or Denmark. For whereas the latter can, if necessary, expand their industrial production without much difficulty and so dispense with our exports, we are far less able to expand our production of food and raw materials.

8. CONCLUSION AND SUMMARY

The general conclusion of this note is that our bargaining power as a large importer is not so great as is sometimes thought. There are many countries — important markets for our exports — that do not depend greatly on the United Kingdom market for the sale of their exports, or that depend even more on the market of the United States; and nearly all countries depend even less on our market for the maintenance of their standard of living and level of employment. Thus many countries would not be susceptible to pressure by us.

It is true that we take a high proportion of world exports of many important commodities. We might hope that their producers would bring pressure to bear on their governments to give concessions to Britain. But there are many other important commodities of which Britain takes only a small proportion of world exports. Although these are relatively unimportant in our import pattern, their producers form a large part of the world's purchasers of manufactured goods — our main export. Countries in which these producers are the most influential would not be very susceptible to pressure by us.

Even where we take a high proportion of world exports of a commodity, our bargaining power with its producers is not likely to be so great as appears at first sight, for two reasons.

First, a large part of the production is often consumed within the producing country. Secondly, we could often not wholly dispense with even the relatively small part exported to Britain, so dependent are we on a few countries for the bulk of our imports of most commodities.

Thus only a limited number of countries would be susceptible to our bargaining power as a large importer, and in many of these we have already exploited fairly fully the market for our manufactured goods. Our bargaining power, too, might in some instances prove short-lived. Nor is it likely to have increased on balance since 1938.

It does not follow, of course, that we should in no circumstances use what bargaining power we have. The general conclusion is merely that we should not exaggerate its importance when framing our commercial policy.

9 Imperial preference: a quantitative analysis[1]

INTRODUCTION

THE NEED FOR QUANTITATIVE ANALYSIS

Much has been written, and perhaps even more spoken aloud, on the subject of Imperial Preference. But the discussion has been to a large extent theoretical and political rather than quantitative. There have, it is true, been analyses of the changing pattern of Commonwealth trade after Ottawa. But the figures are not easy to interpret, since the changes recorded are by no means wholly the result of Imperial Preference. There has been little attempt to analyse in a systematic way the proportion of trade enjoying preference and the size of the preferential margins. Information on such matters would seem to be essential in any attempt to assess the changing importance of Imperial Preference in Commonwealth trade over the past twenty-five years, and the main object of the present study is to provide some of the relevant orders of magnitude. Some of the more detailed results obtained are also given in the hope that they may be of value in the study of particular problems, but these are in general subject to a wider margin of error. No attempt has been made here to relate the results obtained to changes in Commonwealth trade; that would require much further research.

THE CHOICE OF YEARS

The statistical work involved in a study of this sort is very considerable; detailed analyses have to be made of the trade returns and tariff lists of a large number of countries. Only a few years could therefore be studied, and those selected were: 1929, to represent the position before Ottawa; 1937, as a typical year after Ottawa but before the process of extending preferences went into reverse; 1948, as a post-war year.

[1] *Economic Journal,* June 1954, with Rosemary Hutt. We are indebted to the Oxford University Institute of Statistics for technical assistance and to government officials and others in many countries for valuable help and advice.

1937 was chosen partly because work had already been done on this year in connection with an earlier article,[2] but it is probably as good a year as could be found for the purpose. The Ottawa Agreements of 1932 involved the overhaul of Dominion tariffs, and this was a lengthy task; nor was the extension of preference by the Colonies completed for several years after Ottawa. It would thus have been unwise to select a year before, say, 1936; and the U.S./U.K. Trade Agreement of 1938 is sometimes regarded as an important landmark in the 'retreat' from Imperial Preference.

1929 was the latest pre-Ottawa year which it was thought fit to compare with the relatively prosperous 1937; 1930 and 1931 were years of depression.

1948 was the latest post-war year for which reasonably complete information was available when the calculations were made. But it is a useful year to take. By then a large part of the reduction in Imperial Preference that has occurred since 1937 had taken place. The tariff lists we have used in calculating the figures for 1948 incorporate most of the reduced preferences resulting from the negotiations at Geneva under G.A.T.T. in 1947; subsequent reductions have been less important. And by 1948 a large part of the rise in prices that has greatly reduced the *ad valorem* incidence of specific preferences since 1937 had already taken place. In a later section some broad indications are given of what is likely to be the present position (1953).

SCOPE AND DEFINITIONS

The study covers U.K. exports to and imports from the Commonwealth, but not trade between Commonwealth countries other than the U.K.[3] The 'Commonwealth' is defined to cover all countries classified as 'British' in the U.K. trade returns for the three years, but to include Burma in 1948 as preference continued to be given; under this definition Eire is included throughout.

The analysis of U.K. exports does not include our trade with some of the least important Colonies, but covers countries that took some 95% of our total exports to the Commonwealth. Only tariff preferences are considered, and no account is taken of the preferential effects of other trade and financial measures.

For Commonwealth imports from the U.K., the margin of preference *on any item* is defined as the difference between the percentage duty paid on it when imported from the U.K. and the

---

[2] *Economic Journal,* September 1952.
[3] Trade of the latter type comprised about one-sixth of total intra-Commonwealth trade in 1929, one-fifth in 1937 and one-quarter in 1948.

percentage it would have paid had it come from the U.S., specific duties being reduced to their *ad valorem* equivalents. The margin is reckoned as a percentage of the import value excluding duty; had it been based on the value including duty, which is more relevant when assessing competitive power, the figures would have been lower. The comparison was made with the U.S., since the practice in some Dominions of charging different rates of duty on goods from different foreign countries made some such clear-cut definition necessary; and the U.S., as our largest competitor in the world market for manufactures to-day, seemed the most interesting country to choose. Where statistical difficulties necessitated departure from the strict definition this has been mentioned in the notes to the tables concerned.

The margin of preference *on a country's total imports from the U.K.* is the average of the margins on all the items weighted by the value of imports of each from the U.K. The average margin of preference *on the U.K.'s exports to the Commonwealth as a whole* is likewise the average of the margins granted by the various countries weighted by the value of U.K. exports to each.

The method of calculation used may, incidentally, tend to overstate the average margins of preference, since the existence of preference tends to increase the proportion of U.K. exports enjoying higher preferences and to reduce the proportion enjoying lower preferences or none at all.[4]

For each country the average margin of preference is in fact the difference between the total duty paid on imports from Britain and the total duty that would have been paid had the goods been American, expressed as a percentage of the total value of imports from Britain. This is, of course, not at all the same as the difference between the average rates of duty actually paid on imports from the U.K. and from the U.S. in any year. For example, between 1900 and 1932, although Canada granted preference to Britain, the average rate of duty paid on Canadian imports from the U.S. was consistently below that paid on imports from the U.K.; Canada took large imports of heavily taxed alcoholic beverages from the U.K. and large imports of raw materials and semi-manufactures from the U.S., which paid low duties or none at all.

For U.K. imports from the Commonwealth the margins of preference are defined in a similar way.

---

[4] See *Economic Journal,* September 1952, p. 519.

THE TABLES

Table I shows, for each year, for each country and for all countries taken together: (*a*) the proportion of imports from the U.K. enjoying preference; (*b*) the average margin of preference on such 'preferred goods'; and (*c*) the average margin on all imports from the U.K., including those enjoying no preference. (Outside limits are sometimes given instead of precise figures; this is usually where it has been impossible to reconcile the tariff lists with the trade returns for particular items.) Table II gives a fuller picture of the amounts of trade passing at different rates, and the chart a summary for U.K. exports to the Commonwealth as a whole. The main results in these tables are brought together in Summary Table A, which also gives similar figures for U.K. imports from the Commonwealth not included in Table I.

Summary Table B attempts to show how far the changes that occurred between 1929 and 1937 and between 1937 and 1948 in the proportion of trade enjoying preference and in the average rates of preference were the result of: (*a*) changes in the pattern of trade,

SUMMARY TABLE A

Proportion of Trade Enjoying Preference and Margins of Preference

	U.K. exports to Commonwealth			U.K. imports from Commonwealth		
	1929	1937	1948	1929	1937	1948
Percentage enjoying preference	35–36	55–57	49–51	7	60–61	54–56
Of which enjoying preferential margins of:						
10% or less	9	18	19	2	27	39
Over 10%, not over 20%	24	18	22	1	24	12
Over 20%	3	20	9	4	9	4
Average percentage margin of preference:						
On goods enjoying preference	13	19–20	14–15	29–49	17–20	11–13
On all goods	5	10–11	7	2–3	10–12	6–7

Notes: 1. See Tables I and II for further details and explanations.

2. To obtain the figures showing percentage of trade enjoying various rates of preference, the more detailed information contained in Table II has been adjusted:

    (*a*) to allow so far as possible for extra information contained in footnotes to Table II;

    (*b*) to be consistent with figures in first line of above table, which are based on fuller information.

3. The figures for U.K. imports cover 98% of imports from the Commonwealth in 1929 and 1937, and 100% in 1948, except the figures showing percentage of trade enjoying various rates of preference, which are based on less complete information (see Table II).

SUMMARY TABLE B
Analysis of Changes Shown in Summary Table A

	U.K. exports to Commonwealth			U.K. imports from Commonwealth		
		Average percentage margin of preference			Average percentage margin of preference	
	Percentage enjoying preference	On goods enjoying preference	On all goods	Percentage enjoying preference	On goods enjoying preference	On all goods
1. 1929 actual	35–36	13	5	7	29–49*	2–3
2. 1937 if there had been no change in individual *percentage* margins of preference since 1929	39–41	12–14	5	7	38–66*	3–4
3. 1937 if there had been no change in *tariff rates* since 1929	39–41	12–14	5	7	47–80*	3–5
4. 1937 actual	55–57	19–20	10–11	60–61	17–20	10–12
5. 1948 if there had been no change in individual *percentage* margins of preference since 1937	52–55	21–23	11–12	63–65	21–27	14–18
6. 1948 if there had been no change in *tariff rates* since 1937	52–55	17–18	9–10	63–65	14–17	9–11
7. 1948 actual	49–51	14–15	7	54–56	11–13	6–7

*These figures have no great significance as so few goods are involved.

GENERAL NOTES TO SUMMARY TABLE B

Change from 1 to 2 and from 4 to 5 reflects change in trade pattern (commodity-wise and country-wise).

Change from 2 to 3 and from 5 to 6 reflects change in prices which affect *ad valorem* incidence of specific duties).

Change from 3 to 4 and from 6 to 7 reflects change in tariff rates.

Lines 1, 4 and 7. As in Summary Table A.

Line 2. Figures obtained by weighting 1929 *percentage* margins of preference on each item by value of trade in each item in 1937.

Similarly *Line 5.*

Line 3. Figures obtained by applying 1929 *tariff rates* to the 1937 trade. This would give the same result as in line 2 if all duties were *ad valorem*. But in fact the percentage margins of preference are now different for all items subject to specific duties where prices have changed between 1929 and 1937.

Similarly *Line 6.*

This particular method of separating the effects of changes in trade patterns, prices and tariff rates was chosen largely for its statistical convenience. Other, equally plausible, methods might give different results. In particular, it will be noted that the method used in Summary Table C and in Table III differs from that used in Summary Table B, and does not always refer to the same categories of goods.

SUMMARY TABLE C
Changes in Tariff Levels

A. U.K. EXPORTS TO COMMONWEALTH

1. 1929–37

Goods first granted a preference between 1929 and 1937	%
Total value of exports of such goods in 1937	100
Of which goods subjected to:	
(i) Reduction in U.K. rate; no change in U.S. rate	5[1]
(ii) Reduction in U.K. rate; increase in U.S. rate	5[1]
(iii) No change in U.K. rate; increase in U.S. rate	30[1]
(iv) Increase in U.K. rate; increase in U.S. rate	60[1]

Goods already enjoying preference in 1929 (1929 pattern of trade)	Average percentage rate of duty	
	Goods from the U.K. (U.K. rate).	Had goods been from the U.S. (U.S. rate).
(a) 1929 tariff rates, 1929 prices	13–16	25–30
(b) 1937 tariff rates, 1929 prices	14–16	33–36
(c) 1937 tariff rates, 1937 prices	17–19	37–41

2. 1937–48

Goods still enjoying preference in 1948 (1948 pattern of trade)		
(a) 1937 tariff rates, 1937 prices	17–20	38–43
(b) 1948 tariff rates, 1937 prices	24–26	42–47
(c) 1948 tariff rates, 1948 prices	14	27–29

B. U.K. IMPORTS FROM COMMONWEALTH 1937–48

Goods still enjoying preference in 1948 (1948 pattern of trade)	Average percentage rate of duty	
	Goods from Commonwealth	Had goods been from the U.S.
Including excise duties { (a) 1937 tariff rates, 1937 prices	45–58	63–81
(b) 1948 tariff rates, 1937 prices	206–216	226–239
(c) 1948 tariff rates, 1948 prices	75–79	86–92
Excluding excise duties { (a) 1937 tariff rates, 1937 prices	6–10	24–33
(b) 1948 tariff rates, 1937 prices	7–11	27–34
(c) 1948 tariff rates, 1948 prices	2–4	13–16

[1] Based on five countries only, but includes 85%, by value, of goods concerned; round figures.

GENERAL NOTES TO SUMMARY TABLE C

1. No analysis is given of:
   (i) U.K. imports first granted a preference between 1929 and 1937. Such preferences were granted largely by imposing duties on non-Commonwealth goods.
   (ii) U.K. imports already enjoying a preference in 1929, U.K. imports and U.K. exports that lost preference between 1937 and 1948. Such goods were relatively unimportant.

2. Changes from (a) to (b) reflect changes in tariff rates.
   Changes from (b) to (c) reflect changes in prices.

3. In calculating lines (a), (b) and (c), the 1929 or 1948 values of imports have been used throughout. The reference in some of the lines to 1937 prices means only that these have been used in calculating the ad valorem incidence of specific duties.

4. Only the figures in lines A1(a), A2(c) and B(c) (both) are comparable with any of the figures in Summary Table B.

both commodity-wise and country-wise; (*b*) changes in prices[5] which altered the *ad valorem* incidence of specific duties; and (*c*) changes by governments in tariff rates. To save space, no table is given of the figures for each country obtained in the course of this calculation; but some interesting cases where changes in the pattern of trade or in prices were important are mentioned in the footnotes to Table I.

Finally, Table III and Summary Table C give some details which help us to discover how far the intensification of Imperial Preference between 1929 and 1937 was brought about by reducing tariff rates on trade between Commonwealth countries and how far by increasing rates on foreign goods. Some similar figures are given for 1937–48.

The order of countries in the tables corresponds to the value of U.K. exports to them in 1937.

The rest of the article describes the main findings.

THE RESULTS

THE POSITION IN 1929

(a) Preferences Accorded U.K. Goods in British Countries in 1929

In 1929 preferences enjoyed by U.K exports were already fairly widespread. Canada had introduced preference in 1898, New Zealand and South Africa in 1903, Australia in 1908 and India in 1927, while U.K. exports to the Irish Free State enjoyed preferences from the inception of a separate Customs administration in the latter part of 1923. By 1929 Britain was thus receiving preferences in all the most important trading countries of the Commonwealth. They applied to over 80% of our trade to Australia and New Zealand, over 60% of our trade to Canada, but under 30% of our exports to South Africa and less than 10% of our exports to India and Eire. Among the smaller countries, we had preferences covering a substantial part of our exports to the West Indies and British Guiana and to the Rhodesias, but, partly as a result of treaty obligations, partly for other reasons, few preferences of much importance in the rest of Africa or elsewhere.[6]

All told, rather more than one-third of U.K. exports to British

---

[5] Strictly speaking, 'average values'; but, for the sake of brevity, we refer to changes in 'prices' throughout this Study.

[6] The only other countries covered by our calculations that granted preferences in 1929 were Gibraltar (on drink and tobacco) and the Channel Islands, but preferences were also granted by a number of smaller trading countries such as North Borneo, Fiji, Mauritius and Somaliland.

countries enjoyed preferences. The great bulk of these were of not more than 20% — under 3% of our trade to the Commonwealth did better than this — and the average preferential margin on goods enjoying preference worked out at 13%. As, however, this applied to little more than one-third of the total trade, the average margin of preference received by all our exports to the Commonwealth was only 5%.

Even where U.K. goods enjoyed a preference, they often had to pay substantial duties, the average rate on such goods being 13—16%; had the goods been American they would have paid, on average, 25—30%. Many of these duties were, of course, imposed primarily to raise revenue rather than to protect domestic producers.

(b) Preferences Accorded by the U.K. on imports from British Countries in 1929
Preferences were introduced into the McKenna duties in 1919 and into the Key Industry duties in 1921, but with few exceptions the goods concerned were not important in Commonwealth trade. In 1929 preferences were granted on only 7% of U.K. imports from British countries, among the most important being those on sugar, cocoa, coffee, preserved fruits, spirits, wines, tobacco and road vehicles.

Many of the preferences granted were high, and averaged between about 30% and 50% (owing to statistical difficulties the margin of error is here unusually great), but as so few goods were involved, the average margin of preference on all U.K. imports from British countries was only 2—3%, well below the average preference enjoyed by British exports to the Commonwealth as a whole, and very much less than the preferences accorded by countries such as Australia and New Zealand, which, even in 1929, averaged 13—14% and 16% respectively. It would, however, be unwise to make too much of these comparisons, since, among other things, the conditions governing markets for primary products and for manufactures are very different.

The goods that enjoyed preference often had to pay a high rate of duty, usually of a revenue nature. The average worked out at about 100%, so that the margin of preference reckoned as a percentage of price *including* duty on Commonwealth goods was much lower than the figure of 30—50% given in the last paragraph.

THE POSITION IN 1937

(a) Preferences Accorded U.K. goods in British Countries in 1937
Between 1932 and 1935 many British countries introduced pre-

Studies in Political Economy

TABLE I *Proportion of Trade Enjoying Preference*

	A. Percentage of total U.K. exports to British[1] countries			B. Percentage of total imports from the U.K. covered in calculation		
	1929	1937	1948	1929	1937	1948
Union of South Africa	10.0	16.5	14.2	100.0	98.8	100.0
Australia[4]	16.7	14.9	17.1	99.2	92.8	99.0
India	22.2	14.2	13.4[17]	99.4	99.1	100.0
Canada	10.8	10.9	8.3	100.0	99.7	99.6
Eire	11.1	8.6	8.9	99.7	99.3	98.8
New Zealand	6.6	8.0	6.2	99.3	100.0	79.1[23]
Straits Settlements[28]	3.8	3.4	2.4[16]	100.0	100.0	100.0[16]
Channel Islands[5]	1.1	2.2	1.8	100.0	61.0	80.5
Ceylon	1.8	1.6	1.5	100.0	97.2	97.1
Hong Kong[28]	1.9	1.3	2.4	100.0	100.0	100.0
Burma[29]	1.9	1.3	1.7	–	98.6	95.0
Southern Rhodesia	0.6	1.2	1.8	99.8	99.5	99.6
Federated Malay States	1.0	1.2	1.9[12]	100.0	97.9	99.9[12]
Trinidad and Tobago	0.5	1.0	1.0	98.6	99.4	–
Jamaica	0.5	0.8	0.8	99.7	99.9	–
Malta	0.4	0.5	0.8	100.0	100.0	100.0
British Guiana	0.3	0.5	0.4	97.9	99.8	–
Gibraltar[26]	0.2	0.4	0.4	100.0	100.0	–
Northern Rhodesia	0.1	0.4	0.4	99.9	99.8	97.1
Territories granting no preference in 1948[20]	6.1	8.2	10.4	100.0	100.0	100.0
Total of above	97.6	97.1	95.8			
Weighted average						

[1] Includes Burma after it left the Commonwealth, as preference continued to be granted. Otherwise 'British' is defined as in the U.K. Trade Returns.

[2] Includes results of Geneva tariff negotiations under G.A.T.T. in 1947 (cf. footnote 11; also footnote 10 of this study).

[3] Allows for surtax on U.S. goods of 9/40 or 1/20 of duty. Also allows for provisions relating to exchange depreciation. About half of the fall in the percentage margins of preference between 1937 and 1948 is due to changes in the pattern of trade.

[4] In 1929 and 1937 margins are expressed as a percentage of the f.o.b. value of imports in terms of Australian currency in order to achieve comparability with 1948. This involved reducing 1937 margins of preference and tariff rates as shown in the tariff list in the ratio of 125:110 and increasing 1929 margins and rates in the ratio 100:110. In 1937 and 1948 allowance was made for primage duty and also for the Exchange Adjustment Act in 1937.

[5] Preference granted by charging same duties as the U.K. on U.S. goods and admitting U.K. goods free of duty.

[6] High because spirits and tobacco formed so large a proportion of dutiable imports.

[7] Allows for surtax of 30% of duty on most goods from the U.K. and the U.S.

[8] Allows for discount of 10% of duties of over 15% on U.K. goods. The change in the pattern of trade between 1937 and 1948 tended to increase the average margin of preference on all imports from the U.K., and the true fall was thus larger, say 24% to

and Average Margins of Preference

C. Percentage of imports from the U.K. enjoying preference[22]			D. Percentage average margin of preference on goods enjoying preference			E. Percentage average margin of preference on all imports from the U.K.		
1929	1937	1948[2]	1929	1937	1948[2]	1929	1937	1948[2]
28–29	40–43[25]	32–34[25]	5	7	4–5	1	3[19]	1–2
90–93	88–91	88–91	14–16	22	15–16	13–14	19–20	13–14
6–8	50	24–25[18]	7–8	12	11–12[18]	0–1	6	3[18]
62–63[8]	88[9]	85–87[8]	11[8]	23[9]	12–13[8]	7[8]	20[9]	10–11[8]
8	10–12[13]	29–31[14]	9–10	13–31[13]	16–17[14]	1	1–2[15]	5[14]
83–86	88–90	90–91	18–19	26[3]	18[3]	16	23–25[3]	16–17[3]
0	24	23[16]	–	13	16[16]	0	3	4[16]
8	74–87	86–93	92–99[6]	34–44	33–38	7	26–39	29–35
0	70–86	65–68[11]	–	9–10	8–9[11]	0	7–8	5–6[11]
0	5	7	–	15	16–24	0	1	1–2
–[29]	62–92	61	–[29]	14	17	–[29]	9–13	11
93–94	96	97[27]	6–7	19–20	15[27]	6	19	14–15[27]
0	44–58	36[12]	–	14–15	13–14[12]	0	6–8	5[12]
90	64[24]		11–16	19[10]		10–14	12[10]	
84	83		9	15		7	12–13	
0	70	76	–	12	13	0	8	10
90	93		17	18[7]		15	17[7]	
5	5–7		13	34–39		1	2	
42	93–97	98[27]	10–11	9–10	10[27]	4	9–10	10[27]
0	0	0	–	–	–	0	0	0
35–36	55–57	49–51[21]	13	19–20	14–15[21]	5	10–11	7[21]

10–11%. Of this fall nearly one-half was due to price changes. See also footnote 10 of this study.

[9] Allows for discount of 10% of duties of over 15% on U.K. goods and for excise duty of 3% on U.S. goods. Of the large rise between 1929 and 1937 in the percentage of imports from the U.K. given preference, 6 points are due to the change in the pattern of trade.

[10] Allows for surtax of 15% of duty on certain goods from the U.K. and the U.S.

[11] Does not include results of Geneva tariff negotiations in 1947.

[12] Malayan Union.

[13] Takes no account of additional 10% duty on certain U.K. goods.

[14] 1948 rates weighted by 1947 values (latest available when calculations made).

[15] Allows for additional 10% duty on certain U.K. goods.

[16] Singapore only.

[17] Includes Pakistan.

[18] 1948 rates weighted by 1947–48 values (latest available when calculations made). Includes Pakistan up to August 14, 1947, only. Weighted average thus assumes that Pakistan granted preference to same proportion of U.K. imports and granted same average margin of preference in the period August 15, 1947–March 31, 1948, as India. Of the fall in the percentage of imports from the U.K. given preference between 1937 and 1948, 10 points are due to the change in the pattern of trade.

Notes continued p. 254

GENERAL NOTES TO TABLE I

In calculating the margins of preference it was sometimes necessary to give upper and lower limits for a small percentage of items for which it was impossible to reconcile the classifications in the trade returns with those in the tariff lists. This kind of difficulty accounts for the outside limits in columns C, D and E, which take the place of precise figures. It also, together with rounding, accounts for the apparent slight inconsistencies between columns C, D and E and for the fact that the figures in column B are sometimes less than 100%.

Calculations for Australia and South Africa to replace the figures taken from *Official Year Books*, and slight revisions elsewhere account for the discrepancies between the figures for 1937 given here and those in the table published in the *Economic Journal* for September 1952 (G. D. A. MacDougall, 'British and American Exports: A Study Suggested by the Theory of Comparative Costs.' Part II, Appendix E.).

Column A: Calculated from *Annual Statement of Trade of the U.K.*

Columns B—D: Financial years beginning July 1 for Australia and April 1 for India and for Canada 1929—30 and 1937—38. Calendar years for Canada 1948 and for all other countries.

Weighting: The margin of preference on each country's total imports from the U.K. is the mean of the margins of preference on each item weighted as follows:

(*a*) New Zealand, Australia, Northern and Southern Rhodesia, South Africa and Malta for all years; British Guiana, Eire and Hong Kong for 1937; Eire and Ceylon for 1948: value of imports originating in the U.K.

(*b*) Channel Islands, Federated Malay States, Gibraltar and Straits Settlements for all years; Burma and Ceylon for 1937; Hong Kong and Burma for 1948: U.K. exports of 'U.K. produce and manufactures.'

---

[19] *Official Year Book* figure is 3.8, compared with 3.4 obtained by this calculation.

[20] Nigeria (including British Cameroons), Gold Coast (including Togoland), Kenya, Uganda, Tanganyika, Zanzibar, Nyasaland, Anglo-Egyptian Sudan, Palestine, Aden, New Guinea and Papua.

[21] Figures for countries for which 1948 material was not available assumed to have changed since 1937 in same proportion as average of rest.

[22] Refers to imports from the U.K. that were covered in this calculation.

[23] This figure is relatively low because *Report on Trade and Shipping of the Dominion of New Zealand 1948* was not available when the calculations were made. See footnote 1 to Table II.

[24] Fall from 1929 due wholly to change in pattern of trade.

[25] Large part of rise 1929—37 and fall 1937—48 due to changes in pattern of trade (see also footnote 9 of this study).

[26] Duties are levied only on intoxicating liquors and tobacco.

[27] In 1948 some of the duties listed in the printed Customs tariffs were wholly or partially suspended. Allowing for these suspensions the figures in columns C—E would be approximately:

	C.	D.	E.
Southern Rhodesia	92	13	12
Northern Rhodesia	59	8	5

[28] In Singapore the only Customs duties levied are on intoxicating liquors, tobacco and petroleum. In Singapore and Hong Kong there is also a 'first registration fee' of 15% on motor vehicles not of British Commonwealth origin. This was treated as a preference of 15%.

[29] Included in India for 1929 in respect of C, D and E.

(c) India for all years; Eire for 1929; Canada for 1948: value of imports consigned from the U.K.

(d) Canada, Jamaica, Trinidad and Tobago for 1929 and 1937; British Guiana for 1929: margins of preference on each item were weighted by the value of imports from the U.K. actually admitted at preferential rates and then to obtain the average margin of preference on all imports from the U.K. the total of the margins so weighted was expressed as a percentage of the total value of imports consigned from the U.K. (for Canada, British Guiana and Trinidad 1929 and Canada 1937) or of the total value of imports originating in the U.K. (for the others). For these countries therefore some of the figures in columns C and E have a slight downward bias relatively to the others, since the weight given to items having no preference includes goods which did not qualify for preferential treatment because an insufficient percentage of their value was the result of British labour. This is not sufficient to affect the general picture.

To obtain average figures for all British countries covered, the figures for each country were weighted according to the value of exports of U.K. produce and manufactures to it (column A), except column D, which was weighted according to the value of exports of U.K. produce granted preference by each country.

The comparability of margins of preference for different countries is slightly reduced by differences in methods of valuing imports (c.i.f., f.o.b., etc.); but this does not affect the general picture.

Trinidad, Jamaica, British Guiana, Gibraltar: No calculations made for 1948; no sufficiently recent trade returns available when work was done.

ferences on U.K. goods for the first time. These included the Straits Settlements, the Federated Malay States, Hong Kong, Ceylon and Malta among the countries included in our calculations, and other small trading countries such as Gambia, Sierra Leone, St. Helena, Seychelles, Gilbert and Ellice Islands, Solomons and Tonga. In addition, many countries that had already been granting preference in 1929 widened the range of their imports from Britain on which preference was given.

By 1937 the proportion of U.K. exports to the Commonwealth enjoying preference had, according to our calculations, risen to about 56%, compared with about 36% in 1929. This increase is due in part to a change in the pattern of trade, which would have raised the 1929 figure of 36% to about 40% in 1937, even if there had been no extension of preference;[7] but the great bulk of the rise to 56% is the result of new preferences. Those granted by India and Canada were of major importance.

Alongside the rise in the proportion of U.K. goods enjoying preference, there were substantial increases in the margins of preference on preferred goods. The proportion of U.K. exports to the Commonwealth enjoying preferences of over 20% jumped from

[7] In particular, a large part of the rise in the proportion of South African imports from the U.K. granted preference from about 28% in 1929 to 40% or more in 1937 can be accounted for by the change in the pattern of trade, while the surprising fall in the percentage for Trinidad and Tobago is entirely due to the change in the trade pattern.

one-fortieth in 1929 to one-fifth in 1937. The average preference on goods receiving preference rose from 13% to 19–20%.

As a result of these two developments — new preferences and increases in the margins — the average rate of preference on all U.K. exports to the Commonwealth rose from 5% in 1929 to 10–11% in 1937. Not much of this rise can be accounted for by changes in the pattern of trade or by changes in prices that altered the *ad valorem* incidence of specific duties. It was mainly the result of changes in rates of duty.

How far were these results accomplished by reducing rates of duty on U.K. goods, and how far by increasing the rates on goods from other countries (represented by the United States according to our definition)? It is convenient to consider separately the manner in which: (i) margins of preference were widened on goods already enjoying preference in 1929; (ii) preferences were accorded to new goods.

(i) *Goods already enjoying preference in 1929.* We have worked out for 1929 the average rate of duty on U.K. goods (the U.K. rate) and the rate they would have paid had they been American (the U.S. rate). We have also worked out for comparison what the U.K. and U.S. rates would have been if the 1937 tariff lists had been operative in 1929, *i.e.,* we have applied the 1937 tariff rates to the 1929 trade. In this way we can eliminate the effects of changes in the pattern of trade and in prices, and are left with the effects of changes in tariff lists on the U.S. and U.K. rates.

Preference enjoyed by U.K. Exports to the Commonwealth.

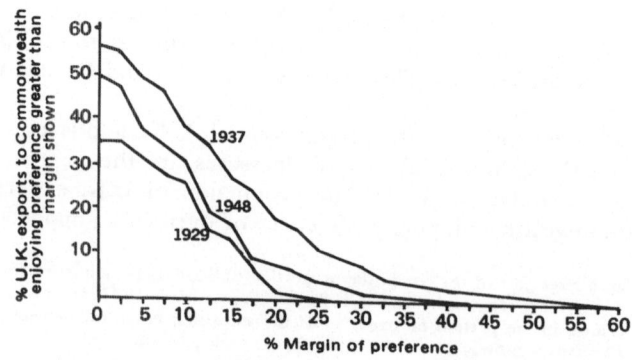

In most countries the U.S. rate for 1937 is higher than that for 1929, and for all countries taken together it rises from 25–30% in 1929 to 33–36% in 1937. The average U.K. rate remained at around 15% in each year. However, the fall in prices between 1929 and 1937 raised the percentage rate on U.K. goods to 17–19%, and that on U.S. goods was raised further to 37–41%.

(ii) *Goods First Granted a Preference between 1929 and 1937.* On only one-tenth of these goods, by value, was the rate payable on U.K. goods reduced. On 95% the rate on U.S. goods was increased and on no less than 60% the rate on U.K. goods was increased as well.

The increase in preference accorded to U.K. goods in British countries during this period was thus achieved very largely by increasing the rates on foreign goods, and only in minor degree by reducing the rates on U.K. goods; on the contrary, these tended to be increased as well.

(b) Preferences accorded by U.K. on Imports from British countries in 1937.
The Import Duties Act and the Ottawa Agreements greatly widened the scope of preference on U.K. imports from the Commonwealth. By 1937 over 60% of such imports enjoyed preference, compared with only 7% in 1929.

The average margin on goods accorded preference fell greatly, but this has no significance, since the high level in 1929 reflected exceptional margins on a very few items, and the great bulk of the new preferences were of not more than 20%.

The average margin on all U.K. imports from British Countries was raised from 2–3% to 10–12%, *i.e.*, to roughly the same average level as that enjoyed by U.K. exports to the Commonwealth as a whole.

A large part of this increase was, of course, achieved by imposing a tariff on foreign goods while retaining duty-free entry for goods from British countries. Taken in conjunction with the results obtained for U.K. exports to the Commonwealth, this means that the intensification of Imperial Preference during the thirties was achieved largely by increasing tariffs against the outside world, rather than by reducing tariffs between Commonwealth countries.

THE POSITION IN 1948
Between 1937 and 1948 there were important reductions in Imperial Preference. The average percentage margins of preference fell at least half-way back to the pre-Ottawa level. This was the result partly of the large rise in prices which reduced the *ad valorem* incidence of specific duties and partly of alterations in rates of duty made at the Geneva Tariff Negotiations under G.A.T.T. in 1947 and, for

TABLE II
% Distribution of British Countries' Imports from the U.K. According to Margin of Preference Granted

Percentage margin	South Africa 1929	South Africa 1937	South Africa 1948	Australia[16] 1929	Australia[16] 1937	Australia[16] 1948	India 1929	India 1937	India 1948	Canada 1929	Canada 1937	Canada 1948	Eire 1929	Eire 1937	Eire 1948
Coverage, %:	99.5	95.8	96.6	85.3[6]	86.3[7]	93.1	97.0	99.1	98.7	100.0	99.2	96.9	98.9	89.0[10]	96.8
0	71.9	59.4	68.3	7.5	12.7	10.7	94.3	49.8	76.0	37.8	12.6	12.9	92.3	84.8	72.3
Up to 2.5	0.1	0.2	2.7	0.2	0.0	6.9	—	2.6	1.7	2.1	0.2	6.4	0.1	0.1	0.3
2.6– 5.0	25.5	27.9	27.9	0.4	0.4	8.1	—	0.4	—	5.2	0.9	6.2	2.2	1.0	0.5
5.1– 7.5	1.3	1.4	0.1	5.7	0.1	3.5	5.4	4.3	5.3	3.0	4.4	18.7	0.0	0.0	3.3
7.6–10.0	1.2	1.6	0.9	0.5	1.3	3.9	—	30.2	1.2	8.7	—	10.6	0.1	0.6	2.9
10.1–12.5	—	0.0	0.0	30.3	2.9	26.9	—	2.0	13.5	30.6	7.4	4.7	5.2	0.8	11.1
12.6–15.0	—	9.2	—	3.2	18.1	6.0	0.3	1.0	—	8.1	9.4	4.7	—	0.5	0.7
15.1–17.5	—	0.2	—	37.8	10.5	12.2	—	—	—	3.9	8.9	20.6	—	2.1	2.3
17.6–20.0	0.0	0.0	—	3.4	14.0	0.5	—	0.2	—	0.5	13.8	4.1	—	0.4	1.0
20.1–22.5	—	—	—	3.3	11.5	4.1	—	—	0.0	0.1	2.6	4.2	0.0	0.9	0.1
22.6–25.0	—	0.1	—	0.0	1.0	5.6	—	9.5	0.8	0.0	12.6	6.0	0.1	0.6	2.9
25.1–27.5	—	—	—	3.2	9.3	3.9	—	—	—	—	2.6	0.8	—	—	0.0
27.6–30.0	—	—	—	0.1	3.4	2.8	—	—	0.0	0.0	4.3	0.1	0.0	0.0	0.1
30.1–32.5	—	—	0.0	2.5	6.2	2.1	—	—	—	—	8.4	—	—	0.0	—
32.6–35.0	—	0.0	0.1	0.3	1.6	0.2	—	—	—	0.0	1.2	0.0	—	0.0	0.0
35.1–37.5	—	—	—	0.4	0.6	0.4	—	—	—	0.0	0.9	0.0	—	—	—
37.6–40.0	—	—	—	0.2	1.1	0.6	—	—	0.3	0.0	3.9	0.0	—	0.0	0.6
40.1–42.5	—	—	—	0.4	0.7	0.0	—	—	1.2	—	0.5	0.0	0.0	0.0	0.1
42.6–45.0	—	—	—	0.6	0.2	0.3	—	—	—	—	0.8	0.0	—	—	0.6
45.1–47.5	—	—	—	—	0.1	0.0	—	—	—	—	0.2	—	—	—	0.0
47.6–50.0	—	—	—	0.0	0.1	0.1	—	—	—	—	—	—	—	—	—
50.1–52.5	—	—	—	0.0	3.0	0.6	—	—	—	—	0.1	—	—	—	—
52.6–55.0	—	—	—	0.0	0.1	0.5	—	—	—	0.0	0.8	—	—	—	0.1
55.1–57.5	—	—	—	—	0.3	0.1	—	—	—	—	0.1	—	—	—	0.6
57.6–60.0	—	—	—	—	0.1	—	—	—	—	—	0.0	—	—	—	0.2
60.1 and over	—	—	—	—	0.7	0.0	—	—	—	—	3.4	—	—	—	0.3
	100.0	100.0	100.0	100.0	100.0	100.0	100.0	100.0	100.0	100.0	100.0	100.0	100.0	91.8[3]	100.0

Percentage margin	New Zealand 1929	New Zealand 1937	New Zealand 1948	Straits Settlements 1929	Straits Settlements 1937	Straits Settlements 1948	Ceylon 1929	Ceylon 1937	Ceylon 1948	Hong Kong 1929	Hong Kong 1937	Hong Kong 1948	Southern Rhodesia 1929	Southern Rhodesia 1937	Southern Rhodesia 1948
Coverage %:	96.3	94.8	67.4[1]	100.0	100.0	99.6	100.0	81.8[a]	96.6	100.0	100.0	100.0	95.7	97.5	97.6
0	14.4	10.8	10.4	100.0	76.5	77.1	100.0	17.1	35.4	100.0	95.2	92.8	5.3	4.1	2.7
Up to 2.5	0.0	0.1	0.0	—	—	—	—	0.1	0.2	—	—	—	1.1	0.4	0.9
2.6– 5.0	0.1	0.3	0.1	—	—	—	—	19.4	12.8	—	—	—	48.2	30.2	33.4
5.1– 7.5	0.9	6.7	3.0	—	—	0.3	—	10.8	13.1	—	0.2	0.3	18.7	1.6	0.8
7.6–10.0	7.1	3.1	9.0	—	14.9	—	—	47.9	38.4	—	—	—	0.1	20.4	8.7
10.1–12.5	0.4	8.7	12.2	—	—	8.1	—	—	0.0	—	—	—	21.2	5.2	3.8
12.6–15.0	10.9	0.7	1.9	—	—	14.5	—	0.5	0.0	—	3.1	—	0.4	9.6	17.4
15.1–17.5	0.3	2.6	31.4	—	—	—	—	3.8	—	—	—	6.3	2.6	0.0	0.4
17.6–20.0	58.0	9.5	0.0	—	8.6	—	—	—	0.1	—	1.5	—	0.3	6.7	23.8
20.1–22.5	0.0	4.5	2.8	—	—	—	—	—	—	—	—	—	1.8	0.0	0.0
22.6–25.0	4.5	10.8	7.4	—	—	—	—	0.4	—	—	—	—	—	2.0	2.8
25.1–27.5	—	0.7	0.0	—	—	—	—	—	—	—	—	—	0.1	—	—
27.6–30.0	3.0	18.4	11.8	—	—	—	—	—	—	—	—	—	—	1.9	1.2
30.1–32.5	—	1.5	3.7	—	—	—	—	—	—	—	—	—	0.1	0.1	—
32.6–35.0	—	7.7	2.2	—	—	—	—	—	—	—	—	—	—	0.7	1.2
35.1–37.5	—	0.4	0.0	—	—	—	—	—	—	—	—	—	—	—	—
37.6–40.0	—	0.3	0.0	—	—	—	—	—	—	—	—	—	—	0.2	—
40.1–42.5	—	0.1	0.7	—	—	—	—	—	—	—	—	0.6	—	0.0	—
42.6–45.0	0.3	—	2.7	—	—	—	—	—	—	—	—	—	—	—	—
45.1–47.5	—	13.1	0.0	—	—	—	—	—	—	—	—	—	—	0.1	—
47.6–50.0	0.1	0.0	0.7	—	—	—	—	—	—	—	—	—	—	—	—
50.1–52.5	—	—	—	—	—	—	—	—	—	—	—	—	—	—	—
52.6–55.0	—	—	—	—	—	—	—	—	—	—	—	—	—	12.7	—
55.1–57.5	—	—	—	—	—	—	—	—	—	—	—	—	—	—	—
57.6–60.0	—	—	—	—	—	—	—	—	—	—	—	—	—	0.1	—
60.1 and over	0.0	0.0	—	—	—	—	—	—	—	—	—	—	0.1	4.0	2.9
	100.0	100.0	100.0	100.0	100.0	100.0	100.0	100.0	100.0	100.0	100.0	100.0	100.0	100.0	100.0

TABLE II (*continued*)

Percentage margin	Federated Malay States			Trinidad and Tobago			Jamaica			Malta			British Guiana		
	1929	1937	1948	1929	1937	1948[2]	1929	1937	1948[2]	1929	1937	1948	1929	1937	1948[2]
Coverage, %:	100.0	85.3[a]	99.1	93.8	99.4	—	99.7	93.9	—	100.0	100.0	96.4	97.9	98.6	—
0	100.0	48.8	64.0	10.7	36.3		16.5	18.4		100.0	29.9	24.7	10.1	7.5	
Up to 2.5	—	0.6	—	2.1	0.3		0.2	0.2		—	0.1	0.1	—	0.0	
2.6– 5.0	—	—	7.3	4.2	0.4		56.9	36.7		—	2.7	8.5	10.3	8.8	
5.1– 7.5	—	6.4	0.1	10.4	1.5		0.1	0.1		—	0.8	0.9	18.5	20.2	
7.6–10.0	—	28.0	9.4	21.2	8.9		19.4	26.6		—	52.3	6.9	3.9	8.7	
10.1–12.5		—	0.0	38.4	39.2		1.5	4.5		—	1.1	4.7	2.1	3.3	
12.6–15.0		—	1.3	0.3	0.5		0.2	1.6		—	1.2	51.4	2.8	12.9	
15.1–17.5		—	1.1	0.3	1.9		0.0	1.7		—	3.5	0.4	29.9	24.9	
17.6–20.0		8.2	16.2	3.3	1.6		0.1	4.1		—	5.0	1.2	6.8	2.7	
20.1–22.5		—	—	7.3	2.9		0.0	0.1		—	—	1.2	4.2	0.1	
22.6–25.0		—	0.6	0.7	2.3		0.1	0.2		—	—	—	4.2	0.2	
25.1–27.5		—	—	0.8	0.6		0.2	0.2		—	3.3	—	0.1	0.8	
27.6–30.0		6.9	—	0.2	0.1		—	1.7		—	—	—	0.7	0.6	
30.1–32.5		—	—	0.1	0.0		—	—		—	—	0.0	0.1	0.0	
32.6–35.0		—	—	—	—		0.0	2.0		—	—	—	0.8	0.0	
35.1–37.5		—	—	0.0	0.1		—	0.0		—	0.0	—	0.0	2.0	
37.6–40.0		—	—	0.0	0.0		2.0	0.6		—	—	—	0.0	0.0	
40.1–42.5		—	—	—	—		—	0.2		—	—	0.0	0.0	0.1	
42.6–45.0		—	—	0.0	0.9		—	0.5		—	—	—	0.0	—	
45.1–47.5		—	—	—	0.0		—	—		—	—	—	—	—	
47.6–50.0		—	—	—	—		—	0.1		—	—	—	0.0	—	
50.1–52.5		—	—	—	0.0		—	—		—	—	—	0.0	—	
52.6–55.0		—	—	—	0.0		—	—		—	—	—	—	0.2	
55.1–57.5		—	—	0.0	0.2		—	—		—	—	—	0.4	0.5	
57.6–60.0		—	—	—	0.0		—	—		—	—	—	0.2	—	
60.1 and over		1.1	—	0.0	2.3		2.8	0.5		—	0.1	—	4.7	6.5	
	100.0	100.0	100.0	100.0	100.0	100.0	100.0	100.0		100.0	100.0	100.0	100.0	100.0	100.0

Percentage margin	Gibraltar 1929	Gibraltar 1937	Gibraltar 1948[2]	Northern Rhodesia 1929	Northern Rhodesia 1937	Northern Rhodesia 1948[5]	All British countries covered[11] 1929	All British countries covered[11] 1937	All British countries covered[11] 1948	Percentage distribution of U.K. imports from British countries according to margin of preference granted 1929[13]	1937[14]	1948[14]
Coverage, %:	100.0	100.0	—	99.3	84.0[4]	88.3[5]				96.3[13]	91.0[14]	90.4[14]
0	95.3	95.0	—	58.2	4.2	2.4	64.8	46.3[12]	51.7	96.5	41.4	49.7
Up to 2.5	—	—	—	1.8	1.4	0.3	0.3	0.5	2.6	0.4	—	3.0
2.6– 5.0	—	—	—	2.1	40.4	22.0	3.9	6.2	7.8	1.1	10.6	0.2
5.1– 7.5	—	—	—	7.2	0.1	0.2	3.0	1.9	3.2	0.1	—	15.7
7.6–10.0	—	—	—	2.7	16.9	63.5	1.7	8.5	4.8	0.0	19.4	22.7
10.1–12.5	1.6	1.7	—	20.4	13.7	0.1	9.7	2.7	9.9	0.5	0.2	1.0
12.6–15.0	3.1	—	—	0.0	20.2	6.5	2.3	6.3	2.9	—	17.5	4.3
15.1–17.5	—	—	—	7.0	0.4	—	7.1	5.3	7.2	0.7	1.9	0.2
17.6–20.0	—	—	—	0.6	0.3	0.7	4.7	5.5	1.4	—	4.7	4.3
20.1–22.5	—	—	—	—	—	—	0.6	2.7	1.4	0.0	0.0	0.7
22.6–25.0	—	—	—	—	—	—	0.3	4.2	2.6	—	0.1	0.0
25.1–27.5	—	—	—	—	—	—	0.6	1.9	0.8	—	0.1	—
27.6–30.0	—	—	—	0.0	—	—	0.2	2.8	1.4	—	0.4	0.1
30.1–32.5	—	—	—	—	—	—	0.4	2.2	0.7	—	0.2	0.0
32.6–35.0	—	—	—	—	0.1	—	0.1	1.1	0.2	0.1	1.2	0.1
35.1–37.5	—	—	—	—	2.3	—	0.1	0.2	0.1	—	0.5	—
37.6–40.0	—	—	—	—	—	4.3	0.0	0.7	0.2	—	—	—
40.1–42.5	—	—	—	—	—	—	0.1	0.2	0.2	—	—	—
42.6–45.0	—	—	—	—	—	—	0.1	0.1	0.3	—	—	—
45.1–47.5	—	—	—	—	—	—	—	1.2	0.1	0.1	0.2	0.0
47.6–50.0	—	—	—	—	—	—	0.0	0.0	0.0	—	—	—
50.1–52.5	—	—	—	—	—	—	—	0.5	0.1	—		
52.6–55.0	—	3.3	—	—	—	—	—	0.3	0.1	—	1.6	
55.1–57.5	—	—	—	—	—	—	—	0.1	0.1	—		
57.6–60.0	—	—	—	—	—	—	—	0.0	0.0	—		
60.1 and over	—	—	—	—	—	—	0.0	0.6	0.1	0.5		
	100.0	100.0	—	100.0	100.0	100.0	100.0	100.0	100.0	100.0	100.0	100.0

example, in the Trade Agreements between the U.K. and the U.S. (1938), the U.S. and Canada (1938)[8] and the U.K. and India (1939). (On the other hand, increased preferences were obtained under the U.K./Eire Agreement of 1938.) But while the average rate of preference was markedly reduced, the general structure of preference

[8] This agreement made various changes which reduced the preference accorded to U.K. over U.S. goods, including the removal of a special excise tax on a long list of goods imported from non-British countries.

GENERAL NOTES TO TABLE II

In Table I outside limits were given instead of precise figures where it was impossible to reconcile the tariff list with the trade return for particular items. These imprecise items have been omitted from the frequency distributions in Table II so as to obtain a clearer presentation of the data, and the coverage for the frequency distributions is therefore less good than for the calculations whose results are shown in Table I. The coverage is, however, given for each distribution, and it will be seen that it is generally sufficient to give a fairly complete picture of amounts of preference granted. Where coverage is definitely insufficient (Channel Islands and Burma) distributions have not been constructed.

For reasons of presentation, figures are given to one decimal point, but this degree of precision should not be taken as an indication of the margin of error involved. See also notes to Table I.

FOOTNOTES TO TABLE II

[1] Calculation made from *External Trade 1948* (Census and Statistics Department, Wellington, N.Z., 1951), as *Report on Trade and Shipping of the Dominion of New Zealand 1948* was not available when the calculations were made. Of trade omitted at least 12% (of imports from U.K.), probably much more, granted preferences of 7.6—17.5%.

[2] Sufficiently recent trade figures not available when calculation was made.

[3] Additional duty of 10% on 8.2% of goods imported from the U.K.

[4] Over half trade omitted granted preference of 5% or 10%. The rest was granted none or preferences of up to 25%.

[5] Trade omitted was mostly granted 5% or 10% preference.

[6] Of trade omitted 7% (of imports from U.K.) was granted preference of 11—15%. Rest was granted none or preferences of up to 85%.

[7] Of trade omitted 4% (of imports from the U.K.) was granted preference of 13—22%. Rest was granted none or preferences of up to and over 100%.

[8] Most of trade omitted was either granted no preference or a preference of 10%.

[9] Most of trade omitted was either granted no preference or preferences of up to 15%.

[10] Preference on trade omitted varied between −10% (see note 3) and over 100%.

[11] Excluding British Guiana, Jamaica, Trinidad and Tobago and Gibraltar. Including territories granting no preference in 1948.

[12] Including 0.8 exports to Eire, on which additional duty of 10%.

[13] Of trade omitted 2.7% was granted preference of between 27% and 61%, 0.4% was granted preference of between 2% and 10%. The preference granted on the rest varied up to over 200%.

[14] Of trade omitted, at least 4.1% was granted preference at rates well above 30%, and at least a further 1.4% at rates above 15%. The rest was granted either no preference or preferences varying up to 25%.

[15] Of trade omitted, at least 3% was granted preference of 20% or less. A further 1.5% was granted either no preference or various rates up to 33.3%. A further 3% was granted preference of between 9% and 28%, and nearly a further 2% was granted preference of 47—53%.

[16] See footnote 4 to Table I.

was not seriously modified; the proportion of intra-Commonwealth trade enjoying preference did not fall greatly.

(a) Preferences Accorded U.K. goods in British Countries in 1948

The proportion of U.K. exports to British countries enjoying preference fell from about 56% in 1937 to about 50% in 1948, and a significant part of this fall can be explained by changes in the pattern of trade. The elimination of preferences was thus relatively unimportant. The proportion of trade enjoying preference fell quite markedly in South Africa, but this was largely the result of changes in the trade pattern.[9] India is the only important country where the elimination of preferences was of major significance (partly as a result of the 1939 Trade Agreement with the U.K.); the proportion of trade accorded preference fell from 50% in 1937 to about 25% in 1948, but even here some 10 points of the fall was the result of changes in the pattern of trade.[10]

But while comparatively few preferences were eliminated between 1937 and 1948, there were large falls in many percentage rates of preference. The average rate on goods receiving preference fell from 19–20% to 14–15%; and as changes in the trade pattern tended to increase the average rate, the true fall on a comparable basis was larger, and probably about one-third (roughly from 22% to 14%). High preferences became much less important; the proportion of Britain's exports to the Commonwealth enjoying preferences of over 20% fell from one-fifth in 1937 to under one-tenth in 1948.

The average margin of preference on *all* U.K. exports to the Commonwealth fell from 10–11% to 7% and by rather more assuming a constant pattern of trade. Of this fall about half seems to have been due to the rise in prices and about half to tariff changes.

The fall in margins of preference was on balance, but not in all countries, associated with reductions in *percentage* rates of duty both on U.K. and on U.S. goods. There were, it is true, steep increases in the *tariff rates* charged by some of the Colonies, partly no doubt to maintain the real value of revenue from specific duties in the face of rising prices; and for all countries taken together we find some increase in the average U.K. and U.S. rates on goods enjoying preference in 1948 when the effects of changes in prices and in the

[9] We are advised that these changes were temporary and resulted from Britain's inability to supply South Africa with many goods on which preferences were granted.
[10] The Geneva Agreement of 1947 scheduled the elimination of preferences on 8% of Canada's imports from the U.K. (1937 trade), but 7% of this consisted of items on which the duty on the U.K. product was to be raised. This required specific legislation which was not completed until 1949. Its effect does not therefore appear in the 1948 figures given here.

TABLE III *Average Rates of Duty*

	Goods already enjoying preference in 1929 (1929 pattern of trade)				
	1929 tariff rates, 1929 prices	1937 tariff rates			
		1929 prices		1937 prices	
	(1)	(2)		(3)	
	U.K. rate	U.S. rate	U.K. rate	U.S. rate	U.K. rate	U.S. rate
Union of South Africa	3	7	6–7	12–15	6–7	12–15
Australia (c)	14–23	29–39	17–20	37–43	18–21	39–45
India	11–17	18–26	7–8	11–13	9–10	14–16
Canada	17	28	18	42–43	18	42–43
Eire	31–37	40–45	77–90	106–126	92–108	127–150
New Zealand	10–11	29–30	9	32–33	9	33
Straits Settlements	(b)	(b)	(b)	(b)	(b)	(b)
Channel Islands	0	92–99	0	82–94	0	105–121
Ceylon	(b)	(b)	(b)	(b)	(b)	(b)
Hong Kong	(b)	(b)	(b)	(b)	(b)	(b)
Burma	Included in India					
Southern Rhodesia	5	12	4–5	18–19	5	19–20
Federated Malay States	(b)	(b)	(b)	(b)	(b)	(b)
Trinidad and Tobago	9–12	20–27	12–13	30–31	14	34–35
Jamaica	23	31	19–20	32–34	20–21	34–36
Malta	(b)	(b)	(b)	(b)	(b)	(b)
British Guiana	16	32	23–24	44–47	27–29	53–56
Gibraltar	40	53	40	53	51	68
Northern Rhodesia	9–10	19	9–10	20–22	9–11	21–23
Weighted average	13–16	25–30	14–16	33–36	17–19	37–41

U.K. rate: average percentage rate of duty on goods from the U.K.
U.S. rate: average percentage rate of duty had goods been from the U.S.
Change from (1) to (2) and from (4) to (5) reflects change in tariff rates.
Change from (2) to (3) and from (5) to (6) reflects change in prices (which affects *ad valorem* incidence of specific duties).
The high average rates of duty shown for some countries (such as Straits Settlements, Hong Kong, Federated Malay States and Gibraltar) are attributable in large part to the limited range of goods that enjoy tariff preferences and to the high level of duties on intoxicating liquors and tobacco (which are preferential).

pattern of trade have been eliminated. But the rise in prices more than offset these increases in tariff rates. The net result was that, for all countries taken together, the U.K. rate fell from 17–20% in 1937 to 14% in 1948 and the U.S. rate from 38–43% to 27–29% (based on the 1948 pattern of trade throughout).

(b) Preferences Accorded by the U.K. on Imports from British Countries in 1948
Between 1937 and 1948 there was some fall in the proportion of

on Goods Enjoying Preference

	Goods still enjoying preference in 1948 (1948 pattern of trade)				
	1937 tariff rates, 1937 prices	1948 tariff rates			
		1937 prices		1948 prices	
	(4)		(5)		(6)
	U.K. rate	U.S. rate	U.K. rate	U.S. rate	U.K. rate	U.S. rate
Union of South Africa	3	8–11	3	8–9	2–3	7
Australia (c)	18–20	42–46	15–16	37–41	9	23–25
India	22	32	26–27	38–39	25–26	38–39
Canada	15	41	13	28	10	22
Eire	68–103	95–145	72–79	96–107	35–38	50–55
New Zealand	7–8	30–32	7–8	25–26	6–8	24–26
Straits Settlements	60	72	296	331	108	124
Channel Islands	0	36–45	0	62–65	0	33–38
Ceylon	14–15	22–24	26–27	35–36	23–24	31–32
Hong Kong	30–34	45–48	96–109	136–137	59–68	83–84
Burma	20–26	32–40	24–25	42–43	24	41
Southern Rhodesia	5	25	5	20	5	20
Federated Malay States	32	44	284–286	317–319	96	109–110
Trinidad and Tobago	(a)	(a)	(a)	(a)	(a)	(a)
Jamaica	(a)	(a)	(a)	(a)	(a)	(a)
Malta	12–13	24	27–29	41–42	19–20	33
British Guiana	(a)	(a)	(a)	(a)	(a)	(a)
Gibraltar	(a)	(a)	(a)	(a)	(a)	(a)
Northern Rhodesia	6–7	17–19	14–15	30–39	7–8	17–18
Weighted average	17–20	38–43	24–26	42–47	14	27–29

The figures for India, Burma and the Channel Islands are subject to particularly wide margins of error, possibly wider than those shown in the table.
See also notes to Summary Table C and to Table I.
(a) Not calculated; no sufficiently recent trade returns available when work was done.
(b) No preference in 1929.
(c) In all years amounts of duty paid were expressed as a percentage of the f.o.b. value of imports in terms of Australian currency in order to achieve comparability between the years (see footnote 4 to Table I).

U.K. imports from the Commonwealth enjoying preference — roughly from 60% to 55%. Since the change in the pattern of trade tended to increase this proportion, the true fall was larger.

There was a large fall in the average margin of preference on goods receiving preference, from 17–20% to 11–13%; and, as the change in the trade pattern tended to increase the average margin, the true fall was greater, and probably about one-half. The proportion of trade enjoying preferences of over 10% fell from one-third to one-sixth.

The average rate on all imports fell from 10—12% to 6—7%. Using the 1948 pattern of trade throughout, the fall is greater, from 14—18% to 6—7%. Of this fall well under one-half seems to have been due to tariff changes, and well over one-half to the rise in prices which reduced the *ad valorem* incidence of specific duties; U.K. import prices in general nearly trebled between 1937 and 1948, and specific duties were of importance for many imports from British countries.

The fall in preferential margins was accompanied by large increases in rates of Customs duty, which were not wholly offset by the effects of higher prices, on imports from both Commonwealth and non-Commonwealth countries. But many of these increases were imposed for revenue purposes, and were largely matched by increases in excise duty. The average rate of Customs duty less excise duty on goods enjoying preference in 1948 fell from 6—10% to 2—4% for imports from Commonwealth countries and from 24—33% to 13—16% for imports from other sources (based on the 1948 pattern of trade throughout). These falls reflect wholly the effect of the rise in prices on the *ad valorem* incidence of specific duties.

Thus, for trade in each direction between Britain and the Commonwealth, the reduction in Imperial Preference between 1937 and 1948 was accompanied by a general fall in percentage rates of duty (net of excise duty for U.K. imports), just as the increase in preference in the thirties had been accompanied by a general rise.

THE PRESENT POSITION (MID-1953)

Five years have elapsed since 1948, the latest year for which calculations have been made. Since then there have been further reductions in Imperial Preference, although the general picture given for 1948 cannot have been radically modified.

Probably the most important change has been the reduction in the *ad valorem* incidence of specific margins caused by a further rise in prices — British import and export prices in general have risen by around 25—30%. The results of the Annecy and Torquay tariff negotiations under G.A.T.T. in 1949 and 1951 scarcely affect our average figures, and it is unlikely that the reduction of preferences brought about in other ways has been much more important. The pattern of trade has also altered. We have not calculated the effect, beyond establishing that the shift in U.K. exports between Commonwealth countries granting different average margins of preference has on balance been of no importance.

It is impossible to give any precise details of the present position, but what rough calculations we have been able to make suggest that the following broad picture is unlikely to be very wide of the mark.

Something like one-half of both British exports to and imports from the Commonwealth enjoy preference, but in some Commonwealth markets for U.K. exports the proportion is much higher. Well under one-tenth of the trade in either direction enjoys preferences of over 20%, although there are still a few very high preferences of 50% or more. The average percentage margin of preference on all U.K trade with the Commonwealth has been greatly reduced since the late thirties, and is now probably in the neighbourhood of 6% in either direction. The margin is still smaller — probably around 5% on U.K. exports to the Commonwealth — if it is reckoned as a percentage of the value of trade *including* duty on British goods, which is more relevant when assessing competitive power.

A figure of 5% may seem surprisingly low to those with experience of very high preferential margins; but such margins, as we have seen, are few and far between. There is no doubt that preferences are of very considerable importance in certain trades, where the rate is relatively high or the market highly competitive and sensitive to price differentials. For many years tariff preferences were overshadowed by direct trade and exchange controls and by the existence of sellers' markets. They will regain importance to the extent that these conditions change. But the effect of preferences on our total export trade cannot be more than marginal. Following a rough method of calculation used in an earlier article,[11] it seems unlikely that an average preference of around 5% on our exports to the Commonwealth can make a difference of more than, say, 5% in our total exports to the world as a whole — although even marginal exports of this size can, of course, be of crucial importance while the balance of payments remains precarious. It is certain that the effect of Imperial Preference on the total sales of U.S. manufacturers is entirely negligible.

SUMMARY OF MAIN RESULTS

Even before Ottawa, Britain was enjoying an average preference of 13% on over one-third of her exports to British countries, giving an average preference of 5% on all her exports to the Commonwealth. In return she gave preferences (admittedly high ones) on only 7% of her imports from the Commonwealth, making an average rate of preference of 2—3% on all her imports from British countries.

By 1937, mainly as a result of the Ottawa Agreements, the proportion of trade enjoying preference had risen to well over

---

[11] *Economic Journal*, September 1952, p. 509.

one-half in each direction, and many old preferences had been increased. This intensification of Imperial Preference, which was considerably more important for Britain's imports than for her exports, raised the average margin of preference to 10—12% on all trade in each direction. It was achieved largely by raising tariff rates on foreign goods and not by reducing rates on intra-Commonwealth trade; the latter, on the contrary, tended to rise as well.

Since 1937 there has been a large reduction in Imperial Preference. The proportion of trade enjoying preference has not fallen greatly, and is still about one-half in each direction. But the average rate has fallen to about 6% on both imports and exports. (The rate is, of course, about twice as high on goods enjoying preference, and higher still on many items.) The reduction in Imperial Preference since 1937 has been the result, first, of tariff changes, including those negotiated under G.A.T.T. and in other Trade Agreements, and secondly — probably more important — of the very large rise in prices which has reduced the *ad valorem* incidence of specific margins. The rise in prices has also brought about a substantial fall in percentage rates of protective duty, both on intra-Commonwealth trade and on similar goods imported from outside the Commonwealth.

Index

The letter 't' following a page number indicates that the reference is to a table or diagram.